RESULTS ON INTERNET

ROI

Secrets of Successful Business Websites

The Only Book You Need
to Produce, Manage and Market
Your Company's Website
and Achieve Your Business Goals

ANDREW KUCHERIAVY

authorHOUSE®

AuthorHouse™
1663 Liberty Drive
Bloomington, IN 47403
www.authorhouse.com
Phone: 1-800-839-8640

Edited by Diane Pearson
Illustrations and cover design by Alex Noio

Published by AuthorHouse 10/10/2014

ISBN: 978-1-4969-3353-9 (sc)
ISBN: 978-1-4969-3352-2 (hc)
ISBN: 978-1-4969-3351-5 (e)

Library of Congress Control Number: 2014914537

This book is dedicated to my parents

TABLE OF CONTENTS

WHY THIS BOOK?

Read this book before you begin your website project. You will be glad you did.

I've been building websites for over eighteen years. *Intechnic*, the Chicago-based agency that I founded in 1997, is responsible for thousands of successful websites. We are also known for pioneering a results-driven approach in web development – something we call *"Results on Internet"* or ROI, which also happens to be the title of this book.

Over the years, I became increasingly frustrated with industry methods used in building websites. I also realized that most business people don't understand what it takes to produce, manage and market a successful website. Through their lack of experience they directly contribute to these failures by hiring the wrong web developer, micromanaging their work or taking an insufficient leadership role on the project. Poor decisions are made, important steps are overlooked and mistakes are made along the way, all resulting in websites that underperform and will never realize their true potential.

You don't need to be a web developer to guarantee the successful outcome of your website project. You must be informed and educated. You should understand what works and what doesn't. This book was written to help you make the right choices, manage the website project correctly, and avoid costly mistakes.

Read this book, and let it guide you toward achieving your own *Results on Internet*.

Andrew Kucheriavy

CEO and Founder of Intechnic

WHO SHOULD READ THIS BOOK?

If you own or manage a website, you should read this book! It gives you the building blocks to successfully produce, manage and market your website. Whether you are in management, marketing or IT, struggling with an underperforming website, or starting from scratch, this book will ensure your new website meets your business objectives.

This book is written in plain English. You don't need technical or creative skills to take full advantage of the recommendations in this book. It is not written for web developers, and by reading it you won't become one. However, you will learn everything you need to know to select the right web developer and properly manage and market your website to produce successful results.

HOW TO USE THIS BOOK?

I encourage you to read *Results On Internet* as you progress through your website project. The book is written in sequential order and is designed to guide you through each step to build an effective website. There are hundreds of recommendations and examples to apply to your project. Also included are mistakes to avoid. Keep this book handy, and use it as reference tool throughout your project to ensure the successful outcome.

This book is organized into three parts:

- **Part I** shows how to set proper business objectives for your website and helps you choose the right web developer for your project.

- **Part II** outlines the best methods to manage your project, maintain deadlines, operate within your budget and ensure that your website is built to meet and exceed your business goals.

- **Part III** provides methods to measure the performance of your website, offers marketing strategies to multiply traffic, and focuses on increasing your website's performance following its launch.

ABOUT THE AUTHOR

Andrew Kucheriavy is the Founder and CEO of *Intechnic*, a leading web design agency with locations and clientele in North America, Europe and Australia.

With eighteen years of experience and thousands of completed websites, Andrew's team has worked with some of the world's largest brands, including Google, Microsoft, Facebook, Disney and Sony.

Every day millions of people use websites developed by Andrew and his team. The "results driven" approach described in this book helped many companies worldwide reach their full potential.

For more information and downloadable materials, visit the book's website:

www.ResultsOnInternet.com

Part I:
Starting Your Website Project the Right Way

Today's websites are complex and sophisticated systems that can take many months and considerable resources to produce. Unfortunately, many websites are set up to fail before their production begins. Lack of proper research and planning can result in websites that do not deliver business results.

The purpose of Part I is not only to prevent disaster caused by underperforming websites, but also to set up a foundation into a powerful business tool that contributes to the growth and success of your business. This part of the book will guide you through every step—from setting proper business objectives to hiring the right web developer.

"Always do right – this will gratify some and astonish the rest."

Mark Twain

2

Chapter 1 – Choosing the Right Partner

A successful website can literally turn your business around. It can help boost sales, build awareness, enhance customer experience, reduce costs, improve workflow, and grow your business beyond your wildest dreams and expectations. On the other hand, a poorly designed website can cost your company more than your initial investment. It can cost you your job or lead to your business's failure.

No one person can successfully achieve all aspects of planning, design, development and maintenance of a modern business website. Having a reliable and experienced web development company by your side is critical to the success of your business. You want someone who is experienced, dependable and vested in your success. You want a reliable partner who will work hard as an extension of your team.

Finding the right company to build and manage a successful business website may not be easy, but if you invest the time and follow the advice laid out in *Results On Internet*, the efforts and research you employ initially will save you from headaches, disappointments and financial losses down the road.

Cutting Corners May Lead to Costly Mistakes

A web development company is one of the most important vendors you will ever hire for your business. Selecting the wrong web developer is an expensive, time-consuming and sometimes irreparable mistake. Businesses often underestimate the potential consequences of choosing the wrong web development partner. Worse, many settle for mediocre results. Consider this example:

Meet John and Jen. They work in the same industry and in similarly sized companies. They were each responsible for their respective company's website. A year ago, it became clear to the business management of both companies that their websites were underperforming and were ineffective in generating leads and in converting visitors into customers. John and Jen were each tasked with having their websites redesigned.

Jen took the time and followed the steps fully explained in this book to hire the best web developer her company could afford. After creating a comprehensive plan, Jen's company retained a web developer for $100K and worked closely with the team to build and market a website that was specifically designed to increase the company's sales within six months following its launch.

John took a different approach. Without doing his homework, he quickly looked at a couple of firms and selected a developer who offered a "simpler" solution at the lowest price of $10K. John thought the web developer he selected was adequate to achieve expected results.

After six months, Jen's new website had generated $500K in additional sales, where John's had generated an extra $10K. The difference in their website-generated sales was due to the sales and marketing performance of the websites. Remember, Jen took the time and effort to select the right web developer and worked hard with them to design an effective website that targeted John's ideal customer base. John used a hands-off approach, deferring completely to his sub-standard web developer, who gave him a generic, template-based website, which ultimately did not deliver expected results.

At first glance, after spending $10K for the website it might appear that John broke even. In reality, John's company suffered a significant loss. When Jon's lost sales are brought into the calculation and the cost of redesign by a better website developer, the actual loss is clear in the analysis below:

	Jen	John
Initial Investment (Cost)	($100,000)	($10,000)
Website-Generated Sales (Gross Revenue)	$500,000	$10,000
Return on Investment (ROI)	$400,000	$0
Cost of John's Lost Opportunity		($490,000)
Cost of John's New Website Upgrade		($100,000)
Net Profit (Loss)	$400,000	($590,000)

At this point Jen is enjoying a $400K return on investment, where John's haste has cost her company $140K. The difference in their bottom lines is a staggering $1 million. Beyond the monetary loss, John has realized an irretrievable loss of time, reputation, his company's stunted growth, and countless lost business opportunities.

What Type of Web Developer Is Right for Your Business?

Throughout the book I will be referring to your website partner as a "web developer". While terms "web developer" and "web designer" are often used interchangeably, there is a subtle but important difference between these roles. Web designers traditionally focus on the design and visual aspects of the website, where web developers also focus on the underlying technology in addition to web design. Often web designers come to web developers to help turn their vision into a technical reality. Since most websites today are complex systems that require a great deal of technical skill, I prefer the term "web developer" as a more encompassing description of the right vendor for your website.

Before you start your search for a web developer, it is important that you understand the fundamental differences among types of firms. If you don't understand how web developers are designed to operate, you risk hiring a firm that is not compatible with your project's needs. If you hire the wrong web developer, the company will not meet your expectations, and you will incur additional overhead—bridging gaps in qualifications and communication.

How would you like your website?
(You may only pick 2)

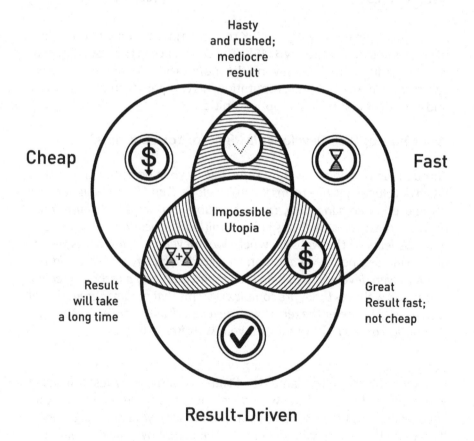

It is important to understand that there is no right or wrong web developer style or type. Your decision in selecting a company should be based on a number of factors, including the skill set and capabilities your business requires to reach its objectives, budget, and compatibility between the main contact of this firm and your project manager.

Let's compare types of web developers so that you can determine which one is the best match for your project:

Freelancers vs. Full-Service Agencies

Building a world-class website requires a team of experts with many areas of expertise. One person simply cannot do it all (or cannot excel in all areas). Why? Here is an example. Would you hire just one person to build an entire house for you from the ground up: obtaining permits, architectural design, foundation, plumbing, electrical, roofing, painting and decorating? Can you imagine the finished home at the hand of one individual attempting to fulfill all these elements of construction?

A world-class website, the kind of website that can actually achieve your business goals, is not a one-man job. It takes a small army of professionals, each with their specialty, working compatibly over an extended amount of time.

Successful business websites require business-minded project managers who can delegate projects effectively. They work with market research professionals who study the needs of your customers. The team often includes copywriters, who design customer-centric messaging based on conducted research. Usability experts create user-centric experiences. Following this phase, art directors and designers transform these plans into effective designs. Coders and programmers convert designs into a functional website, which, in turn, is tested by quality assurance teams. Driving traffic to a website is the job of Search Engine Optimization (SEO) and Social Media Optimization (SMO) specialists. System administrators ensure the website is fully operational around the clock, and account executives manage client communications. Some projects may require additional services from photographers, illustrators, videographers, voice-over artists, post-production specialists, animators, data entry personnel, mobile marketers, IT strategists and security experts. The list of specialists grows depending on the complexity of the project.

Similar to building a house, building a world-class website requires at least a dozen professionals, each hand picked for their expertise. Most projects require even more skill sets and resources. While it is feasible that one person can be functional in all of these areas, it is unlikely that this person will be an expert in all and able to multi-task effectively and efficiently. Professionals devote their careers perfecting one skill, and when they are placed in a team, the collective talents of these world-class skills blend into a world-class website creation.

Your website's production is only as strong as its weakest link. If you hire a single individual to complete your entire project, it is likely they will have to outsource some of the tasks. If they focus strictly on cost-effective measures and cut corners on talent and resources, the unfavorable result will fall on your shoulders. You may find yourself managing efforts in an industry where you lack expertise.

A classic conundrum is a company trying to improve its website by tasking an in-house "all-around website expert," who will be responsible for the entire website. Let's call him "Bob." Bob is tasked with all aspects of project management from inception to completion with little or no assistance from other staff or outside professionals. Would you trust Bob with all the vital functions of your business? Many businesses make this mistake.

It is wise to hire outside professionals for the expertise you don't have in-house, but don't do it blindly or hastily. Ensure clarity on courses of action in all phases of project management and full skill sets of all parties involved, including vendors and subcontractors.

Unlike freelancers, agencies are full-service strategic communication firms that employ a range of professionals with top-notch levels of expertise to achieve a successful website. A full-service agency should capably manage all your site development needs, allowing you the time to manage your company operations.

Working with an agency is typically more expensive. An agency has employees and a greater overhead, so more expense is incurred, but in doing so, you are hiring a managed and controlled team of professionals who should deliver professional results. Because agencies typically offer the greatest depth and range of experience in multiple disciplines, it is well worth the investment.

There is a third course of action. You may choose to act as the project manager of several freelancers. In this scenario, you will hire, supervise and trouble-shoot all aspects of the process. Project Management is a skill itself and requires sound communication, resource management and technical expertise.

The bottom line: Many brilliant people possess the above-mentioned skills, but cannot effectively create a world-class website on their own. If you want spectacular results, you must insist on stellar qualifications in all aspects of your web project. When Intechnic was in the start-up phase, I was building websites from ground up. I had skills in design and programming, and created websites from inception to launch, but I quickly learned that there were subject matter experts who were better qualified in specific areas. I started to delegate some phases of the process in order to grow with continued success. I had to find and retain these experts and then manage their efforts. As a result, our collective body of work has thrived, we have grown exponentially, and each new endeavor produces websites that deliver business results. The most important advice I can offer is to acquire an experienced team, where all members possess empirically superior skills.

Graphic Designers vs. Technology Firms

Have you ever heard people say they are more right-brain or left-brain thinkers? The theory of right-brain/left-brain dominance was presented in 1981 by Nobel Prize winner, Roger W. Sperry. His theory[1] claims that creativity, communication and marketing tend to be right-brain activities, while technology, analytical thinking, and programming are more left-brain functions.

---

[1] http://www.nobelprize.org/educational/medicine/split-brain/background.html

Although the theory was recently debunked[2], many professionals in the industry state that they are "more creative" or "more technical". The same applies to cultures within web development firms. There are "creative" companies that specialize in design, marketing and communications and "technical" companies that specialize in programming and technology implementation. This is largely due to companies expanding their teams by hiring people who think and perform like their leaders.

My company, Intechnic, began as a strictly "technical" company. As we expanded, we hired right-brain thinkers to improve our design and marketing capabilities.

Let me begin with creative companies for the following reason: with the growth of the Internet, many design firms that traditionally specialized in print became web designers overnight. Designing for print versus designing for the Web are quite different. What looks great on paper does not necessarily look and function well on a website. This is especially true for websites that require interactive, advanced functionality. Because of their extensive experience designing for static media (paper), many graphic designers struggle to master working with dynamic media (the Internet). They often lack the fundamentals for creating online interfaces and the technical skills required to create what cannot be done on paper. For example, a website designed with the "print" ideology may appear great on the graphic designer's printouts but will not display well on smart phones and tablets, and conversely, an e-commerce store might take on the appearance of a paper catalog. You can often identify such companies by their own websites. They focus on design and marketing and look more like online brochures as opposed to having interactive functionality.

The dirty little industry secret is that technical work is often outsourced to freelancers or partnering technology firms outside their clients' knowledge. Although a graphic design firm might fully understand the marketing and communication aspects of a website, behind the scenes the technical implementation may be outsourced.

---

[2] http://healthcare.utah.edu/publicaffairs/news/current/08-14-2013_brain _personality_traits.php

The technology-oriented companies often have the opposite problem. These companies usually specialize in the implementation of IT strategies, infrastructure and software development. IT companies have strong backgrounds in technology and programming, and unlike design companies, they are quick to incorporate the latest and greatest technology, but they are lacking in design and marketing skills. If a website was designed by a programmer (left-brain dominance), the website will function flawlessly but will not provide results in operational growth or increased revenue. You can recognize such companies by their own websites; they understand the functionality, but they don't know how to make the visceral or emotional connection with the visitor.

Technology companies also try to compensate for what they lack by outsourcing their design and marketing work to creative firms. The problem with this approach (and the converse as well) is that two separate teams work on your project, and the end result is directly related to how well these entities communicated. Unfortunately, communication is often lost in the abyss. Sometimes right-brain and left-brain differences are so vast that teams don't even understand each other, let alone produce effectively as a cohesive team.

Consider this analogy. Imagine having an artist (Susan) and a rocket scientist (Frank) working on John's new website. Jen tells the team she wants a world-class website. There is only one problem—Susan and Frank have different pictures of a world-class website. Susan is inspired by the opportunity to create a masterpiece. She already has visuals and contemplates styles, colors and aesthetics for a true work of art website. Meanwhile, Frank is thinking horsepower. His website must be powered by the latest propulsion system—exactly what will make it world-class in his opinion. Frank needs room for his big engine and is annoyed by Susan's "artsy stuff" bogging down his speed. They both want to do a good job for John, but their visions are polarized, and they struggle to find common ground. Susan's arguments are not well received by Frank because he insists the website should be powerful and functional (like NASA's rockets). Susan perceives the visitor's experience as joyful and aesthetically rich (like a museum piece). Eventually Susan or Frank will have to bridge this chasm, but, will compromise on both sides produce a website that is ugly or dysfunctional...or both?

Many creative and technology company partnerships do succeed. They establish effective lines of communication and deliver effective results. This level of communication often comes at a price, which is ultimately transferred to you. Prepare to pay for redundancies like multiple project managers and account executives on both sides. You will have two sets of managers working on the same phases of production, and the challenge of merging their work results in an additional expense because of these duplicated efforts.

Full service agencies have left-brain/right-brain issues as well, but they are on the same team and under the same management. They follow the same procedures and protocols, which facilitate cost-effective management and produces better results. In fact, that's the whole idea about full-service agencies. They specialize in cohesively managing creative and technical people under the same roof.

Local vs. Remote

The obvious benefit of a local vendor is that you can meet face-to-face with their team. Some people prefer to do business locally. It promotes a sense of confidence in the project to be able to view the on-site operation and meet staff.

There is added benefit to shopping for a vendor out of your geographical area in that the pool of candidates is virtually limitless. There may not be a web developer of the right caliber in your area. Do not settle for a company because it is geographically convenient. Websites are tools that allow your business to communicate with customers internationally. Website developers need to be specialists in communicating effectively. They must have online systems for project management, file sharing, customer feedback and project delivery, so close proximity to your company is not an issue.

While many prefer doing business face-to-face, the savvy business owner must make a choice based on the caliber of the developer he selects. Peace of mind is directly proportionate to the effectiveness of the team you select, regardless of location. My agency, for example, has experience delivering results throughout the U.S. and internationally, with no compromise in product or service quality.

If face-to-face communication is required, international travel is well worth the investment of both time and money.

Out of Country and Offshore Development

If your business is in North America, hire a developer in the U.S. or Canada. There is also great work done for U.S. firms by web developers in the U.K. and Australia.

When working with companies overseas, consider the following important factors: a firm in India may offer top-notch talent and a phenomenal price for your project, but these savings may accompany significant risks. Cultural differences are vast. If your target market is a customer base in Mumbai, an Indian firm would best serve your needs. Can a web developer in Mumbai create an experience that will cater to customers in Boston, New York, or Chicago? Do they fully understand the nuances of connecting with customers across cultures? The price of that question can be the cost of missed sales opportunities. Great websites are created by overseas companies that conform to the very letter of the contract, but depending on the product or service, they may not make a connection with American customers.

Another important issue often overlooked is legal protection. In the U.S. your company's interests are represented by the contract you sign, and you are protected by state and federal laws. If a legal matter arises in the business relationship, you have the option to defend your interests in court. This may not be feasible or affordable in another country. While there are services that offer international mediations, if litigation cannot be avoided, favorable settlement can be challenging.

When communicating internationally, there is the inconvenience of time zones. It can mean a wait of several hours to get responses or feedback.

Finally, language barriers and cultural differences can pose a problem in communication and writing style. If your website developer speaks English as a second language, it is imperative that the copy be written by an expert writer with a full command of English grammar and sentence structure. Stilted or awkwardly composed text clearly shows the reader that the copywriter does not have command of the English language. Poorly written copy (even the slightest nuance of incorrect wording) kills the credibility of the website, and worse, may offend or mislead the reader.

Ten Things Every Company Must Do Before Hiring a Web Developer

Listed below are solutions that address common mistakes that people make when starting their web developer search. Identifying these pitfalls before embarking on your research is key to your success:

1. **Research several companies.** Many companies rush into hiring the first web developer they find without due diligence. Sufficient time and effort must be invested in the *beginning* of the project to insure against lost time and money in the end.

2. **Define clear and specific business website objectives.** A business owner needs to be fully cognizant of what is expected from the website, or it will fail. "Building a better-designed website" is not a specific objective. Website objectives must always be specific and measurable.

3. **Create a thorough written RFP.** A request for proposal (RFP) helps you define and outline your business objectives. It communicates your objectives to prospective vendors and provides a benchmark for selecting the appropriate web developer. If an RFP is not in place, the selection process may be more time-consuming and less effective.

4. **Establish a full understanding of your web developer's methods of operation** (freelancer vs. agency, creative vs. technical, local vs. out of area). There must be a clear understanding of the variables in web developers and

details showing how these variables may affect all aspects of the project. If clarity is lacking on this level, the results may not be cost-effective and efficient, and may cause additional recuperative overhead.

5. **Retain a developer with a full range of qualifications and expertise.** Building a successful business website requires a team of experts across multiple fields. Your website is only as strong as its weakest link. Hiring someone who lacks the proper expertise or experience will result in either the project's failure or additional resources and time in reparation.

6. **Invest sufficient time and research in making this important decision after fully determining all qualification criteria.** Making a decision purely on a proposal while overlooking other important factors (such as web developer's own website or recommendations) may result in hiring a firm that is not the best match for your project. You should always set your own criteria for objective evaluation and an effective decision making process.

7. **Hire a company that has a broad range of specialties.** Beware of a web development company that specializes in just one or two industries and builds canned and generic websites. Many such companies are "one-trick ponies" that use templates and offer cookie-cutter solutions.

8. **Ask for recommendations.** How can you be sure that the experience promised in the presentation will be the same after the contract is signed? Your prospective web developer's previous clients will agree to provide references if their experience went well.

9. **Get it in writing.** A written contract protects both parties and helps ensure there are no surprises or potential disasters as you embark on this working relationship. A contract is necessary to prevent exposure to risks.

10. **Budget appropriately to your expectations.** While the budget is a major concern, it should not be the main criterion for selecting your web developer. The old adage is true: "You get what you pay for." Do not make your decision solely on price, but hire the best professional within the constraints of your budget.

Chapter 2 – Defining Business Requirements

Long before you choose a web developer, the fate of your website is determined. Knowing your organization and setting clear goals are prerequisites for success. There must be clarity in your goals and desired results from your website, or it will fail.

Setting S.M.A.R.T. Business Objectives

Saying "I want a website" is like saying, "I want a house" or "I want a car." This mistake was illustrated in the previous example of John's experience. Would John ever shop this way for a house or a car? Probably not, yet many managers make this hasty mistake their business websites.

Your website, like any other business tool, must consistently produce a Return on Investment (ROI). A great website will not only pay for itself through the increase in traffic, conversions and sales, but it will also help your business grow and prosper. Unless you are building a website simply for the sake of having a website, there must be a clear objective in place.

John learned the hard way that simply stating he needed a business website was not an adequate objective. To set a business objective you must determine the ways your website can grow your business, enhance customer satisfaction, improve workflow, support your brand, and reduce expenses. Be as specific as possible.

A good test for your website's business objectives is the S.M.A.R.T. Model, which is often used for goal setting in project management. S.M.A.R.T. is a mnemonic for Specific, Measurable, Attainable, Relevant, and Timely. This Model guides you to in setting goals in a way that promotes achievement.

SMART Business Objectives

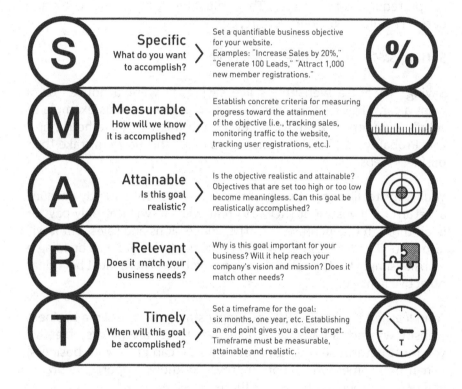

Specific
What do you want
to accomplish?

Set a quantifiable business objective
for your website.
Examples: "Increase Sales by 20%,"
"Generate 100 Leads," "Attract 1,000
new member registrations."

Measurable
How will we know
it is accomplished?

Establish concrete criteria for measuring
progress toward the attainment
of the objective (i.e., tracking sales,
monitoring traffic to the website,
tracking user registrations, etc.).

Attainable
Is this goal
realistic?

Is the objective realistic and attainable?
Objectives that are set too high or too low
become meaningless. Can this goal be
realistically accomplished?

Relevant
Does it match your
business needs?

Why is this goal important for your
business? Will it help reach your
company's vision and mission? Does it
match other needs?

Timely
When will this goal
be accomplished?

Set a timeframe for the goal:
six months, one year, etc. Establishing
an end point gives you a clear target.
Timeframe must be measurable,
attainable and realistic.

If we go back to Jen's website objective—simply creating a website, the S.M.A.R.T. objective would be "I need a website that will increase my sales by $60K in 12 months by targeting my ideal customers."

✳ *Download: You may download the S.M.A.R.T. Objectives Worksheet at* www.ResultsOnInternet.com *to see how John defined new goals for His website. You can also use the same template to set and test your own website's objectives.*

Deciding on the Budget

Asking how much a website will cost is similar to asking how much a house will cost. You cannot answer the question without evaluating a myriad of factors: How many stories and bedrooms do you want? What materials would you like to use? Do you own the land?

The cost of your website is ultimately determined by its size, complexity and essential components as required by your business objectives. For example, a website that requires custom photography, video production and copywriting will obviously cost more than a template-based website with stock photography. Remember, this is a service industry so there is no fixed "widget price" unless you are purchasing a DIY (do-it-yourself) website which should not be considered by any serious business.

Most web developers use an hourly rate to calculate the cost of the project but quote a fixed price. Many factors determine web developers' prices: location, size, reputation, level of experience and the talents they employ. Presently, in the United States rates are as low as $50/hour from freelancers to over $300/hour from some of the largest and well-established agencies.

Hourly rate alone is meaningless. You must determine skill level, quality and efficiency of the developer. A developer who charges $75 per hour may provide a quote of 10 hours for the same task that would be performed in less than 2 hours by a $200 per hour developer. A vendor should not be selected solely based on rates. An hourly rate is not the slide rule of quality.

How Much Should You Pay?

Hire the best web developer you can afford.

If you are serious about your business and want a website that can achieve your business objectives, you need to retain the services of the best professionals. Their expertise will deliver proven business results, and they will produce a fast return on investment.

Do not cut corners. You do not bargain-hunt when you seek the services of a heart surgeon or an attorney. You hire the best professional or service to achieve your goal. The analogy is clear. A top cardiologist can save the life of a patient. A top web developer can save the life of your under-achieving website. Every business wants a world-class website. Every business wants to be the best in their industry and retain the best tools and services that will increase their sales, improve customer satisfaction and enhance their brand.

The budget is an important issue, but it should not be the bottom-line criterion for retaining a vendor as important as a web developer.

What Can You Expect to Get with Your Budget

As previously stated, no two websites are the same, so you cannot put the same price tag on all websites. However, you need to understand what you can expect to get with a certain budget.

To learn more about budget ranges and what they offer, look at price ranges of various websites in the United States at the time of the writing of this book.

Under $5,000

This budget is generally considered entry level and is offered by freelancers or small teams. You can expect a "basic" website that will use stock photography, often based on templates and with limited design and programming. Websites in this budget typically look and function like ordinary websites and appear cloned because they often are.

This budget is often insufficient to create measureable results. A website in this budget will include basic features: an image slider, a contact form and a blog, but not much more. This budget would typically include a free basic Content Management platform like WordPress with little or no customization.

Bottom Line: you will probably have to provide marketing and business direction as well as content for a site in this budget. Expect to closely manage the vendor almost to the point of "designing your own website." This budget is often insufficient to achieve a successful business website for a company of any size.

$5,000 - $15,000

This budget typically allows room for a more custom and better-equipped website. Most small design firms offer this caliber of websites. With this budget you can count on design that is more tailored to you; however, it would still rely on stock photography and somewhat generic templates.

This budget may include some custom functionality, such as limited interactive features, but this will be a "hands on" experience where you work integrally with the developer through all stages of the project.

Case study: John's initial website was built in this price range (his budget was $10,000). The website was produced by a three person team: project manager, designer and programmer. The primary focus was on the visuals, and there was no budget for market research of any kind. With John's hand-off approach and without solid understanding of his business or customers' needs, the web development team produced a website that was generic, and it did not target John's customers. Six months after the launch the website failed to attract any significant leads or convert them into customers.

Bottom line: the web developer may be well equipped to produce your website, but won't necessarily be knowledgeable about your business, so you will have to fill in gaps in marketing and business direction. This budget is also insufficient to properly support and promote your brand, product or service on a large scale. This budget may produce a website that is inferior to your competition.

$15,000 - $30,000

In this range, you can expect a bit more handholding. This is a good starting range for most small business websites. This budget will support limited market and competitive research, which essentially means your web developer will look at your competitors and attempt to improve on *their* websites. This is also a good starting range for e-commerce websites or those designed to engage visitors and convert them into customers. This budget range allows for custom design that matches your business needs and extensive programming. You may also have a copywriter to produce content.

Bottom line: you will get a fair to a good website with this budget (one that is perfectly acceptable to most small businesses), but the results still may not be adequate to win the hearts and wallets of your customers.

$30,000 - $50,000

In this range, you can expect a robust website that is built specifically to meet your business objectives. Larger corporate websites or sites with advanced functionality often fall into this range. You will probably have a team of a dozen professionals working on your project. This budget will adequately serve a larger, more established firm or agency, where a project manager will oversee the efforts of the team members. Expect solid marketing and business advice, art direction, usability testing and proper quality assurance. The design will be custom and may include logo design, branding and complete copywriting. You can also expect interactive and dynamic features, a customized Content Management System, integration with third party APIs, such as your CRM and Inventory Management.

Bottom line: you will see a unique project specification detailing the thorough plan of action. You can expect substantial leadership and direction from your developer throughout the project. Many corporate entities and online retailers have their websites built in this price range.

$50,000 - $100,000

In this range, you can expect the Cadillac of web design—a top-notch performer, a website that is specifically designed to blow your competition out of the water. You can expect it all: custom photography, video production, responsive design, SEO, social media strategy, and more. Websites built in this price range often stand out and win awards and recognition if they are designed properly. More importantly, your website show significant improvement in performance. It will generate maximum leads and sales, and it will represent the company in the best possible professional manner.

A website in this budget range should be built with the highest standards. It should incorporate thorough market research, customer interviews, and a solid plan to achieve your business objectives.

Case study: Jen and her team were initially hesitant to spend $100,000 on a website when all other quotes were much lower. They did, however, see the value of working with a large, experienced agency with a proven track record and a team of some of the best professionals in the industry. The agency demonstrated an in-depth understanding of the business, and it conducted market research, customer interviews, and competitive analysis to create a website designed to blow Jen's competition out of the water. Over a dozen team members worked on the project, including a business-oriented project manager, a marketing MBA, a copyrighter, a usability expert, a photographer, a cameraman, a post production specialist, an SEO expert, an SMO expert, as well as several designers and programmers. Six months following its launch, the new website helped to establish a strong presence in the industry while attracting new leads (including former clients of competitors with weaker online presences) and converting them into Jen's customers. The website generated a quick return on investment.

Bottom line: if you are a corporate entity, a retailer, distributor or manufacturer who wants to dominate the competitive landscape, you must be in this budget range. This is the budget where the right team can produce a website that is a guaranteed game changer.

$100,000+

This is the budget of a unique, ambitious, one-of-a-kind website that operates on a world scale and has national or global recognition. This budget may include multi-lingual websites for large international corporations and world-class brands, large online retailers, and custom-built social networks or major online service providers. If your website's target audience or sales numbers are measured in millions, your budget will be in hundreds of thousands or millions.

Very few web development firms have proven themselves in successfully building and managing these types of websites. These high-tier projects require teams of dozens (sometimes hundreds) of world-class professionals that few web development firms can bring to the table.

Bottom line: in this range, the sky is the limit. If you are a Fortune 500 company that wishes to dominate on a state, national or international level, or if you want to build the next Facebook, expect your budget to be in the hundreds of thousands or millions, and reach for the stars.

Chapter 3 – Writing an Effective Request for Proposal (RFP)

A Request for Proposal (RFP) is a document that is written by your company and provided to prospective web developers. An RFP is an invitation to bid on your project, and it outlines your website requirements, existing challenges, and business objectives.

There are three reasons why a written RFP is strongly recommended. I call them the three C's of RFPs: clarify, communicate and compare.

1) Clarify. The RFP is a process that facilitates design and definition of your business objectives and requirements. By writing an RFP, you will compile thoughts, outline your needs and ensure that all aspects of the project are detailed thoroughly.

2) Communicate. The RFP clearly communicates business goals, objectives and requirements to prospects. It also provides a paper trail and avoids misunderstandings.

3) Compare. Finally, the RFP creates a thorough point of reference for comparing and contrasting all proposals. By providing all candidates with the same RFP, proposal comparisons are easily done.

An effective RFP should be worded clearly and directly. Its purpose is to provide specific business goals. Compose the RFP with clarity, and ensure that the content details the objectives, deadlines and budget.

Many experienced web development companies offer specialized worksheets and questionnaires that are designed to aid in this process. I advise that you request these documents in order to shed more light on their plan for your project. The framework in their form's content will reveal the web developer's experience and capabilities. If a web developer doesn't have a procedure at the outset of the project, or if they do not pose a series of questions, it should raise some red flags about the distinction and quality of this organization.

✳ **Download:** *You may download the following website RFP template as an example for your project:* www.ResultsOnInternet.com. *I've used John's project as a template for his improved website.*

The following outline will help you put together an effective RFP. Start with your general company information, and then focus on the project and business needs. Skip any items that are not applicable to your project.

Business Overview

- Describe your business. Describe the products and/or services that you offer and whether you market to other businesses, consumers or both.

- Describe your industry.

- Who are some of your major competitors? List their website URLs.

- What sets you apart from the competition? What is the competitive edge that makes your products or services unique, i.e., price point, features, value?

- Do you already have a website? If yes, what is the URL, and what are the known problems or issues with it? What do you like and dislike about it? Can you provide visitor analytics?

Website Business Objectives

- Why is the project necessary?

- List S.M.A.R.T. business objectives for the website. Test each objective against the S.M.A.R.T. model and provide details (see the previous section).

- What is your budget for the project? You may be reluctant to disclose this, but an approximate budget will help web developers propose optimal and realistic solutions within the confines of the budget. You may also learn your budget is not adequate for your expectations. It is better to include at least an "up to" number or a ballpark range. If you are seeking a true professional, fully disclose this information with your expectations. They also want to know that you are serious about the project and that you will see it through to completion. If you begin the relationship with a forthright delivery, it will help to cement the long-term, positive relationship with your developer.

- What is your timeframe for the project? Include the deadline for the proposal submission, expected turnaround time for decision, and anticipated start and completion dates. Be sure to indicate any critical (hard-stop) deadlines in the project time line.

Target Audience and Experience

- Who is your target audience? Describe your ideal customer. What are your ideal customer's demographics?

- What actions do you want users to take when visiting your site? Examples: make a purchase, request information, call, register, sign-up for a newsletter.

- How do you want your audience to perceive your brand? Describe the image you want the user to identify with your brand (reputable, dependable, innovative, prestigious, fun, cutting edge).

- Why should your potential customers choose to do business with you? Why should your customers care about what you have to offer? What are the benefits to them? How do your products or services help improve their lives?

- Is there a common problem or an industry pain that your products or services help solve? What is your solution?

- What is the single most important message your website visitors should take away? It is your most important BIG IDEA.

- How can this message be made believable? What support can you provide to lend credence to this message? Are there any visuals, charts, analogies, metaphors, testimonials or any other data, props or tools that can be used to project credibility and enhance your message?

Website Requirements

- Color scheme: Do you have corporate or preferred colors? Do you have a branding guide? If yes, include it with the RFP.

- Are there any existing assets that should be used in the new website (logo, branding guidelines, screen mockups, copywriting, photography, videos)?

- What are some websites that inspire you? Describe what you like about them. Give examples (provide URLs), and be specific.

- When you close your eyes and visualize your site, what do you see?

- What do you dislike on websites and want to avoid? Give examples (provide URL), and be specific.

- Are there any specific functions or features that you would like to see on your website? Examples: product catalog, shopping cart, mailing list, user registration, blog, information request form.

- Are you going to be managing the content for the website? If yes, how will the content be provided? What type of data do you have? How much content do you have?

- Are you going to be managing the updates to the website in-house? If yes, how often would you make updates? Do you have any requirements for the Content Management System (CMS)?

- What type and depth of ongoing support and maintenance will you need or expect the web developer to provide?

- Are there any technical requirements or limitations (hosting considerations, database, programming language)? You may want to confer with your IT Department.

- Are there any legal or compliance requirements such as HIPAA, PCI or accessibility (508)?

- Do you need a responsive (mobile-friendly) support or your website?

- Will you be managing the hosting of the website, or will you require the web developer to provide or assist with hosting services?

- Will you be managing the marketing and Search Engine Optimization (SEO) of the website, or do you require the web developer to provide or assist with marketing and SEO?

- Are there any other issues that should be taken into consideration? List any concerns, challenges or limitations that you would like to be addressed.

Proposals Requirements and Vendor Guidelines

- List any requirements or expectations you may have for the companies that will be bidding on your project (areas of expertise, capabilities, background and history, staff, support process, references, years of experience).

- List any special requirements you may have for the proposal, including how and when it needs to be submitted. Include a deadline for the proposal submissions.

- Include explanation of how the decision making process will be made. This will allow web developers to tailor the proposals to address your concerns and requirements.

- Who is going to be the main point of contact in your organization? If there are two or more contacts with specific roles, list all names. Also list third parties or subcontractors, if applicable.

- In the event that prospective web developers have additional questions, include detailed contact information as well as instructions on how to submit questions.

Chapter 4 – Searching for Web Developers

Once you complete the Request for Proposal (RFP), you are ready to start your search process for the right web developer. Assemble a short list of no more than five to seven candidates. This section will focus on methods to select your candidates for this short list.

Establish your goals, and clearly convey them to your candidates. If your goals are vague, go back to the previous step and review your RFP. You must have clarity and certainty at this point to ensure your project is successful.

Setting Baseline Qualification Criteria

During your search, you are sure to meet hundreds of web developers. The best way to determine the strongest candidates is to establish baseline qualification criteria. Without these criteria in place, you cannot proceed.

The following worksheet will help you evaluate web developers before approaching them with your RFP. Give each potential vendor a score on a scale from 0 to 10 for each of the following criteria, and select five to seven companies with the highest scores.

✳ **Download:** *The Web Developer Score Card is available for download as an Excel spreadsheet from* www.ResultsOnInternet.com.

How Effective Is the Web Developer's Own Website?

If a web developer's own website doesn't impress you, move on. If you have any doubts, move on. If their website doesn't make you excited about working with them, move on. The effectiveness of a developer's website is one of the most reliable indicators of their potential.

Points to consider when reviewing web developers' websites:

- Do you need what they are selling? You do not want just any website; you want a business tool that produces business

31

results. A company that promises "modern design," "latest technology" and "interactive experience" will deliver just that. Is that all you need to achieve your business objectives? No.

- How effective are their presentations? Go with your first impression (as most customers will when viewing your website). Did they "wow" you? Did they stand out from the competition? If yes, how did they accomplish this? Pay attention to their message delivery (taglines, visuals, videos, etc.). If they have achieved this on their website, it is likely they will do the same for you.

- Poor grammar, spelling mistakes, and typos are not acceptable. Any reputable web development firm works with copywriters and editors who ensure empirically perfect copy and effective message delivery.

- Look for components of their website that are out of order: inconsistencies, layouts in disarray, broken links—anything missing or out of place. If there are technical issues, it may be an indicator of poor QA (quality assurance) in the web developer's company.

How Diverse Is the Web Developer's Portfolio?

Beware of companies that have a portfolio with no variation in style and have completed projects for only one industry. If you see several websites in the portfolio that look similar, there is a strong possibility the web developer could be a one-trick pony. Don't hire a firm that uses templates and offers cookie-cutter solutions. You want a web developer who approaches each project based on the business needs of the particular customer and designs websites that promote companies with a dynamic style.

Your business needs individual and specialized attention. The web developer must go the extra mile to deliver a unique, innovative style that will blow away the competition.

32

Does the Web Developer Have the Experience in the Type of the Website I Need?

All websites are not created equal. Just as websites differ by their business objectives, purpose, and function, the skills and expertise required to build successful websites differ as well. If you need a corporate website, someone with experience in a single-faceted, social network development is probably not a good match. However, if you are developing a social network, retain a developer with that skill set.

Following are the basic website types to help you find the web developer who specializes in the website you need.

- **Corporate B2B / Corporate B2C** websites are designed to represent companies in the promotion of their services and/or products.

- **E-commerce and retail** websites are designed to effectively sell products online and maximize conversions.

- **Consumer and direct marketing** websites are designed to generate consumer loyalty and to support consumer brands.

- **Promotional micro sites** are typically smaller or temporary websites that supplement a company's primary website to promote specific products, services or offerings.

- **Entertainment** websites are designed to create engaging and long-lasting experiences for films, TV and music.

- **Online services** are websites that provide valuable services (paid or free) to their members.

- **Social networks and community** websites offer a variety of ways to interact, collaborate and share common interests.

- **Information portals** are directories, catalogs or repositories that offer search, sort and organization of large amounts of data.

- **Enterprise intranets** / extranets are internal (secure) websites that provide information exchange and collaboration between offices, dealers, vendors, affiliates, and employees in the field.

- **Custom web applications** are uniquely designed online programs that feature advanced functionality.

Is the Web Developer Showing a Proven Track Record?

Does the web developer have a client list published on their website? Do you recognize any of their clients?

Are their existing clients similar to your company, or do they cater to a similar customer base? Are there case studies of past projects? Do they provide client testimonials with names and contact information?

Large companies tend to have very strict and refined processes for hiring vendors, so if well-established companies appear in the web developer's portfolio, the web developer has been vetted by these companies.

Also, check for performance awards, recognitions, endorsements or memberships in professional associations. This connotes success in their work.

How Long Has the Web Developer Been in Business?

A proven track record is an important indicator, but when you factor in the age of the company, you have a better perspective of how well established they are and their level of experience in the industry.

Web development (and technology in general) is a very competitive, volatile industry. A developer must continuously learn, innovate and ratchet up the bar in cutting-edge technology, or they are lost in the shuffle. Most web development firms fail within two years.

Any web development company in business for more than five years has proven itself. Companies that are in the industry 10 years or more are considered seasoned veterans. They survived the infamous dot-com bubble and other volatile periods. They are most likely going to remain in existence and can offer you more experience and longer-term support than younger firms.

On the other hand, many young, talented firms should not be overlooked. They have demonstrated amazing short-term success and exhibit multi-talented teams. However, as any seasoned business professional knows, short-term success does not necessarily translate to staying on top of their game. Hire a company whose website reflects its success and has a sustained history of satisfied customers with unwavering quality and delivery.

What's Wrong with Them?

You need to scrutinize the company closely on several levels. If there are traces of negativity, if suspicion about their reputation is raised in your mind, or if their content or images are incongruous, it pays to stop and analyze further. The truth is—no one is perfect. There are always areas in which a company can improve. The goal is to research your prospective vendor thoroughly, so there are no game-stoppers that will impact your project.

Look for negative feedback; check the company's Better Business Bureau and YELP ratings, or pull up their DUNS profile. If you are working with a freelancer through a facilitating service, like Elance.com, check that they have extensive positive feedback, substantial earnings and a large number of high-caliber, completed jobs. It is safe to use the vetting approach with freelancers as though you were buying from them on eBay.

One negative comment doesn't necessarily mean you should automatically disqualify the web developer. Some unreasonable customers cannot be satisfied. Scrutinize the detail behind the negative comment: what really happened, and how was the issue resolved. Beware of patterns (trends) in complaints from different sources. This should raise a red flag that this firm has service issues.

Can the Web Developer Handle All of Your Needs? Are They the Right Fit?

When shopping for a developer, focus on the companies that demonstrate capabilities in all components of the project. For example, if you are certain you will host your own website and that you do not need SEO, you will not be concerned if the web developer offers these services. However, if at some point you see the need for hosting service, the burden falls on you to acquire and manage these resources.

RFI (Request for Information)

When hiring a web developer (or any vendor for that matter), some companies submit a Request for Information (RFI). This pre-RFP document poses the same questions to all candidates, and when collected, it provides a structured side-by-side comparison tool. This enables you to narrow your pool of candidates in a controlled and timesaving manner.

Similar to an RFP, the idea is to put all your questions to potential vendors in a single document and have each vendor complete the form. Then, based on the responses, the choice will be clear as to whom you want to submit an RFP. Think of the RFI as a pre-screening step that will facilitate a smaller pool of the best candidates in a controlled and structured way. This is a huge time saver.

Asking for Recommendations

The best way to begin your search for a web developer is to request recommendations from colleagues. Referrals are always a much lower risk, so exhaust that route before you begin cold call research.

Ask the source of the referral lots of questions, such as:

- Did the web developer fully meet expectations?

- Did the website achieve stated business objectives?

- Was the project completed on time and on budget?

- Would they hire this web developer again?

- How responsive and reliable was the web developer? Was the working relationship pleasant?

- Ask for positive and negative aspects of the experience. When embarking on a large, complex project, there will be inevitable problems at some point, so inquire what steps this developer took to remedy the issue.

Competitive Research

Do you have a competitor whose website blows your socks off? If so, ask for the name of their developer. If you are not comfortable pursuing a competitor for this information, research tangent markets or geographic areas outside your direct interest? Seek companies that sell slightly different products or companies that cater to a different demographic. For example, if your website needs to serve as a retail clothing sales platform, look at retail clothing websites that cater to a slightly different audience, but remain within your industry. If your business targets other businesses, look for other B2B sites.

There are several advantages to conducting this specialized and detailed research. A developer who has done an outstanding job in your industry is likely to repeat this success for you.

If you hire the same company that created a website for your competition, there is no need for concern if you have a Non-Disclosure Agreement (NDA) in place. The developer's projects are kept completely separate, and everything outside the publicly accessible sections of the website is kept strictly confidential. You may want to ask the web developer about their procedures and protocols where it pertains to working with customers who are direct competitors. Most reputable firms have an ethics code that requires them to notify their existing clients; however, the developer will accept your business and take every precaution to protect the confidential information of all clientele.

The idea above applies to companies outside your industry as well. Have you seen other business websites that look great and perform well, and in your opinion are effective in message delivery?

Researching Competitor's Web Developer

There are several methods to acquire this information:

- Look for credits. Many web development companies place their credit in the footer of the website.

- Right-click on the webpage. Select "View Page Source." Search for "Author" in the code, and look for company name. Some web developers insert credits in the website's HTML.

- Also check the WHOIS lookup of the website's domain name (http://www.networksolutions.com/whois/), where you can get the name of the hosting company. However, the host may not be the company that developed the website.

- Finally, many web developers have case studies for their projects or at least a client list. Google "company +case study" or "company +web design" to see if a specific web developer's website appears in the search results.

Using Search Engines and Directories

Google remains a dynamic tool for conducting research. For a list of local web developers, you can always search for phrases like "Chicago web development" or "Boston web design" and browse the first couple pages of search results. This approach also reveals their effectiveness in Search Engine Optimization (SEO). If you can find them through a search engine, chances are they can do the same for your business.

The opposite is also true—many companies that you consider to have strength in SEO may lack skill sets in other major aspects of website development. Explore thoroughly, and analyze each candidate for all areas of expertise necessary for your project. If a web developer's own site is not engaging, it is a given that your targeted base will not engage in your website either. Eliminate them from you developer candidate list immediately.

Finally, search engine results vary over time, and based on your geographical location search results will evolve as well. The fields of web design and web development are equally competitive. If you limit your search only to the first page of results, you may miss some great companies. Filter by different criteria, and review the first several pages (a minimum of fifty search results), and look closer at those companies.

There are specialized websites and directories that list well-known and respected web development companies and agencies. One such directory is www.sortfolio.com. If you are seeking freelancers, check out www.elance.com, www.freelance.com and www.odesk.com.

Chapter 5 – Hiring the Right Web Developer

At this stage, you should have a short list of between five and seven web development companies that meet your baseline criteria. It is now time to contact these companies, request proposals, and carefully select the one that is the perfect fit for you.

The worksheet provided below will assist you in evaluating each web developer on your short list. I have designed the worksheet in three sections: Communications, Referrals and the Proposal. Your task is to give each prospective vendor a score between 0 and 10 for each line item (0 being the poorest and 10 being the best). The worksheet will provide clear indications of which prospects should be in your final pool of candidates.

✳ **Download:** *You may download and complete the Web Developer Score Card as an Excel spreadsheet from:* www.ResultsOnInternet.com

Communications: Pay Attention to Early Signs

When you approach a prospective web developer, it is in your best interest to be thorough in your communication. Since communication is a two-way street, you have to convey your exact expectations carefully. Detail your goals explicitly, and state what you expect from the website. Proceed only when you have a mutual understanding.

At this point, do not offer all the specifics. It is web developers' job to ask questions and offer solutions. You can then assess the responsiveness and expertise of each web developer based on each presentation.

After you have provided your goals, they will create a proposal. Their proposal needs to outline clearly how they can assist in reaching your objectives.

Your initial communication with prospective web developers gives great insight into the energy they will put into your project. Communicate,

communicate, and communicate more by phone, e-mails and face-to-face. Ask questions and pay attention to nuance in their responses. This is your opportunity to screen thoroughly in making your decision.

Score each vendor (using a table or chart) on a scale from 0 to 10 for each of the following criteria:

- Do they have a thorough understanding of your business objectives? Do they demonstrate an in-depth understanding of your needs?

- Have they identified and offered adequate solutions to your specific issues and concerns?

- If you already have a website, have they identified shortcomings and recommended areas of improvement? Were they able to think on their feet, show abundant energy and readily offer appropriate analysis and solutions?

- Did they appear professional, credible and knowledgeable? Did they represent themselves as true experts in the field of web design and development

- Did they agree with everything you said, or did they offer alternative courses of action? Were they resolute in their suggestions even if you posed resistance?

- Did they communicate clearly? Did you achieve a mutual understanding? Were they attentive to your comments and ideas? Are you able to envision a productive relationship with them and realize a successful product?

- Were they informative and generous with preliminary ideas? Did they offer innovative and exciting insights that are compatible with your goals? Did they satisfactorily answer all your questions?

- Did they ask you the right questions, and were the inquiries relevant and insightful? A web developer who has few or no questions will most likely not produce great results.

- Did they show a process or methodology (worksheets, questionnaires, interviews) to help assess your needs and ensure you have the same vision? Most reputable firms do have processes in place to achieve this goal.

- What is their turnaround time for returning your calls and e-mails? Are they prompt with feedback to your questions? A good indicator of their future availability throughout the project is their responsiveness during the sales process.

Sending Out Requests for Proposal

If you feel that any of the companies on your short list failed the initial communication test, eliminate these candidates, regardless of how impressive their proposal appears. You don't even need to request a proposal. Effective communication is paramount to any project. Failure to communicate clearly at the beginning is a red flag that communication problems will most likely continue for the duration of the project.

Send the remaining candidates your RFP and be sure to indicate the deadline for the proposal and full submission instructions. Also, include detailed contact information for follow-up inquiries.

Finally, make yourself available to your prospects if they have questions. You are equally responsible for providing pertinent information a web developer candidate needs to complete the proposal. Give all potential candidates an equal playing field by answering all questions promptly and diligently. If some questions are better answered by members of your team, make the connection so the developer's questions are answered thoroughly and accurately.

Protecting Your Confidential Information

In "Chapter 6 – Executing a Written Contract" we discuss the importance of protecting your confidential information before your project begins. If your project or RFP contains any proprietary or sensitive information (such as a unique idea, business methodologies, trade secrets, etc.), you must request a Non-Disclosure Agreement (NDA) from each vendor before disclosing any details or sending your RFP.

The NDA protects you by prohibiting use and disclosure of your confidential information outside your working relationship. Many vendors have their own NDAs, but it is wise to have your attorney prepare an NDA that fully protects you.

Asking for References and Examples of Work

While prospective web developers are working diligently on their proposals, ask for their references. You should check the references for valuable information about your prospective web developer. Experience, reputation and a positive track record are three essential attributes that should factor into your decision. It is in your best interest to assemble a full profile on the company so you can make an educated decision.

When you request examples of work from your prospects, ask for a diversified portfolio. You want to see a broad spectrum of their work so you can compare and contrast their results. You want be confident that the vendor has the expertise and the skill set to fully achieve your specific business results and that the company is not a one-trick pony. Reviewing the varieties of their work provides certain exposure to subtle and stark distinctions in diverse businesses. Examples of their work should parallel your vision.

If they cannot provide references, or if they do not have at least three websites for your review, beware. Any established, reputable developer should be able to fill this request. Contacting the references can be done immediately or following your determination that this is the vendor you want to offer the job. Devote adequate time to this step. It may be time-consuming, but it should be the preliminary and major contributing factor to your decision.

When you contact a prospect's clients, do not limit your inquiries to their satisfaction level of the website. Ask how the developer handled the unexpected issues along the way, how they resolved the problems, and was their approach collaborative. Get a full assessment of the developer's efforts from start to finish.

On a separate sheet or table, score each vendor on a scale from 0 to 10 for each of the following criteria:

Portfolio Overview

- Were examples/references provided relevant or similar to your business objectives?

- Was the vendor quick to offer references? Was there any reluctance or resistance?

- Were you impressed with the examples and websites they provided? Were there any issues or aspects of websites they produced that were a cause for concern (outdated or ineffective websites, lacking functionality, etc.). These website are supposed to represent the web developer's best work.

References Evaluations

Ask each of the reference contacts the following questions and score their answers with your notes:

- Did the vendor fully meet their expectations? Did the website achieve their business objective?

- Was the website completed on time and on budget?

- Would they hire this web developer again? Why or why not?

- How responsive and reliable was the web developer to this client? Were they congenial and pleasant throughout the process?

- Were there unanticipated charges?

- Were there problems that were directly caused by vendor? How were problems addressed in general (regardless of origin or cause)?

Evaluating Website Proposals and Making the Decision

You should have received multiple proposals from different web development companies. It is always a good idea to schedule a phone call or a meeting with each web developer to review and discuss the proposal in detail. This provides the perfect opportunity for you to examine and explore all aspects of this company and the proposal. You may also request information about a Content Management System (CMS), examples of additional websites and any other useful documentation.

Your decision should be based on the compilation of the prospect's presentation, their overall response time to requests for information or communication and the collective feedback from references. They may have a stellar presentation, but if they are slow to respond and lack good references, can you be sure they can walk the walk?

Your chances of selecting the best developer for your website will greatly improve if you make your decision as objectively as possible. You must examine all criteria of the presentations. While the proposal may remain the primary decisive factor, it should not be the only one. Do not make your decision solely based on the quoted price (we will cover this separately).

As everyone's proposal will vary in levels of detail, price and style, you may find it difficult to compare proposals side by side. You will see a wide range of styles, from inspiring designs and creative taglines to technical jargon and marketing plans. The following worksheet will help you parallel and extract the important information and objectively evaluate each of the proposals despite the differences in the presentation style.

On a separate sheet or table, score each proposal on a scale from 0 to 10 (0 being the worst, and 10 being the best) for each of the following criteria:

✳ *Download: You may download the Proposal Score Card as an Excel spreadsheet at* www.ResultsOnInternet.com

- Did you like the proposal and the presentation? Your overall first impression is very important. A well-written proposal is in many ways like a well-designed website. After all, a proposal's objective is to sell web developer's services to you, just as your website will sell your products and services to your customers. If a web developer has effective sales presentations, they probably have a solid grasp on sales and marketing, which are necessary disciplines to build a successful business website.

- Does the proposal accurately, clearly and completely identify your business objectives? Did the vendor fully understand your requirements and address issues effectively?

- Does the proposal include a specific plan of action to meet the objectives? How would the vendor approach the goals to ensure they are met? Do you think the plan is solid and realistic?

- Are these goals S.M.A.R.T. (Specific, Measurable, Attainable, Relevant and Timely) or the equivalent? Remember, you want specifics. Don't settle for goals just to "increase your sales." Seek goals that are specific with an appropriate timeframe.

- Does the proposal address all the points and requirements listed in your RFP? Is this a well-constructed, informative and impressive response to your request for proposal?

47

- Is the proposal "on target" with your company's needs? Does it appear to be a generic, template-based proposal, or did the company actually make an effort to construct it specifically for your business and your project?

- Does the proposal give you confidence that the web developer understands your business and your industry adequately to successfully market and sell your products or services to your customers?

- Overall, how do you rate the web developer's marketing and sales skills based on the proposal/presentation, examples provided and the effectiveness of their own website?

- How do you rate the web developer's design and creative skills based on what they have demonstrated: their presentation, examples provided, and their own website?

- How do you rate the web developer's technical skills based on the demonstrated understanding of technical issues, examples of work and their own website?

- Does the proposal explain the project flow, steps or methodology the web developer is employing for your project? Does it appear complete, and does it make sense? This is where you will see how web developers differ vastly. Look for steps that ensure smooth project flow and quality control, and guarantee better results. (More on project flow later.)

- Does the proposal include all the services that are essential to your website? On a scale of 0 to 10, rate the value of each of the proposed services (as separate criterion), their importance and your confidence in web developer's abilities to provide these services successfully:

  - Content Management System
  - E-commerce / Payment processing
  - Hosting

- Mobile support
- Search Engine Optimization (SEO)
- Social Media Optimization (SMO)
- Copywriting
- Photography
- Video production

- Does the proposal indicate who specifically will work on your project? Does it appear to be a complete team with all the skill sets required by your project? Will the vendor assign a dedicated account executive or a project manager? Have you met that person?

- Are the quote and payment terms within the parameters of your budget? Read the section "How Much Should I Pay for My Website" (page 20) before making this assessment.

- Do they explain what is included in the quote and why they believe it's necessary? Does it provide a full breakdown with no combined budget items? Can they justify the quote? Is the hourly rate acceptable? Pay attention, not only to the initial quote for the project, but also to the hourly rate, which will come into play for additional work outside of the original contract.

- Is the proposed timeframe parallel with your desired "go-live" date? Does the proposal clearly state project schedule and a full breakdown of milestones?

- Does the proposal outline warranty and post-launch support of the website?

- Does the project include training? For example, will the web developer provide training to your team on CMS (Content Management System)? If so, is there a separate and additional cost?

After evaluating each of the proposals using this score card you should reach a final score for each web developer. This will allow you to objectively compare vendors side by side to make your final selection. Remember, your decision should be made not only on the proposal, but also on the overall experience preceding the proposal.

Once you have made the decision, the courtesy is to notify all of the vendors who submitted proposals. Some companies may ask you for the reasoning behind your decision to not go with them. This information allows companies to improve, so offer it if you desire to do so.

The last step is to notify the vendor you selected, and request their contract. This will be the focus of the next chapter.

Chapter 6 – Executing a Written Contract

No one enters a business relationship expecting to have problems. Unfortunately, if anything goes wrong, your contract will be put to the test. A well-written contract protects both parties and helps ensure that you and the web developer are on the same page throughout the project. A man much wiser than I once said, "Paperwork will make us friends."

Most web developers will provide a separate contract for each project. Some will ask you to sign their proposal as the main contract. Either way, you should begin the project only when you have fully reviewed the terms of your relationship in writing. Embarking on a project without a signed contract is just too risky and not sound business practice.

These recommendations are not intended as legal advice. Ask your attorney to review the contract before you sign it.

The following essential elements should be included in every contract for a website project, so get the assurance of your attorney that these clauses are covered:

What Is and Isn't Included?

Details of important services and features to your business need to be included in your contract. Devote sufficient time to incorporating every detail into your contract. Web developers will quote the project based on their understanding of the scope of work. It is important that you have a clear, mutually understood plan from the beginning of the project. Your web developer cannot be held responsible for something that is not in writing.

Our friend John learned it the hard way. He realized midway into the project that many important services were not included. For example, he would have additional charges for SEO, he would have to write his own copy for the new website, and cover his licensing fees for stock photography. This came as a costly surprise, and John learned the deal was insufficient for his needs.

Your contract should clearly state the detailed services and features. It is your responsibility to ensure that your contract is all-inclusive. Get it in writing. You may even want to list specific optional aspects of the project for future consideration, so it will be clear to both sides that these aspects of the project will not be billed separately.

How Are Changes and Additions Handled

Websites evolve naturally, so you will have changes or additions to your project that were not included in the original contract. In fact, you can almost count on having a need for extra work as your project progresses. Successful websites need to be maintained and updated so they can accommodate the true growth and expansion of your business. Expect an ongoing relationship with your web developer.

When changes to the project occur, the web developer will most likely charge a fee for the added work. Establish an agreement on the hourly rate for all such work.

Following commencement of the project, you must provide your web developer with consistent direction and feedback. If you change direction or provide contradicting instructions, the web developer may charge extra for the resulting inefficiencies. You must establish a mutual understanding on the policies throughout the course of your project, including the cost structure. Many web developers limit the number of design revisions. This should be agreeable to both parties and be detailed in the contract.

What Are the Milestones and Deliverables?

A website project should have milestones regardless of its size. Detail deliverables and milestone deadlines in the contract. This will facilitate the flow of the project, meet deadlines and reduce the risk of major problems.

Indicate what is to be delivered at the completion of each milestone: designs, copy, functioning website, etc., and as each milestone date approaches, see that deliverables are provided in a timely fashion.

In addition to tracking actions of the web developer, your own responsibilities should be in your focus as well, such as reviewing and signing off on work, providing feedback, and so on. Delays on your end will cause delays on the web developer's side.

Milestone planning depends on the project itself. For most websites I recommend the following four standard milestones:

What Are the Payment Terms?

Your contract should state the hourly rate and the total cost of the project. It should also show the payment timeline. The project should be divided into milestones. Payments should be scheduled at the completion and delivery of each milestone.

Most web development companies require a deposit at the beginning of a project. This amount should not exceed 50% of the project's total. The reason for assigning payment milestones is to ensure prompt delivery, as the web developer will have an incentive to complete work on time.

The contract must state the due date and the method of payment. Ensure that your funding source can accommodate these payment terms, so project work is not delayed.

Is There a Warranty and What's Covered?

What happens if something on the website is not working after the project is completed? Are you required to pay for the repair work? You may want to see that all work is covered by a warranty. This means that if an error, a glitch or a flaw in logic is discovered post-launch, it will be fixed in a timely fashion by the developer at no cost.

The contact should clearly state what is and is not covered and if there are restrictions. Reasonable warranty terms are 1-3 years, and it is generally accepted that if a third party tampers with the website, it voids the web developer's warranty.

Milestone	Activities	Deliverables	Payment
Discovery	This phase includes all the activities in the beginning of the project such as the schedule, competitive analysis, kick-off meetings and interviews.	- Project Proposal - Contract	Deposit is due prior to commencement of work.
Design	This project phase focuses on the structure, flow, look and feel of the new website, such as the sitemap, wireframes and mock-ups, as well as the completed designs. Often this phase includes copywriting as well.	- Site Map - Wireframes - Completed Designs - Copy	2nd payment is due when the design is completed and approved.
Development	This phase focuses on implementing the design and programming functions and features of the website.	- Functional Website	3rd payment is due when the functional website can be reviewed and tested.
Launch	This phase provides for website testing and preparation for launch.	- Finalized Website	Final payment is due when the website is launched.

Who Owns the Website?

An intellectual property dispute could be a potential cause of conflict between your company and the web developer. This is why it is recommended to address the issue of the website ownership prior to commencement.

Most companies assume they own their entire website. This is not necessarily the case. Today's websites are complex systems that consist of multiple components, such as databases, servers, platforms and other tools that cannot be owned. Instead, you own a combination of these components, or the "finished assembled work" that comprises your website.

To understand what you can and can't own, let's look at some of the components separately:

What You Own

- Design and Visuals – the combination of visual assets that makes up your website is what you own, such as your brand, colors, interfaces, typography, images and any other visual components.

- Content – all of the text content on the website, including any multimedia, such as photography and videos are also components you should own. Stock photography should be licensed to your company, meaning that you have a license to use photographs, but you don't own them.

- HTML, CSS and JavaScript are building blocks of any website. This is what essentially makes up your website and makes it unique.

What You Typically Don't Own

- Domain Name – this may come as a surprise, but you do not own your domain name. Even though you are a registered owner, the domain registrar gives you an exclusive right of its use, similar to a phone number.

- Web Server – unless you actually purchase your server and collocate it with a hosting company, you are renting a server or a shared space on a server. You do not own it.

- Web Stack – this software runs on a server so your website can function. You do not own it. Common web stacks on which most websites run are Windows (IIS, ASP .NET and MS SQL) or LAMP (Linux, Apache, MySQL and PHP).

- Database – this software allows your data to be stored on a server (such as MySQL, Oracle, and MS SQL). You own the data but not the software.

- Content Management System (CMS) – this application allows you to update and manage content on your website. The CMS is owned by the web developer or a software company (or by a community, if it is open-source). You own the content but not the software.

- Custom Source Code – in most cases, you do not own the source code that makes up features and functions of the website. Web developers often reuse their own code as well as third party solutions. The benefit to you is that you have solutions that are tested and can be deployed more quickly and cost effectively. The flip side is that no single customer can claim ownership of these solutions. You can specify that the code is "work for hire," which means that technically you do own it. However, it gets very complicated with any code that has been written prior to your project by the web developer (proprietary code), as well as any open source code covered by the GNU General Public License. In most cases, it is impossible to distinguish between custom-written versus proprietary code.

The question of a website's ownership can get very technical. Some of the most seasoned intellectual property attorneys don't fully understand all components and insist on one-sided agreements that would be most likely invalid and unenforceable.

Do not obsess over ownership, as long as the contract unequivocally states that you own the design, the content and the HTML/CSS and JavaScript of the website and have full control over the source code. This is necessary for your company to access and make modifications to the website, if you decide to bring the website in house or switch to another web developer down the road.

If you don't have access to source code, you may be stuck with your web developer. It is imperative that for components of the website you do not own, the web developer provides you a license (or in cases of third party solution, a sub-license) that is worldwide, perpetual, non-exclusive, transferrable, irrevocable and royalty-free. Even though technically you may not own certain website components, there should be nothing preventing your business from making full use of the website. If a web developer cannot provide you with a "license to use," this should raise a red flag.

How Is Confidential Information Protected?

A Non-Disclosure Agreement (NDA) may be a part of the main contract or a separate agreement. It is commonly used to protect a company's confidential or proprietary information (ideas, methodology, concepts, designs or processes).

In the course of working on your project, the web developer will need to have access to information that may be considered confidential. Some examples are: client lists, sales numbers, marketing ideas, and unique concepts (prior to securing patent or copyright protection). An NDA prohibits use and disclosure of such confidential information outside your working relationship.

Legalese and Fine Print

A good contract for a website project may include the some of the following important clauses and provisions. The specific clauses important to your project should be established with your attorney:

What You Own/Don't Own

What You Own

What You Don't Own

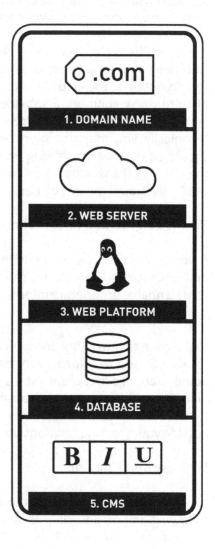

- **Termination** – what happens if your company or the web developer wants to terminate the relationship prior to completing the project?

- **Jurisdiction** – this is especially important when working with a web developer who is out of state or overseas. If issues arise, you need to be aware of governing law of the web developer's state or country.

- **Force Majeure** – what happens if either party cannot meet their responsibilities due to circumstances out of their control?

- **Limitation of Liability** – this limits the liability of the client and the web developer. The maximum amount of liability for both parties should be the amount paid for the project.

- **Severability** – this states that if any portions of the contract are found invalid or unenforceable, the rest of the contract remains in effect.

- **Notices** – this explains how future changes to the contract will be executed, and where notices should be sent.

This chapter is not meant to replace legal advice. Remember to consult with your legal counsel before signing the contract. Depending on the specifics of your project, there may be other necessary clauses or conditions that need to be covered. Having attorneys negotiate contract language could be the least pleasing part of the process, but it will protect both parties from possible issues down the road.

Summary of Part I

Your company's website can be a significant driver of profits, either through direct sales or by attracting and retaining clients. In today's hyper-competitive marketplace, your company or organization needs a strong Internet presence, and if you have a website, you will ultimately need to redesign or upgrade it to accommodate growth, reach a wider audience and address changes in product or service lines. Finding the right web developer is an essential component of this process. The time and effort you invest initially will save you from headaches, disappointments and potential losses later.

The following are the ten key points to remember when hiring a web developer.

1. Do not hire the first web developer without doing due diligence. Cast a wide net.

2. Understand your business needs and set clear and precise business objectives for your website.

3. Write down your business objectives, and compile a request for proposal (RFP) before approaching potential web developers.

4. Differentiate the types of web developers and their methods of operation to ascertain compatibility with your organization and its needs.

5. Carefully evaluate and review the web developer's qualifications, expertise, and experience to ensure that the demands of your project are met.

6. Have a system to evaluate all web developers objectively, and do not rush the decision-making process or base your decision solely on the proposal.

7. Beware of hiring a web developer that specializes in a single industry with a "cookie cutter solution."

8. Always ask for references.

9. Do not begin the project without a contract in writing.

10. To ensure success, have a budget that is adequate for your expectations.

Part II
How to Produce a Results-Driven Website

The contract is signed and you are now ready to embark on the exciting project of building a new website for your business.

This part of the book will take you through each step of managing the project effectively. It outlines the best methods to manage your project, maintain deadlines, operate within your budget and ensure that your website is built to meet and exceed your business goals.

"Coming together is a beginning; keeping together is progress; working together is success."

Henry Ford

Chapter 7 – Fundamental Principles of Creating a Successful Website

A world-class website consists of multiple components that should not be taken for granted. It is essential that you understand these components thoroughly, as some will remain your responsibility, regardless of your web developer's part in the process. Address and incorporate the following principles in your new website, and you will improve its performance greatly.

How You Name a Boat, is How it Will Sail

A domain name (e.g., yourbusiness.com) is your website's "address" on the Internet. Without it, there is no easy way to navigate to your website. Sometimes compared to an international phone number, the domain name system (DNS) is designed to give every Internet website a memorable address. Most often, the domain name is your company name, but actually, it can be any combination of characters (with some restrictions in place). Most American websites use three-letter, top-level domains (TLD), ending with ".com" for instance. Other countries have their own top-level domains (such as "co.uk" in UK or "co.ca" in Canada), but ".com" has the largest presence around the world[3].

If you register a new domain name, register it as ".com." As mentioned above, online users are accustomed to instinctively adding ".com." following business or product names in order to access the company's website. You may get additional domain names (as many as you want) for your website, if necessary or desired. Businesses often get additional domain names for their other trademarks, products, services, common misspellings, or other top-level domains such as ".biz", ".net", ".info" and many others[4]. Additional domains can point to the main website or parts of that website.

---

[3]   http://w3techs.com/technologies/overview/top_level_domain/all
[4]   http://en.wikipedia.org/wiki/List_of_Internet_top-level_domains

You do not own the domain name. You lease it from a Registrar. A Registrar is an organization that has authority to issue and assign the domain name (again, parallel to phone companies and phone numbers).

Just like a phone number, the domain name is a critical component of your website. It needs to be registered and renewed on a regular basis. If you forget to renew the domain name, it can be disabled, which bars user access and receipt of your e-mail, and even worse—another person or company can take over your domain name if they see it available. Most domain names renew annually, but you have the option of paying for a block of years (five, ten or more). I strongly recommend the longer-term payment, because domain name registration is relatively inexpensive. Many companies have lost their domains or had to fight to get them back, simply because they forgot to renew it on time.

Keep a file with the Registrar name, contact information and the date and method of renewal, to make it easy to renew your domain name registration when the time comes. If you do not have Registrar information, you can verify this information through WHOIS lookup of your domain name at: (http://www.networksolutions.com/whois/) or ask your web developer/hosting company for assistance.

Content is King

Good content is what sets your website apart from the masses and delivers the right message into the hearts and minds of your customers. The success of your website is determined primarily by its content. Ultimately, content wins the wallets of your customers. All other components of your website (design, visuals, videos, etc.) provide a secondary support role. If you have effective taglines, great design will only enhance their effectiveness. Design itself does not sell.

The content of your website should always begin with proper market research. First, you should determine your high value customers (HVC) and determine how you will target them. Taglines and slogans that are customer-centric (i.e., focuses on the needs and wants of the customer) are essential to capturing the attention of your prospective customers.

Your taglines must deliver a clear value proposition and include an effective call to action.

The key to a successful website is having clear, relevant and keyword-rich content that delivers the right message with power and conviction. The content on your website should target your audience, engage them and persuade them to take action.

Because good content is so important to the success of your website, consider hiring a professional copywriter to deliver professional copy for your website. *Copywriting* is the process of professionally written content for marketing purposes. It is not to be confused with *copyrighting*–the process of obtaining a *copyright* or legal protection for your unique content (usually done by an intellectual property attorney). It is a good idea to secure both services. Once you invest in professional copywriting, it is recommended that you copyright it with the U.S. Patent Office[5]. You may also consider filing for trademarks for some of your most successful taglines and slogans.

Effective content doesn't always come in the form of text. Videos are changing the way websites communicate important messages. Website visitors expect to get the information they need without effort. Videos provide a great way to engage audiences and drive important messages in a format that requires less effort than reading large amounts of text. In addition, illustrations, infographics, diagrams and interactive presentations are often used to explain difficult concepts and assist users in their decisions.

Effective Design Strengthens Your Message

"A picture is worth a thousand words." In web design, this is particularly the case, as first impressions are most important. Statistics show that your website typically has between one and five seconds to retain your website visitor[6]. This is hardly enough time to read and process any content. This means that you have to find additional methods to retain the visitor's attention or lose them to another website.

---

[5]   http://www.uspto.gov/
[6]   http://www.theguardian.com/media-network/media-network-blog/2012/mar/19/attention-span-internet-consumer

This is where the design and appearance of your website is relevant. It creates the first impression, captures the attention and engages your visitor to read and process your taglines, dive into your website and ultimately help to make purchasing decisions with confidence.

Effective design works in harmony with your copy; it supports your messaging, strengthens it and delivers it in a visual, easy-to-process manner, allowing your customers to connect with your website on a deeper level. Good design also reinforces your company's brand and facilitates purchasing decisions. Design must work in tandem with your branding and content in order to emphasize your strengths and core business values, and ultimately direct users to take action.

Avoid using stock photography as much as possible. You may think a stock picture is a perfect fit for your website, but there are feasibly thousands of other websites using the exact picture. Nothing complements and represents your business more effectively than professional and original photographs of your products, customers, team and facilities. Custom photography makes your website stand out among the rest, and they lend credibility and connect with the visitor on a personal level. Using custom photography also provides the opportunity to incorporate your marketing message and brand into photographs. This will greatly improve the marketing power of your website.

Effective web design is more than just an aesthetically pleasing website. Professional web designers must factor in all design aspects, from the psychology of color and screen resolution to accessibility requirements and typography, in order to engage, excite and inspire. Challenge your web designers, and ask them to explain the rationale of the designs they promote. Don't be afraid to ask questions.

Simpler is Always Better

Research conducted by HubSpot.com reveals that when asked about the most important factor in a website, over 75% of respondents stated[7] they rank ease of finding the information at the top. If you construct your website in a manner that's too complicated to navigate,

---

[7]   http://www.hubspot.com/marketing-statistics

produce content too difficult to comprehend, or design functionality too cumbersome to use, your website will not meet its objectives, and you will lose business.

Usability, or User Experience, is the art of making your website simple, user-friendly and easy to use. Understanding your customer's online behavior gives you insight into what works and what doesn't. One of the best books on Usability is entitled *Don't Make Me Think* by Steve Krug. The title spells out the rule of thumb when designing websites – make it effortless for your users, and they will stay; make it difficult, and they will leave.

Some of the most basic and proven usability tips include proper use of taglines, intuitive navigation, concise content, and strategic use of visuals. Avoid confusing features or functionality. Do links and buttons appear clickable, as they should? Does the website flow logically? Is it abundantly clear where important information can be found? If not, your website has not been designed for usability.

How do you design a user-friendly website? The secret lies in proper planning and thorough testing. Most established companies have a step in their project flow specifically designed to detect and eliminate potential usability issues. This step is called wireframing or prototyping. A wireframe is essentially a schematic, a blueprint or pencil sketch of the website's content. It typically has no design elements or color; rather it focuses on substance. The exclusive focus is on content, structure, flow and functionality without other visuals to distract the eye.

If you are running a government or non-profit website, you may want to look into ADA (Americans with Disabilities Act) compliance that covers many aspects of Web Accessibility, including the look and feel of the website, alternate text for images, and much more. Web Accessibility refers to the practice of designing websites that can be accessed and used more easily by people with varying levels of ability. It is legally required for government websites to be ADA-compliant; however, many experts agree that ADA-compliant site design is a good practice for every website.

There is invaluable feedback in retaining multiple-user reviews of wireframes (or later designs). This feedback can be incorporated into the early stages of the project. If you don't have the budget to retain a professional company to manage focus groups or usability testing, it is easy enough to create one yourself with your customers, or by using an online service. Ask them to review the website and provide feedback on their website experience and its ease of use.

Experiences that Help Your Customers

Successful websites are always customer-oriented at their core. If you help your customers solve a problem or address their pain, they will love the website and reward you with their business. If functionality is added at the expense of ease of use, you will certainly lose more than you will gain.

Every website experience has to be designed specifically to solve a problem in the most effective and user-centric manner. There are many success stories on the web where a website wasn't the first in its category, but its success was the result of being the best at what it does. Facebook wasn't the first social network, but it made staying connected with friends easier than others. Google wasn't the first search engine, but it produced better search results.

Be careful not to overdo it. Ask the question every time you want to add another bell or whistle to your website. Why bother? Why should we add this? How is it going to be of value to our customers? We discuss feature creep later in the book, but be aware that adding features increases complexity. You don't want to solve one problem and create another in the process. Always remember the "simpler is always better" principle when adding new features.

Best experiences are *simple*. For example, Apple products are known around the world for fully featured products that are *easy* to use. iPhone revolutionized the smartphone industry in 2007, but it wasn't only because of its new features. In fact, there were other smartphones containing the same or similar features. Apple made these features easy to use.

Use the same principle in the design of your website to ensure that every feature is carefully implemented to help your customers *more* than your competition does. For example, are you selling a variety of complex products or services? Designing an interactive guide that will help the customer select the right offering, based on his needs may be a game changer for your website.

Mobile Support is No Longer an Option

Have you ever noticed how many times a day you check your e-mail, read news or update your Facebook status on your phone? Next time you're waiting in line, enjoying your morning coffee in a restaurant or taking a walk, look around. How many people do you see staring at their mobile phones?

A recent study[8] reports that the vast majority of mobile users who see a website that is not optimized for their phone will simply move on to the competitor's website.

It doesn't matter what you do, who you are, what your website sells or who it serves. Mobile users are on the go, and they have no time to waste. If they are unable to access the information they are seeking quickly, they will move on.

For the next several years, many businesses can have a competitive edge by building mobile-friendly websites and be ahead of the curve. Several years from now, you will not have a choice. Mobile isn't going away, and ultimately you will be forced to upgrade your website. I strongly urge anyone designing or redesigning a website to consider investing in Responsive Design. It needs to be mobile friendly.

Responsive Design is a practice of building a single website that is optimized for screens of many sizes: smaller smartphones, tablet screens, laptops and large desktop monitors. Unlike the traditional approach of building multiple versions of the same website, responsive websites automatically adapt to screen size and to the capabilities of a mobile device. The benefit of Responsive Design is clear—only one website to build and maintain.

---

[8]   http://blog.kissmetrics.com/wp-content/uploads/2011/09/mobile-mania.pdf

Remaining in Control of Your Website

We already discussed the importance of management and control of the domain name. Several additional key aspects of your website must also be managed continually.

A proper Content Management System (CMS) puts you in control of your website's content. This allows you to update and manage the online content at your convenience and without assistance from your web developer. This allows for a more efficient delivery of mission-critical information and reduces the operating cost of the website.

Before embarking on the project, ensure not only that the website contains a Content Management System, but also that your developer identifies the specific system being used. Then request a demo. The CMS must be easy to use and provide you maximized control of your website, including product/service information, company news and events, job openings, team members, blogs, press releases, testimonials, case studies and more.

Many Content Management Systems are available, so ask for your developer's recommendation on which system will give you the level of control needed. The degree of "control" depends on which projects you will complete in-house as opposed to the project you will assign to your web developer. For example, there are very easy-to-use systems that require zero training but offer limited control within predetermined content placeholders. They also follow predetermined styles and formatting. More advanced CMS's are more difficult to use, but they allow access to advanced features and even permit control of HTML and CSS. Do you want to struggle with advanced features, or would you rather rely on professionals? In either case, discuss the options with your developer.

Every developer has a preferred CMS. You shouldn't insist on a specific system, as you would be limiting your options, and it can pose a detriment to your web developer's efficiency and effectiveness. Both options will deliver inferior results. Also, beware of any proprietary CMS that has hidden licensing fees or protected source code, which will prevent changes or modifications to your website. Ask your developer to explain the levels of access to the recommended CMS and the source code they provide. I am a firm believer in the practice that each business must have *unrestricted* and full access to the source code of their website. If you don't provide this latitude, you are taking the risk of being indefinitely tied to your developer without an easy exit strategy.

Finally, depending on the purpose and the features of the website, you may need more control than the typical CMS offers. One example is an online store, where you will certainly need the ability to change pricing and inventory.

Another example is a social network, where you will need to moderate content or control user accounts. Regardless of the purpose of your website, be assured that you will be in control of all content, functions, components and parameters important to the operation of your website.

Choosing a Reliable Host

In order for your website to work and be accessible on the Internet, you need a reliable hosting provider that actually "hosts" your website or makes it available on the Internet by residing on their servers.

A Hosting service is similar to a phone provider. It is a monthly service that has different options depending on the size, traffic and specific needs of your website. It is important to understand that hosting and web development are two different services that can be provided by different companies. To continue with the phone analogy, your new website is like a phone you purchase from a store (web developer), for which you need phone service (hosting) to make use of it.

Most web developers will be able to host your website, or they will recommend a hosting company, so that's a good place to start. I recommend hosting through your web developer, if that option exists, for one simple reason. It offers a single point of contact. If there are any issues with the website, they are more easily resolved with one company. When you have retained separate services, you may get caught in the middle or be given the runaround.

You can expect to pay more for the convenience of having a single point of contact, but it is often worth the extra money. Hosting through your web developer means they have a hosting environment that is preferred and optimized for their websites, as opposed to a separate hosting provider that may be incompatible with or problematic in supporting the technology and solutions deployed by your developer. Finally, if there are problems, you will have to communicate with your hosting company directly, or worse, pay your developer to work with them on your behalf.

We will talk about hosting and its various options later in the book, but one choice I strongly advise against is hosting your website in-house. Most hosting companies operate out of multi-million dollar data centers designed for redundancy and continuous operations including data backups and security, fire suppression and power management. Many corporate servers and networks are designed for internal needs (such as e-mail and file sharing) and simply lack the level of redundancy and availability required for hosting an external website.

Content Marketing = Customers

You have probably heard the term Content Marketing but may not be sure what it means. Content Marketing involves the creation and sharing of media and publishing content in order to acquire customers. This information can be presented in a variety of formats, including blog posts, news, videos, white papers, infographics, case studies, how-to guides, photos, etc.

Content Marketing is one of the best methodologies for marketing your website and your business. Posting relevant, valuable and frequently updated information on your website will boost search engine optimization (SEO), help position you as an expert, and allow you to build relationships with your audience. All are priceless benefits for any business.

One of the benefits of publishing good content is that it will increase the number of people who find your website through search engines. Search engines love content, especially frequently updated content, and if you want to get people to your site, it's important to provide content that people want to see. Similarly, a search engine's job is to find content for their customers. Consider the following: How many pages do you have detailing your company's products and services on your website? You probably have a limited number. In a blog, for example, you can add fresh, relevant content virtually every day. Every additional page of content is potentially a new entry point (landing page) for your website.

Many companies seek close relationships with their customers. It is wise to post relevant and useful information on your website in the form of blog posts, articles or whitepapers. This provides prospective customers to see you as an expert in your industry and be more inclined to conduct business with you. When you use content marketing, you establish trusted lines of communication with your customers, and build credibility in the process.

One of the best ways to promote your content and generate traffic is through social media. To get the most from your content, you must harness the power of social media. For best results, your content should be syndicated, distributed and promoted through social media sites like Facebook, Twitter, LinkedIn and Google+.

We will be talking more about Content Marketing in Part III.

Organic Traffic is the Healthy Choice

Just like the produce in the organic section at your grocery store, "organic" search traffic has long-term "health" benefits for your website. Organic traffic comes from the listings in search engines that appear because of their relevance to the search terms, as opposed to being paid advertisements.

So what are the benefits of organic traffic over pay-per-click or other forms of paid advertising? First, Internet users tend to trust organic results more than sponsored results, so while paid ads can be an important segment of your marketing strategy, the organic search results will produce better click-through rates. Secondly, your paid advertising campaigns are only as good as the amount of money you invest in them. When payment of advertising stops, the traffic stops.

With organic search results, your website will be getting residual traffic for years to come. Finally, when combined with solid Content Marketing, organic search engines' positions tend to improve over time. This means more "free" and continuous traffic.

In order to achieve favorable positions in search engines, many websites rely on a service called Search Engine Optimization (SEO). SEO isn't an automated one-size-fits-all magic trick; it's a pinpointed strategy formulated specifically for each individual website and it's demographic. The strategy selected depends on the audience you're targeting, as well as the competition, and keywords/phrases that your intended demographic uses.

We will cover SEO in more detail in Part III, but to give you a basic understanding, it usually consists of two parts: content strategy, and ongoing link building and optimization. Before the project begins, it is important to ensure that the website will be "optimized" for search engines to prevent changes in the future. This means that the website must be easily "crawlable" by search engines and be compatible with all the good SEO practices. Furthermore, by optimizing the structure, adjusting content, setting Meta descriptions, and employing a myriad of other techniques while the site is being built, you will ensure a solid foundation for ongoing SEO work.

Your web developer may offer SEO services as part of the project or recommend an SEO company, just as they did with hosting services. In any case, you should discuss SEO at the beginning of the project and work with a developer who can help manage and oversee the SEO effort.

Fundamental Principles of Creating a Successful Website

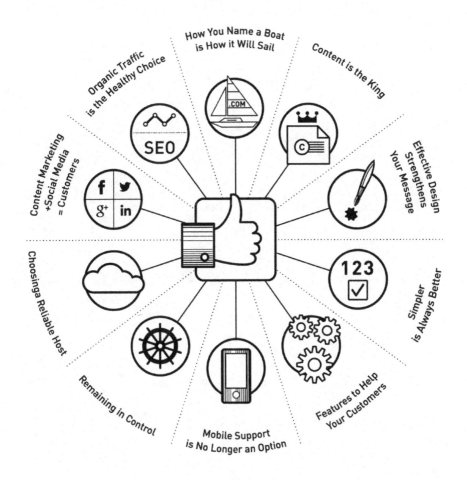

- How You Name a Boat is How it Will Sail
- Content is the King
- Organic Traffic is the Healthy Choice
- Effective Design Strengthens Your Message
- Content Marketing +Social Media = Customers
- Simpler is Always Better
- Choosing a Reliable Host
- Features to Help Your Customers
- Remaining in Control
- Mobile Support is No Longer an Option

Chapter 8 - Things That Drive Everyone Crazy in Website Projects and How to Avoid the Stress

Before you get started on your website project, it is a good idea to look at some of the mistakes that are commonly made in all phases of website projects. If you don't take steps to avoid these mistakes, you will undoubtedly waste time and money. Avoiding these obstacles from the beginning of the project will be conducive to a stress-free, efficiently completed website project.

Not Having a Clear Objective and a Solid Plan of Action

We covered this in Section 1. Stop right here if you don't have S.M.A.R.T. (Specific, Measurable, Attainable, Relevant and Timely) objectives in place (or if you have any doubts about your existing S.M.A.R.T objectives). Any attempt to continue with the project without clearly defined objectives will almost certainly guarantee its failure.

The objective alone, however, is not enough. There has to be solid plan of action designed to achieve the objective. It should be backed by market research, stakeholder and customer interviews, competitive analysis, and more. Your web developer should provide you with a plan of action as part of their proposal. Make sure you read it, understand it and, more importantly, agree with it.

Real Case Study: A customer came to us, and when asked repeatedly about their objective, consistently responded, "...a website that works better for my business." We immediately slammed on the brakes and sent a worksheet to the customer to establish S.M.A.R.T. objectives. Only when concrete business objectives (to double the leads through the website) were set, did we continue. The customer was happy with the outcome, and as we learned later, our project was their fifth website redesign in two years. All previous websites were built with the same "better for my business" objective. None of the previous websites actually improved their business.

Bottom line: Building a website without a proper objective is analogous to driving blindly. How far can your website travel? Ensure that both you and your web developer understand the key objective and that you have a specific and a realistic plan of action to arrive at your "destination."

Micromanaging and Doing your Web Developer's Work

At this point, you should have hired the best professionals you could find to create a world-class website. Let them do their work. When you go to your doctor, you don't tell him or her how to diagnose or treat you, do you? Unfortunately, when it comes to creating websites, many people think they know better. Let's face it, if you are not a professional designer, copywriter or programmer, please don't take on this role for your own project.

Teams of professionals spend their entire careers perfecting their skills. The best thing you can do for your project is let them do their job. Provide constructive, relevant feedback but don't interfere, and don't do the work for them. When in doubt, give your web developer the benefit of the doubt. Listen carefully to what they have to say. After all, you hired them for their expertise.

Real Case Study: A customer took some graphic design classes in college many years ago. When the time came to redesign the company's website, she dusted off her 1996 version of CorelDraw, and every revision of the design we proposed was followed by her rendition. This psychedelic nightmare looked more like a 70's tailgating banner than a modern website. The customer was having fun designing her website. Our design department was weeping and loading up on Prozac. The catastrophe was averted when we asked if we could present her design (for feedback) to an independent expert. Feedback contained mostly expletives. CorelDraw quickly found its place back on the shelf, and the design team finished the project, which was to become an award-winning website.

Bottom line: If you micro-manage your web developer, not only will it wreak havoc with your project, but also it will result in a mediocre, unattractive and dysfunctional website.

80

Designing for You or Your Boss

In addition to the previous mistake, one that unfortunately happens much too often is when the customer undertakes the role of a designer. It seems so easy: "Let's try this picture...Change that color...Move this here." Bad idea. Again, you are not a professional web designer. How much do you know about the psychology of color, accessibility contrast requirements or responsive design breakpoints? Designing a world-class website is a lot more complicated than simply poking around pretty pictures and colors.

Opinions on issues of color and design elements are subjective by nature. It is the matter of one's taste. It is important to understand that the website you are building is not to satisfy your personal taste, or that of your boss. It is designed for your customers. Inevitably, some may not like it, while others will love it. Now is when a web developer's expertise enters the picture. Ask yourself another question: Would you rather have a website that you love and every customer hates, or vice versa? Trust the company you hired. If the design proposed seems too radical, simple, bland, colorful, etc., there is a reason for it. Your customers may like it very much, and trust me when I say that you may also grow to like and appreciate it.

Real Case Study: There are bosses and then there are BOSSES. This one was THE BOSS. From the first meeting we realized it was going to be "my way or the highway." The entire marketing team, led by the Marketing Director (who was in charge of the website project), was scared to think differently than their President (let alone voice their opinions). The President was very opinionated and, even worse, 100% wrong every step of the way. When asked about his responsibilities, the Marketing Director admitted that his head was going to be on a platter if the website didn't perform. We mailed him a nice porcelain plate that said "His Way" on it. It was heard loud and clear, the Marketing Director found a way to take the project into his own hands and followed our lead to a successful outcome.

Bottom line: Do not build a site that you or your top executives will like. They are not your website's target audience. If they insist, give them this chapter to read.

Making Assumptions and Lacking Proper Communication

"But I assumed this was included...I assumed *you* will write and populate the content!"..."We assumed we can change anything we want!" Do these statements sound familiar? Have you ever been in a situation where you and another person are clearly not on the same page? Unfortunately, this also happens with website projects.

Don't assume anything. Talk things over with your vendor, ask a lot of questions and summarize it in writing. It is your responsibility to convey your objectives, requirements and expectations to the developer in a clear and unambiguous manner. Have the vendor address these objectives in their proposal or acknowledge in writing to ensure you agree on all levels.

The last thing you want is a surprise that a feature you feel is essential to the project is actually outside of the project's scope or developer's capability, and it will take extra time and incur greater cost. Think about it this way: Did you communicate to your vendor the specific need or requirement? If not, it is unreasonable to expect that your vendor should understand your expectations. After all, they can only price out and deliver what you requested.

Real Case Study: "Why didn't you tell me it wasn't included?" a customer asked. We inquired,

- "Did you communicate this requirement to us?"

- "Did you see it in the proposal?"

- "Did you ask us to include it in the proposal?"

They responded "No" to every question, and got the point. We quoted and developed the feature separately, and the issue was resolved. We also explained that the customer didn't lose any money, because if they had requested the feature initially, we would have quoted it separately anyway. However, we did lose time, and the customer's expected completion date was not met because of this lack of communication.

Bottom line: Talk to the web developer at every hint that something is not clear or if you feel they are not clear on a particular detail. Don't be afraid to repeat yourself, and summarize what they tell you. At that point, ask them to reiterate their understanding of what you conveyed. You may be surprised how many details are caught in this process.

Changing Your Mind and Getting Hung Up on Details

"Let's remove it...No, put it back...Let's try it in green...No, blue... No, that's too blue...Let's go back green." Not only will you be driving the designer crazy, you are in fact wasting time and money. At some point, most companies would start billing you extra for changes in this manner. What's even worse is that you are throwing a monkey wrench into the entire project flow.

Change of direction is the number one enemy of proper project planning. For some people it has to do with their indecisiveness. Others decide to take the designer role by requesting that their web developer try every possible color combination (see previous section "Micromanaging and Doing your Web Developer's Work").

If you can't adhere to the project flow, you will be going in circles. You will be late and over budget quickly. The solution is simple. If you make a decision, stick to it. If you are not sure, give the professionals you hired the benefit of the doubt because of their expertise.

There is, of course, always a place for perfection. However, ask yourself if that one shade of color worth your website being late by many months because you realized it's a bit off at the end of the project? Is that sense of "Now we got it right!" worth the loss of time, productivity and additional cost? Will this color shade difference impact the success of your business?

Real Case Study: Despite our advice, a customer decided that the way to achieve the best possible logo design was to try all possible combinations of fonts, colors, shapes and taglines. It took them almost six months and thousands of dollars in going back and forth to decide on something... decent. Our designer had already created a logo that blew theirs out of the water in six hours.

Bottom Line: No detail is too small or insignificant. However, obsessing on aspects that are not relevant, have little impact or marginal improvement, may cost you very real time and money.

Nickel and Diming

Would you ever sign a blank check for your website project? Of course you wouldn't. Yet, this is essentially what many companies expect of their web developers when embarking on a website project – the whatever-it-takes approach for one flat fee. The philosophy is "I am paying you a lot as is, so you shouldn't charge me extra for any add-ons."

In my experience, some customers simply do not understand that their requests may be unreasonable or that they would cost the developer a lot of extra time and money. Some understand but choose not to care or acknowledge it.

I always recommend avoiding this approach. Just like any other business relationship, it is symbiotic. You need a quality website, and your developer needs projects like yours to make money. You may think that you have the leverage to pressure your web developer into doing free work, where in reality you are shooting yourself in the foot. Think about it this way: Would you be more likely to go the extra mile for someone who treats you with respect and compensates you fairly for your time and efforts, or for someone who is constantly trying to get you do extra work without compensation?

You, as a customer have to understand that it's likely you are paying a fixed fee for a specific project. This means that the developer evaluated the scope of work and has a certain budget for your project. Asking your web developer to add work outside of that scope will take them quickly over budget, making the project less profitable for them. This will result in a web partner who loses interest in your project.

Real Case Study: Many years ago we were working with a customer who was making highly unreasonable demands that often included adding and changing elements after the job was completed. The customer lacked direction and planned poorly at the outset of the project, so to compensate for this, he employed these tactics at the project's end. These actions were, of course, at our expense. After several additional projects, we flatly refused to do any more work at the fixed quote and offered to transition to an hourly rate. Once faced with additional costs, because he lacked clarity, the customer's planning and communication improved remarkably, as well as the timing and the quality of the resulting product.

Bottom line: No one likes to be nickel-and-dimed. However, it is important to understand that requests for work outside of the project's scope such as additional features, changes of direction, post-approval changes, excessive revisions and "waffling" will result in an increased cost to the developer, which will ultimately be passed on to you. The best way to prevent this conduct in a business relationship is to impose and adopt proper planning and communication from the beginning.

Rushing or Imposing Deadlines

A world-class website requires careful coordination of many, diverse activities performed by different teams at different stages of the project. For example, plans for websites delivered by our team often include as many as thirty to fifty steps and milestones. These steps have to be implemented in sequential order. An example of this is that programming should not begin until designs are completed, and design shouldn't begin until prototyping and wireframing is approved. Using a construction analogy, the workflow out of sequence would be the equivalent of electric work being done before the house is framed.

You also have to factor in proper timing for communication and management, review and feedback by the team on your side, testing and quality control, etc. All these aspects of the project must be given sufficient time. If the project is rushed, or corners are cut, the compromise will most likely be evident in testing and quality. This is a bad idea. By saving a little time now, you will inevitably spend a lot more time (and money) later to fix problems that could have been easily avoided with proper planning and timing of all activities. In the end, rushing a project guarantees a loss. It is not sound business practice to rush a project at the expense of quality. If a cake is taken out of the oven too soon, it won't be done, and if you raise the oven temperature, the cake will burn. You cannot rush a project to completion.

Another mistake to avoid is planning other activities (such as marketing campaigns, product launches or important presentations) that assume the date of completion will be met, without first consulting the developer. By doing so you assume all the risk if the website is not ready by the date you planned. The website project then becomes a point of stress that will incur additional cost in time and money to repair. This is because quality was compromised or corners were cut in order to meet unrealistic deadlines imposed.

Real Case Study: A customer was not happy with the date of completion we set for the project, asking to get it done sooner. None of our arguments worked. "Well, I understand, but why can't you add more programmers?" he kept saying, not realizing what every experienced project manager knows: adding more people to a project often slows it down even further. Then I remembered what my college professor said, and that got my point across. I told him: "It takes a woman and nine months to make a baby. You can't add eight women to make a baby in one month."

Bottom line: Allow the developer a reasonable amount of time to get the job done. Remember, rushing your developer will often be at your cost and peril. On the other hand, deadlines should always be in place. Proper planning and scheduling is vital to every project's success. Have your developer set realistic deadlines, and hold them accountable for meeting them.

Letting IT Call the Shots: Tunnel Vision

IT departments love to put in their two cents when it comes to your company's website. After all, it is their job to review, approve and recommend the best possible technical solutions. There is nothing wrong with that, with one significant exception. Remember, left-brain versus right brain? A modern website is a lot more than a series of code, a database and a Content Management System. While your IT department may understand the technical side of the website very well, they most likely do not fully understand other essential components, such as marketing and design. All are critical to the success of your website.

Never make decisions on your website based solely on the technology. What may work for your IT department may not work for your customers. Please understand that the objective of your IT department is entirely different from that of your website. IT teams do not manage sales or marketing. They are responsible for the company's IT infrastructure and that it is cost-efficient, secure and reliable. These aspects are of paramount importance for any website, but you cannot focus on the technology at the expense of design and marketing. Every web developer has their own tools of their trade, and if you want effective results, you must let them implement the use of their tools.

Real Case Study: The IT department in a medical company was insisting on using a specific programming language and a Content Management System, because they already had it in place. We asked their manager if they tell their doctors which medication to prescribe just because they "have it on the shelf." Our point was made, and we were allowed to select the appropriate medicine for their website.

Bottom Line: If you want consistent, world-class results, don't let your internal teams implement or impose tools, solutions, technologies or otherwise force the hand of your web partner. It will cost you in extra overhead and will not lead to the expected results.

Avoiding Responsibility

Generally speaking the more experienced the web developer is, the more hands-off approach you will need to adopt when working with them. A good firm will know your specific business needs, and they will achieve the goals you set, while holding your hand throughout the process. Less experienced firms will most certainly need more guidance and input from you.

Regardless of the capabilities of your web developer team, you should remain an active participant during the project. Although you should not micro-manage your web developer, you should perform your due diligence and assume responsibility for the following three roles critical to your project's success:

1. Ensure clear communication between all parties, especially on your end.

2. Proactively adhere to milestones and request regular updates to stay informed on progress.

3. Carefully review deliverables, and provide timely feedback so the developer can incorporate it into the project.

No matter how "hands-off" your project is, it's your job to be proactive in seeing that these steps are completed. Avoiding responsibility during the project may result in project failure, and you will have to take on more responsibility later in damage control.

Real Case Study: We were hired to build an internal company's website (an Intranet). A customer representative who is always busy provided us with less than ideal requirements and then quickly approved all of the deliverables. It was clear they didn't take the time to review, so we asked them to review it again. "Everything looks good!" was the answer. Things weren't as good when the end users actually started using the website. Many of the key features they needed were missing. Since this was never communicated to us and wasn't even discovered prior to the website's launch, it required emergency upgrades, costing more money, time and stress for everyone involved.

Bottom line: You are a busy professional, but without your limited guidance and blessing, your project is not likely to succeed. Even the best web development company in the world can't intuitively know that what they've built is exactly what you wanted and needed. Your thorough review and approval of the work is imperative to the success of the website.

Allowing Feature-Creep

Featuritis (or feature creep) is a disease that can bring your project to a screeching halt. This is what the IT industry jokingly calls the tendency of increasing features and uncontrollably adding elements to a project in progress. In web development, Featuritis is typically caused by enthusiastic clients who request additional items be added to the website because they feel the features will improve the website.

Unfortunately, the result is often the opposite. First, the complexity increases as the square of the increase of the features. In other words, if you double the features, you can expect the complexity to quadruple. This could have a similar effect on the project's timeframe and the budget. Secondly, the rule of thumb in web development is always: The simpler the better. Users today expect the website, regardless of the purpose or objective, to be simple to use and understand. This becomes increasingly difficult for websites overloaded with features and various bells-and-whistles added unnecessarily.

Real Case Study: A customer repeatedly added features to a website delaying the project by over four months, and they showed no signs of stopping. We insisted that we finish the current phase and that we go live despite the customer wanting to add more elements. Once the website was live, it quickly became apparent that many of the features the customer initially wanted were not desired by the users. In fact, we received feedback that was quite the opposite of the customer's expectations, and we were able to reroute resources toward the features the users ultimately wanted versus what our customer requested initially.

Bottom line: After you have a well-defined project that contains all the features integral to the concept, you should draw the line. The rule of thumb is to avoid adding elements to a project unless they are necessary to the finished product. The better approach is to break the project into separate phases or iterations. Maintain a "wish list" or a list of ideas and features as they come up, and then reevaluate the need for them following each phase (factoring in your clients' needs and their feedback).

Things That Drive Everyone Crazy in Website Projects and How to Avoid the Stress

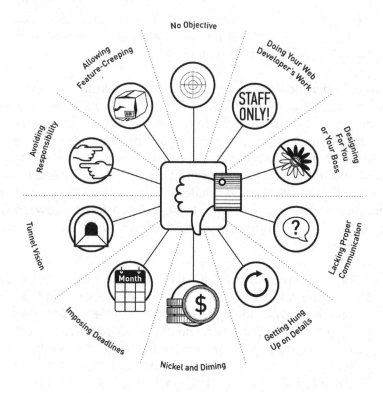

Chapter 9 - Managing Your Website Project the Right Way

So you are finally ready to start on your website project. Read this chapter before diving in. You will be glad you did. Following these simple recommendations will save you time and help to prevent headaches later.

Understand the Project Management Methodology

Project management is the discipline of planning, organizing and controlling inputs and resources to achieve the goals of your project. The primary constraints in project management are scope, time, quality and budget. Why should you care? Well, without proper project management, your website may be late and over budget, so understanding how projects are managed is the key to your success.

There are a great number of project management methodologies. There is no right or wrong methodology for a website project, and every web developer certainly has his own preference. Before you start your project, ask your web developer what methodology they use. Most established companies might even have certifications in project management such as PMP, ISO 9000, PRINCE 2, etc.

For the purpose of this book, we will focus on the two of the most common project methodologies used in web development—Agile and Waterfall. Both have their advantages and disadvantages, and the methodology preferred depends on the detail and scope of your project.

Waterfall Project Methodology

Waterfall is the more traditional project management methodology, in which every phase of the project must be fully completed and signed off before moving forward to the next stage. The Waterfall approach relies on project documentation, such as technical specifications to define the scope of work clearly before it is started. Waterfall is a great methodology for ensuring that all deliverables meet expectations.

The Waterfall approach is recommended for projects that must be completed within a fixed timeframe and do not have the budget for multiple revisions or iterations.

The disadvantage of Waterfall is that it is not flexible. Because it relies on the scope and specifics to be defined up-front, there is little room for change during the project. The limited flexibility is a drawback if any corrections are required during the course of the project (i.e., a specific aspect of the project appears differently than planned). Finally, projects managed under Waterfall methodology generally take much longer since each stage must be fully completed before proceeding to next stage.

For projects managed under Waterfall methodology, you can expect a fixed budget and an accurate timeframe.

Agile Project Methodology

Agile project methodology was developed specifically to address the limitations of Waterfall and other traditional approaches. The concept of Agile methodology is that it is ongoing and is based on principles of interaction and collaboration among team members, where tasks are executed quickly and in an adaptive manner. In other words, there is much less advance planning, and steps are completed as the project requires. The team focuses their efforts on small tasks that require immediate attention without pre-planning the entire project.

This methodology is preferred for projects with limited short-term timeframes where the website (or at least the initial part) must be launched as soon as possible. Agile method also supports quick changes to the scope and direction of the project based on market requirements.

The disadvantage of this methodology is because of its ongoing nature, you can be virtually investing an endless amount of money, time and resources into the project. In addition, because of lack of planning, frequent testing is required, and this commands much more of your involvement. If you prefer a hands-off approach, Agile methodology may not be the best choice.

For projects managed under Agile methodology, you are generally paying for the time spent (e.g., a week's worth of teamwork). It may not be possible to operate within a fixed budget, since the scope of the project is not clearly defined.

Mixed Methodology

You should also know that there are firms who practice the mixed methodology (a combination of both Agile and Waterfall). For example, our firm always starts with the Waterfall approach for the main project, and the uses the Agile methodology where changes and additions are required. This mixed approach allows us to use the advantages of both methodologies, while avoiding the disadvantages.

Define Steps and Project Components

Regardless of what methodology is used for your website project, you should clearly define the stages (phases) of the project and understand what they include and entail. Have your web developer explain the proposed flow and structure of the project. For example, are you going to have to delay programming until all pages of the website are designed, or can the developer start programming them in the order they are approved?

Also, be sure to have an outline of all the components that go into your website. For example, is the web developer providing you with copywriting services, or is the copy provided by you? Will you use custom photography or stock photography? It is very important to understand all the components and flow of the project in order to manage it properly.

Set Deadlines and Define Deliverables

In order to keep the project on track you should set milestones for completing major phases of the project and set tentative dates or

Project Management Methodologies

Waterfall Project Methodology

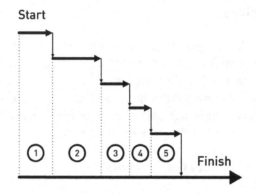

Agile Project Methodology

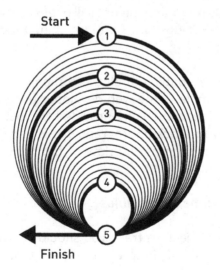

deadlines for each milestone. For example, when does the web developer foresee completion of design, slice-up, programming, etc.?

While you do want to retain some flexibility in the project and some dates may be tentative, it is very important to set projected deadlines and update them throughout the project. Keeping track of milestone deadlines will help you track the completion date for the entire project. For example, if the design completion was two weeks late, does it mean that the entire project will be delayed by two weeks or more?

In order to maintain structure and organization, I recommend a sign-off process at the end of each milestone. I urge adherence to written sign-offs (or documented via e-mail) to provide a paper trail and prevent misunderstandings as the project moves along. If you give your face-to-face or phone approval, make every effort to follow up with a quick e-mail, so you have a paper trail and date stamp of the approval.

It is also a good idea to define deliverables at the end of each phase. Have your web developer explain precisely what will be delivered. For example, "design" can be interpreted in many ways. Are they going to be providing electronic or printed designs? Will they just show you the designs or also provide source files, etc.

Finally, as mentioned in the previous section describing the contract, I recommended tying payments to the completion of specific stages of the project. This will help you control the project flow, meet deadlines and reduce the risk of going over budget.

Agree on Project Roles & Communication

Most problems in project management are the result of inefficient communication or lack of it. In order to prevent issues from occurring, it is a good idea to determine roles of everyone involved at the outset of the project.

I strongly urge assigning a single point of contact on *each* side. This will ensure clear and consistent communications. These individuals can then be responsible for communicating with their respective teams. Having a single point of contact on each side will help avoid contradicting or conflicting communication that often occurs when multiple members on both sides try to communicate effectively. Direct communication among them is acceptable and often productive, but be sure there is consistent and definitive communication between the designated managers.

Project Manager on Your Side

Before embarking on the project, select a Project Manager. This individual will be responsible for communicating with the web developer's team and is responsible for the overall success of the project. Be certain that this individual has sufficient time and resources at their disposal in order to manage communications effectively. Someone who is preoccupied with other projects, lacks the knowledge of the website or lacks authority to make decisions is not the right project manager. In fact, a poor choice here may negatively impact your project, so be thorough and discerning in your decision-making process. Your project manager should have a solid working knowledge of your business, your processes and your current website (if there is one). This individual should have time and resources to manage the project, as well as the authority to make decisions or have a close working relationship with the decision makers.

As part of this process, be sure that the web developer's team has the contact information for your project manager, the decision makers and all team members associated with the project.

Account Executive on the Web Developer's Side

Most web developers will assign an Account Executive as a primary point of contact. This person will manage communications on their side and one who will ultimately be responsible for the successful outcome of the project. In most cases, the Account Executive (AE) will be the same person you communicated with during the sales process.

Larger firms may have account execs on board who specialize in your specific industry and who have practical knowledge in related projects. This individual will coordinate and oversee all the services provided by the web developer and will communicate with all team members, including any consultants or third parties who are participating in the project.

An effective Account Executive should be responsive and reliable and have excellent communication, leadership, human capital management skills, as well as have the big picture focus on your project and its goals. You should expect frequent updates from your Account Executive, as well as problem prevention and resolution, quality control, understanding of your needs, attention to detail and ongoing support. If for some reason the individual assigned to you doesn't have these qualities or doesn't provide the level of support you need, it is acceptable to ask that another individual take this role. The outcome of your project is literally dependent on the effort and skills of the Account Executive assigned to you.

Project Manager on the Web Developer's Side

Depending on the project, and on the web developer's team structure, the Account Executive (your main point of contact) and the project manager may or may not be the same individual.

The role of the Project Manager (PM) on the web developer's side is to manage all the web developer's team members and resources, as well as to establish and maintain communication, procedures, tools and methodologies to ensure that your project is managed effectively, and is delivered on time and on budget. Effective PM's develop detailed project plans and schedules that are continually updated throughout the project and used to manage and guide the day-to-day activities. They then identify detailed project tasks, their duration and dependencies. At this time, they establish checkpoints to assess changes in scope preceding or succeeding milestones. The PM usually assumes the leadership role in communicating and coordinating all project activities with all parties involved, and provides periodic status reports to the Account Executive and your team members. Finally, the PM establishes and conducts quality assurance checkpoints throughout the life of the project.

Just like the Account Executive, the PM's role is critical to the success of you project so ensure that the individual assigned to your project has the experience and the qualities necessary to manage your project.

Set Up Channels & Tools for Collaboration

The success of your website project largely depends on the effective communication and collaboration among all team members, from your initial kick-off meeting, to the final website presentation. This is a good time to agree on communication channels and protocols: How often and when will the team meet? How often will you receive status updates? How will you be able to review work in progress and provide feedback? What will be the sign-off process?

My recommendation is to have the most important communications documented in writing (such as feedback, change requests and approvals). E-mail is probably the easiest option, but for larger projects, it can become difficult to locate notes, document versions or set priorities with thousands of e-mails going back and forth. This is why most companies use collaborative tools for project updates, schedules, team discussions, delegating tasks, tracking resources as well as cloud storage for documents and materials. Some of the most popular collaboration tools include BaseCamp, Huddle, Confluence, Teambox, ActiveCollab, and others. Some tools for exchanging files have benefits over e-mail are Google Drive and DropBox. Ask your web developer what tool they use and if it has a capabilities to share progress updates, transfer files and track issues that would be accessible by your team.

Communication by phone is often the quickest and most effective way to clarify and resolve issues or answer questions, but be sure that you routinely follow up with an e-mail when a phone conversation involves approvals or sign-offs. Remember that the phone has limitations. For example, design collaboration over the phone could be difficult but not impossible. Ask your web developer to e-mail or upload design files for you to review and simultaneously walk you through the details by telephone. Also, consider tools like Skype, GoToMeeting or Google Hangouts that allow sharing computer screens.

Face-to-face meetings (if geographically possible) are always valuable to your project. When we confer with a person, we interact with them verbally but also read body language and establish eye contact, which facilitates optimum communication. We can use tools at our meetings such as charts, visuals, props, sketches or designs on big screen for everyone to review. This face-to-face collaboration is not as important when these tools are available in a digital environment.

While face-to-face meetings are a great way to communicate and collaborate on a project, there are also limitations such as conflicting schedules and travel arrangements. Meetings generally take more time and require effort to schedule. Following are recommendations to maximize your meeting:

- Prepare an agenda for every meeting and send it well in advance of the meeting date and time.

- Prepare for your meetings: list questions or issues you want addressed.

- Set a time limit for each meeting. I recommend each meeting to be no longer than 1-1.5 hours.

- Have someone take notes at meetings, and distribute to attendees shortly after the meeting.

Discuss Project Changes

It should be clear to you that your website will have changes throughout the course of the project. Ask your web developer before the project starts how changes will be handled.

Changes during the project have measurable impact on the project and the deliverables of the project as well. These changes will necessitate modified estimates and task reassignments. Most often, a change is defined by a perceived shortcoming of a project deliverable that would require modification to the meaning or intended outcome, particularly scope, budget and schedule. In many cases, a small change in a current phase of the project may lead to large changes in subsequent work.

You shouldn't be afraid of changes. Changes to your website are not necessarily negative experiences; when properly planned and implemented, improvements will make your website better. In fact, Agile project methodology discussed earlier in this chapter is designed to support continuous improvement of your website. I personally recommend Agile methodology for implementing changes in your project.

Changes and additions to your project will inevitably result in additional time and cost. After all, you are asking the web developer to change a phase of the project that has been completed or approved, or perhaps you want to add an element that wasn't part of the original scope. This will results in additional work for the web developer, the cost of which will be passed to you.

When deciding whether to implement a change or addition to the project, use the following criteria:

- How much is it going to cost, and is it worth the benefit that will be realized from the change?

- How long will it take, and is the delay worth the wait?

- How will this change affect the rest of the project?

Address Quality Assurance

No matter how great your web developer is your website will have bugs, typos, gaps, glitches and other issues. It is impossible to prevent them, but systems should be in place to keep these issues at a minimum. Great project management distinguishes itself from poor management by firmly setting processes and procedures that are designed to control quality. These processes facilitate problem resolution in a timely and efficient manner. This is called Quality Assurance (QA).

Quality Assurance processes ensure that your website meets the highest possible standards on all levels. The QA process covers everything from initial design concepts including functionality and business logic, right down to each line of code that makes the website work.

Ask your web developer in the beginning of the project about their QA process: What do they do to uncover and fix issues so they don't appear on the live website? What kind of testing will be part of the project? What is the process for reporting and turnaround for fixing problems?

Most web developers have some sort of continuous testing built into the life cycle of the project. There are industry standards for Quality Management, such as ISO 9000, and most established companies have Quality Management Systems (QMS) that continuously maintain and monitor the effectiveness and process improvements.

Although types of testing will vary among developers (and depending on their projects' needs), following are several types of testing that can be expected to be part of your project:

- *User Acceptance Testing (UAT)* – determines that the website meets all the established requirements. Many times UAT consists of two stages: Alpha testing conducted in tandem by your team and the developer's internal staff, prior to external release; and Beta testing conducted by a selected group of customers, who sample the website and provide feedback, also prior to external release.

- *User Experience Testing* – establishes how users interact with your website and determines issues or problems they may experience when using your website. This is typically performed with monitored external user groups or focus groups.

- *Browser/Platform/Device Compatibility Testing* – determines that your website performs as planned on different browsers (e.g., Microsoft Internet Explorer, Mozilla Firefox, Google Chrome, Apple's Safari, etc.), Operating Systems (Microsoft Windows, Apple OS) or Devices (desktops, tablets, smartphones).

- *Automated Testing* – creates test cases for automatic test and retest of various cases and functions on your website that would otherwise take extensive manual labor.

- *Regression Testing* – designed to uncover problems by partial retesting of the modified website following every significant change.

- *Penetration/Security/Risk Testing* – determines vulnerability of your website to hacker attacks and unauthorized intrusions that may pose security threats to your website's operation and data.

- *Performance / Load Testing* – determines your website and its hosting behaviors during growth spurts in traffic (planned or unplanned). Can your website handle 1,000 visitors? 10,000? What about a million?

Understand Warranty Limitations

It is a good idea to discuss the project's warranty and its limitations before starting the project. In the previous section of the book that covers contracts, we talked about different warranties. Let's revisit that subject now.

Warranty duration may range from one to three years. The web developer should guarantee that if the website does not perform according to the original specifications (included in the proposal) and in the original environment (including but not limited to the hosting account, operating system, platform, database or scripting language); the necessary repairs will be promptly performed by them at no additional cost. Please note that any tampering of the site's database, code, or components that is not authorized by your web developer may void this warranty.

Talk to your web developer to understand what is and is not included in the warranty coverage, resolution process and related turnaround time. Some web developers may offer an extended warranty at an additional cost.

Agree on Training & Support

An important but often overlooked aspect in developing a website is your team's training and support. It is best to discuss this at the beginning of the project to ensure that you will receive the training and support needed when the time comes.

Is it typical of most development companies to include a specific number of training and support hours with the project, and when this number of hours is exceeded, they will charge extra. Other companies will not include these services in their contract. In any case, all companies will ultimately bill their client for training and support.

Since it is critical for your team to be trained on the new website, be sure to inquire about a training price structure, location and training frequency. It is a good idea to start planning training sessions at the very beginning of the project. You may want to include multiple team members in these sessions to accommodate turnover, vacations, sick leave, etc. Those trained team members who show an aptitude can also assist in training others. Including a greater number of people in your first training session is wise, because they will see the process from the build stage. Keep in mind that retraining or training additional personnel later will not be as cost-effective.

We will talk more about training and support later in the book, but you should understand that the work on the website doesn't end when the website is launched. All websites require ongoing support and maintenance. This is a key component of a successful website that sets it apart from stale, outdated websites. If you want your website to outperform your competition, you should continue working with your web developer to improve your website and have them provide operational, creative and technical support—from simple questions to long-term business strategy and planning.

Most web developers will offer support packages near the completion of the project, at the point when they know more about your project, your needs and your internal capabilities. It is a good idea, however, to inquire about their support programs and packages in the beginning of the project. During the course of the project, you will learn the type and level of support you will need after the website is launched. Also, acquire a thorough understanding of your developer's policy regarding ongoing, post-launch training.

Chapter 10 - Which Technology is Right for My Website?

Modern websites are built using a myriad of technologies. While you don't have to be an expert in these systems to manage your website project properly, it is a good idea to familiarize yourself with the basics of the available technologies and their pros and cons in order to understand the long-term impact they will have on your website.

There is no single "right technology" for building websites. Many factors should be a part of your decision, such as your vendor's experience, vendor's collective team talents, development and licensing costs, as well as your organization's internal guidelines, website performance, maintainability, ease of scalability for growth and more.

You should not impose a specific technology on your developer, especially if it is not their first area of expertise. Your web developer should issue a recommendation with an explanation as to why the technology they recommend is the best choice for you.

At the same time, choosing the wrong technology or the web developer with insufficient experience in the technology can amount to a significant cost. In order to avoid costly mistakes, be sure that the following is true before you embark on the project:

1. You fully understand the choice of technology and its long-term implications on your website. For example, does it pose any limitations or require additional licensing costs?

2. Your web developer is truly an expert in the technology chosen for the project.

The following will help you navigate the sea of modern technologies used in web development:

Website is A Cake of Many Layers

Prior to deciding which technology is right for your website, it is imperative that you understand all building blocks of a website. You can think of a modern website as a cake that has multiple layers. Each layer represents a certain technology. Each "technology layer" has its own function and purpose. Choose them wisely and you have a great-tasting cake. Choose poorly, and your product will be inedible. The following are some of the "layers" you should know:

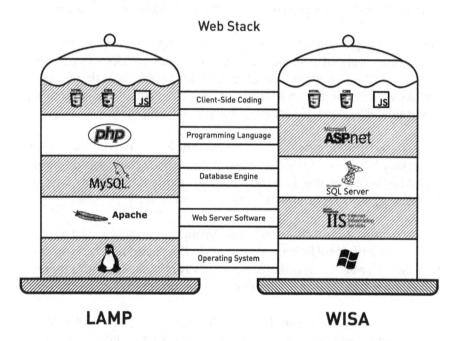

Client-Side Coding

HTML (Hypertext Markup Language), CSS (Cascading Style Sheets) and JavaScript are essential components to your website. They are as important to your website as sugar is to your cake. You can't build a modern website without these components, and your web developer must be an expert in all three.

What do they do? To put things in simple terms: HTML is a language that makes up the content of your website and tells your browser (like

Internet Explorer or Google Chrome) what to show on the website. CSS is a language used to describe the presentation (the look and formatting) of your website, and it tells your browser what to show on your website. JavaScript is a programming language commonly used to create interactive effects within web browsers.

These are *client-side* technologies. Client-side means that when you go to a website, your browser downloads HTML, CSS and JavaScript. At that point your browser renders (or processes) HTML and CSS and executes (or runs) JavaScript. This happens on your computer; therefore, these technologies are client-side. You may hear of other client-side technologies like Ajax or jQuery, which are typically methods or libraries to expand and enhance JavaScript capabilities.

Another client-side technology is Flash. Flash is one client-side technology that should be avoided. Adobe Flash was used historically to create animations and interactive experiences. It has been replaced with HTML5/CSS3 - new versions that have built-in support for functionality that was formerly only possible with Flash. The biggest issue with Flash is that it is not supported by iOS (Apple's operating system) so parts of your website written in Flash won't work on iPhones or iPads. Finally, Flash is also not SEO friendly.

Programming Language

The remaining technology layers that make up your website are *server-side*, meaning that they reside and operate on the server.

In order to program business logic or custom functionality on your website, web developers use programming languages. There are many, but the most common ones are "the top four": PHP, ASP .NET, Java and Ruby. You may have heard of the less common or older languages like Perl, ColdFusion, C/C++ or Python.

What programming language should your web developer use for your website? As long as you have unrestricted access to the source code, I would leave it up to them. My only recommendation is that you stick to one of "the top four". This will make it easier to move to another web developer. Just to give you an idea, below is the breakdown of programming languages used in the world's most popular websites (note that most use more than one, so I am listing the primary languages only):

PHP	Facebook, Yahoo, Google, Wikipedia, WordPress
ASP.NET	Live, MSN.com, Bing
Java	Amazon, eBay, LinkedIn, YouTube
Ruby	Twitter

Framework / Platform

A framework (sometimes referred to as a platform) is the next "layer" in your website. You can think of it as Lego® pieces making up your website. Essentially, a framework is a group of libraries of optimized and field-tested code that provide building blocks you can use to construct a website. They allow reusing code from common functions without "reinventing the wheel". Chances are, your web developer has a framework or platform that they use most often, and I would recommend that you leave this choice to them. Just be sure that the framework/platform is one that other web developers will be able to work with if you should need to move to another web partner.

Most modern complex websites rely on frameworks since they make web development more time- and cost-effective. They routinely have pre-written solutions for most of the functions and features commonly used on websites. Some of the most common frameworks for programming languages are listed below:

PHP	Zend, Yii, Symphony, CodeIgniter, Cake PHP
ASP.NET	C#
Java	Spring/Hibernate, Struts, Tapestry, Scala
Ruby	Rails, Sinatra

Database Engine

A database engine or database server is the underlying component of your website where your entire website's data is stored. This is where your website will store all the information such as products, orders, transactions, user records, etc. You might be surprised to learn that most CMS (Content Management Systems) use databases to store even the content of the website. Yes, this means that even text on your website may be stored in the database as well. The choice of the database engine largely depends on other factors, such as the programming language/framework, web server, etc. The most common databases for web developers are MySQL, Microsoft SQL Server, Oracle and Postgres. The choice is generally dependent on the other technologies covered below. Please note, MySQL and Postgres are generally "free" (open source) database engines, whereas Microsoft SQL and Oracle require licenses that can be expensive.

Web Server Software

The term web server can refer to either the hardware (the physical computer) or the software (the computer application) that helps deliver your website to the end user. Since we are talking about layers of your website's technology cake, we are referring to the software on the server that makes your website work.

The web server is the layer between the Operating System and the rest of the cake. The choice typically depends on what other technologies you are using and where you will be hosting your website.

Two web servers that dominate the landscape of the Internet: Apache (Linux) and IIS (Microsoft).

Operating System

The bottom layer of your website that ultimately "makes everything work" is the Operating System running on the physical server machine. For a vast majority of websites there are two underlying operating systems: Linux and Microsoft Windows.

While Linux is an inherently open source (free) Operating System, it is available in hundreds of different flavors and distributions (Ubuntu, Red Hat, CentOs, SUSE, Debian, Fedora) each supported by different groups and organizations, including distributions and add-ons that may not be free. Windows Server is a Microsoft product that requires a license for purchase.

Web Stack

Now that you understand all the "layers of the cake", there are popular recipes that feature a combination of layers commonly used in conjunction with each other. They are called "stacks". A stack is a combination of technologies or components needed to deliver a fully functioning website.

Most websites fall into two categories: LAMP (Linux-based) or WISA (Windows-based). You can see the expanded acronyms and the individual components below:

	Operating System	Web Server Software	Database Engine	Programming Language
LAMP (Linux-based)	Linux	Apache	MySQL	PHP
WISA (Windows-based)	Windows	IIS	SQL Server	ASP.NET

I will say that both are very popular choices and you can't go wrong with either setup. In fact, most web developers are split between these two camps and build websites under Linux or Microsoft Windows. If you send out an RFP, it is likely you will get bids for both.

Which is the better choice for you, and does it make a difference? Before you can answer this question, let's look at a few other factors.

Content Management System (CMS)

Of all technologies used on your website, the most important one you *must* give primary attention to is the Content Management System (CMS), which is the system used to manage content on your website. It enables your control of the website. A good CMS should easily accommodate the timely updates and management of your entire website without any outside assistance. This CMS will also reduce operating costs. On the other hand, a poorly designed CMS will become a major source of frustration and will drain your time, resources and budget. With no CMS in place, you will have to rely on your web developer for any content changes to your website.

Which Content Management System is Right for My Website?

The answer to this question depends on your needs. Prior to embarking on the project, ask your web developer about the CMS they will be using for your website. Then, request a demo. Make sure that it is easy to use and has all the features that you need.

There are literally thousands of Content Management Systems available, depending on your website's purpose, application and platform chosen. Below are some of the popular choices:

CMS	Platform	Cons / Pros
WordPress	Linux	WordPress is a very popular open source choice for small, simple, entry-level websites. It began as a blogging platform and remains a popular tool for running a blog. It is very user-friendly but not a very good choice for enterprise-level CMS because of known customization, security and scalability issues.
Drupal	Linux	Drupal is a better open source choice for complex / advanced websites or websites that that require complex data organization. It is capable of producing more complex websites but has a reputation of being difficult to work with.
Joomla!	Linux	Designed as an open source community platform, with strong social networking features. Offers more flexibility than WordPress but not as versatile as Drupal.

SharePoint	Windows	While technically not a CMS, Microsoft's SharePoint has a complete set of publishing and collaboration features. It is great for internal intranets, but building a public website requires a great deal of effort and expense.
Sitecore	Windows	Sitecore recently became one of the industry's leading CMS. It is a great enterprise-level .NET CMS that features a Windows-like interface and many features, but it has a relatively high cost of ownership.
Kentico	Windows	Reasonably priced, this easy-to-use and function-friendly growing CMS is quickly becoming a CMS of choice for Windows-based website deployments.

Benefits of a Custom CMS

There are many Content Management Systems, but no single CMS is right for all websites. In fact, you may get an impression that there isn't a single system that does everything you need. If your website requires a great deal of custom functionality, a custom-designed CMS may be the answer.

With a custom CMS, you have the ability to have your website built to the exact requirements of your business. Custom CMS solutions are typically built to be highly flexible, offer integration with third party applications and may better accommodate advanced website functionality.

Ease of Use & Level of Control

The top requirement of any Content Management System is its ease of use and the amount of control you have over your website. If you can't easily update the necessary content, publish timely updates or create new pages on your website on your terms and at your convenience, then having a Content Management System would pointless.

Unfortunately, in the web development industry we see too many Content Management Systems where the website is built around what the CMS does and doesn't support. As a result, users are forced to compromise and settle for inconvenient interfaces, cumbersome update processes and limitations due to "lazy" design. In the process of working with the CMS you might realize it has many shortcomings and limitations. This is unacceptable. A good CMS needs to adapt to your business' standards, processes, and not the other way around.

Ensure that you have a full understanding of the CMS functionality, and insist on the time to test drive an example of the CMS you will be using before it is deployed on your website. Ask your web developer about the level of control that you will have with the CMS. For example, what are the features and components that you will be able to update on your website versus having to involve your web developer? If you foresee a need to update content on your website that the CMS doesn't support, talk to your web developer about providing you with the tools so you can perform this task in house. This will save time and money.

Features of Content Management

The features of each CMS vary, but most include a set of standard features that will either be included with your system or priced individually. This is a good time to review the features you need.

✳ **Download:** *You can download the following CMS Evaluation Sheet an Excel spreadsheet from* www.ResultsOnInternet.com. *This will help you compare systems side-by-side.*

- Level of Automation – does the CMS offer sufficient automation to make updates easy for you? For example, does it automatically update links to newly uploaded or updated content, create image thumbnails or convert uploaded content to the appropriate format? A poorly designed CMS may result in repetitive and duplicate work. A good CMS should make every update quick and effortless.

Features of a CMS

☑		Level of Automation
☑		Navigation & Link Management
☑		Documents & Multimedia Support
☑		Asset Management
☑		Search Capabilities
☑	SEO	SEO Friendly
☑		Editorial Review & Approval
☑	login	Authorized Access
☑		Revision Control
☑		Multi-lingual Support

- Navigation & Link Management – does it automatically support updating links among pages, as well as all forms of navigation on the website?

- Documents & Multimedia Support – can you upload documents of certain formats, embed videos, etc.?

- Asset Management- does the CMS have a central library to store and reuse images, documents, etc.?

- Search Capabilities – does the CMS have search capabilities?

- SEO Friendly – how SEO friendly is the CMS? Does it generate search-engine-friendly URLs?

- Editorial Review & Approval – can you have an editorial review process, where one user prepares an update and another user reviews it before publishing?

- Authorized Access – can you assign user privileges and roles, allowing users to pre-defined levels of access?

- Revision Control – can you quickly revert to a previous version of a page?

- Multi-lingual Support – does the CMS include support for translating the website into multiple languages and allow users to select a language of their choice?

Commercial versus Open Source

When evaluating technology used for your website, there are many factors to consider. One of the biggest decisions you may face is whether to use commercial or open source technology.

In the previous section we discussed the two most commonly used Web Stacks that are popular for web development. The first one (LAMP) is based on open source technologies without licensing costs: Linux operating system, Apache Web server, MySQL database, and PHP programming language. The second choice is commercial software (Microsoft or WISA), which requires the purchase of several additional software licenses: Microsoft Windows operating system, IIS web server, Microsoft SQL Server database and ASP .NET programming language.

Before we compare the two more closely, it is important to understand the fundamental differences between open source and commercial software. Commercial systems are created and supported by for-profit companies (e.g., Microsoft) that typically sell licenses for the use of their software and that are driven by maximizing profits. Open source systems are overseen by dedicated communities of developers who contribute modifications to improve the product continually and who decide on the course of the software based on the needs of the community.

Cost of Ownership

Cost of ownership is one of the biggest factors in deciding whether to use open source or commercial software. Open source software is generally free or has low-cost licensing options. Commercial software, on the other hand, requires purchasing a license. The up-front license cost of a commercial CMS could run from a few thousand dollars to tens or even hundreds of thousands. Most enterprise-level CMS systems also charge significant recurring fees (usually 20% of the initial investment or more) for support and updates. Having said this, an open source solution could provide substantial cost savings to your organization over licensing fees for a commercial solution.

Licensing fees, costs of learning and Microsoft certifications also contribute to the difference in pay between PHP developers and their .NET counterparts. In my experience, developers specializing in Microsoft technologies typically cost around 10-30% more than PHP developers.

There are many web development and hosting companies who would roll various licensing fees into your up-front "consulting fee" and your monthly hosting fees. However, regardless of the payment structure, you should expect to pay significantly more to develop, host and maintain a website utilizing Microsoft technologies or a commercial CMS versus an open source alternative.

The Case for Commercial Technologies

Microsoft Web Stack and a commercial CMS can be a good choice for your organization if the underlying platform (e.g., Microsoft-based technologies) meshes well with other software already used by your organization. For example, if many other solutions utilized by your organization are Microsoft-based, it may be a good idea to stay with a CMS that integrates well with other solutions by Microsoft.

Commercial or proprietary software also equates to better support and typically offers a robust suite of features right out of the box. If your organization's needs are very well planned and documented, your IT favors Microsoft products and commercially supported software, and the up-front budget for software licensing is not a significant concern, then Microsoft web stack and commercial CMS may be a good option for you.

The Case for Open Source Technologies

If your organization doesn't have a specific technology or marketing roadmap in place, but requires a website with virtually unlimited customization possibilities, a custom solution based on LAMP may be a better choice. This solution provides the latitude to modify the website to accommodate the company's changing needs. Another benefit of the open source approach is that you don't have as many limitations on future website expansion and customization, and you can continue improving your website "as you go." In addition, you are not tied to a single web developer using the open source approach, which gives you the flexibility for further development and web partner selection.

Because open source solutions are supported by communities of volunteers, your initial cost may be lower with this choice, but you will most likely need to budget for technical resources to maintain it over time. With a limited budget, however, your financial resources are better directed toward the best possible website as opposed to acquiring licenses and paying mandatory fees for updates.

Commercial versus Open Source

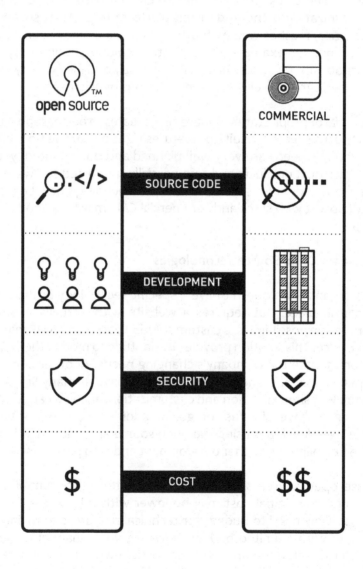

Chapter 11 – Why Mobile is no Longer Just an Option

"We don't really need a mobile website" I often hear. "Yes, you really do!" is always my response. I can bore you with numbers and statistics of growing mobile users, but even more powerful evidence exists to support this argument. Next time you are in a checkout line, on a train or in a coffee shop, look around. How many people do you see with a smartphone in their hands? Chances are you would be looking up from your own phone to answer that question. As I write these statements, my tablet and phone are next to me. I hardly ever take a step without my phone. You and your customers probably do the same.

You Do Need a Mobile Website

Mobile is no longer an option. Mobile is not the future. It is our present reality. It is today's way of life. It doesn't matter what you sell or who your customers are—if you don't have a mobile website, you will lose customers.

If you are designing a new website or currently redesigning your site, you must use this opportunity to build a website that is mobile-friendly. This will allow you to get ahead of the curve, or at least not be left behind. There is no business rationale to delay implementing a mobile-friendly website.

If you are planning to postpone your mobile website development, I urge you to reconsider. Designing a mobile website at this stage will simply be more cost-effective. If you delay the mobile-friendly website, it is just a matter of time before you will need to redesign your website, and of course, additional cost will be incurred.

Furthermore, if you think your website works "well enough" on mobile devices, think again. Research shows that most users opening a website on a mobile device will simply move on at the first sign of unresponsiveness or inconvenience. You probably have a great website with valuable content, but if it is not easy to navigate and experience on a small screen, you will simply lose that visitor permanently.

Responsive Design to the Rescue

Hopefully, you are convinced that you need a mobile website. What are your options in building a mobile-friendly website? The old approach was cumbersome and inefficient. Frankly, you had to build a second mobile version of your original website. Yes, two separate websites to build and maintain.

Luckily, we now have a better solution. It's called responsive design. Responsive websites automatically adapt to the screen size of any device. Using responsive design enables a developer to build websites that work well on all screen sizes – desktops, laptops, tablets and mobile phones. The cost benefit is clear—one website version to build and maintain.

You may have heard the term "adaptive design." You can think of this as an extension of responsive design (which simply adapts to the screen size). The adaptive design can also make use of features available on particular devices, such as GPS and touch-screen capability. This ensures that not only your website looks good on a small screen, but it is also responds to touch events; for example, finger-swipes, pinching to zoom in and out, rotating with your device, and more. For tablet and smartphone users, these actions are becoming second nature to end users, so you want to incorporate them into your mobile website as well.

What Can Be Done with Responsive Design?

A major advantage of responsive design is that it is not tied to a specific device or screen size. This means that a responsive website can technically work on all devices, including devices that will be designed in the future. In a nutshell, the website detects the size of the screen and adapts its design to maximize the experience on the screen. Typically, a responsive website has three built-in screen "modes": larger desktop and notebook screens, smaller tablet screens and the smallest smartphone screens. The website knows what hardware you are using and adapts accordingly (These are called "breakpoints."). Because it doesn't care about the exact resolution of your screen, responsive websites will theoretically work on future devices as well. As screens get smaller (smartwatches) and bigger (ultra-high definition televisions) some future adjustments may be required (for instance, creating additional breakpoints), but you wouldn't have to replace your entire responsive website to accommodate a new screen size.

Geolocation, or geographic location using IP address or GPS, is one of the most exciting features of today's mobile devices. Mobile websites are now capable of having the geolocation feature as well. Mobile websites can have access to the GPS in your device to find business locations closest to you, locate your friends by proximity and incorporate local offers (i.e., events, promotions or announcements for your area).

A mobile device can also link physical media (billboards, business cards, product packaging) to your website by scanning QR (Quick Response) Codes to your mobile website. By linking QR codes to your responsive website, you can enable customers who are "on the go" to order products from your company, contact you, or access your website's general information. This is known as Mobile Commerce, or M-commerce (the next generation of E-commerce).

Today's mobile websites also offer social networking for a new era of global connectivity. Instant communication, augmented reality and location-based services are extensions of mobile and web-based networks, working symbiotically to spread content, increase accessibility and connect users from any location. These functionalities are now available thanks to responsive design.

Do I Need a Mobile Website or an Application?

Before we answer this question, let's make sure we understand the difference between the two, as well as the pros and cons of each.

A mobile website resides on a server and is loaded from the server every time. This means that if you update the website, mobile users will see the same updated version of the website in real time. This makes maintenance of mobile website cost-effective. The responsive website will also work on any device (make, screen size or operating system). However, mobile websites do have limitations. They tend to load slower (over Wi-Fi or cellular connection), and they don't have direct access to all your phone's features such as the camera, alerts and push notifications, phonebook, etc. Another downside of a mobile website is that it cannot be used offline, if you don't have a cell signal, for example.

A mobile application is typically faster, more interactive and can work with a number of phone features that a website might not be able to access. One can also use a mobile application without an Internet connection (limitations apply). The major problem with mobile apps, however, is that they have to be installed. Significantly greater resources are also required to develop and maintain mobile apps. You would essentially have to build a separate application for each major platform: iOS, Android, Windows, etc. This potentially could mean 3-4 applications to develop and maintain. Consider that it also takes time and effort to have apps approved by Apple, Google or Microsoft before they will be available in their stores. Maintenance can also be cumbersome as app updates must be submitted for approval every time. Finally, applications rely on users to accept and install updates.

If you are still deliberating whether to build a mobile website or an application, consider the following: if your primary project is a website, an application will not replace it. In fact, if you are building a website, it is in your best long-term interest to build a website that it responsive. An application, however, could be a nice addition to your website for the reasons mentioned above. Note that I called it an "addition", not a "replacement." Some websites require a mobile application. For example, if you are building a social network or service-providing website, your users may appreciate having a quick access to the website's features through a native application.

Mobile is No Longer An Option

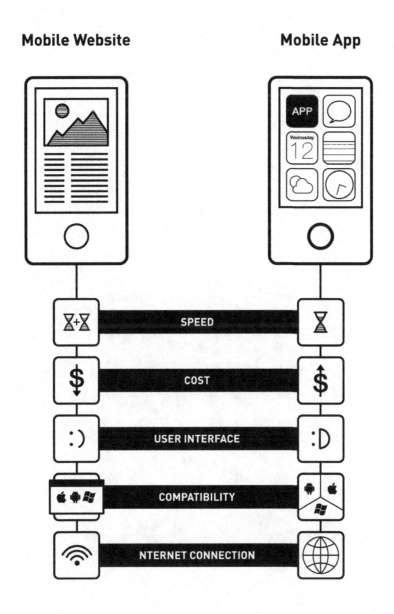

Mobile Website

Mobile App

SPEED

COST

USER INTERFACE

COMPATIBILITY

NTERNET CONNECTION

Chapter 12 - Is Your Website Built to Sell? Proven Ways to Convert Visitors into Customers

Would you rather have a hundred website visitors or a hundred customers? Regardless of the nature of your organization or the purpose of your website, every website must sell. Your website can be literally selling your products or services online, or it can be pitching an idea, supporting an important message or enhancing your brand.

This is not an easy task, and it is where the vast majority of websites fail. Is your website relevant to your customers? What makes your website different from your competition? What makes people go to your website, take out their credit card, pick up the phone or fill out that registration form? If you can't fully answer these questions, your website won't be effective in selling, and it won't fulfill its mission. However, if you get these points right, you will leave your competition in the dust.

The reason most websites are ineffective is because everyone tends to focus on details (aesthetics, content, etc.), but the big picture is often overlooked. First and foremost, your website is a business tool and unfortunately, most web developers don't take the time and effort to understand the business side of your website. This often becomes your responsibility, and since your website's ability to sell is critical to its success, the following recommendations will help you get the most out of your new website:

Always Know Your HVC

Do you really know your customers, or are you mistaken? Do you know your HVC (or High Value Customers)? These are customers who are vital to the survival and growth of your business. When was the last time you interviewed customers about their experience? Do you know exactly why they chose to do business with you? What are the values that you offer, and what are areas for improvement?

Interview Your Customers

When answering these questions, you must not guess or assume the answers. In fact, you need to know exactly what your customers think. You want to get inside your customers' heads. The best way to achieve this is to interview a good sampling of your customers. Ideally, you would want the interviews to be conducted by an unbiased third party. Naturally, when discussing an experience about their interaction with your company, your customers would be more likely to open up to someone who is not part of your organization. Such interviews could be amazingly revealing, as you are likely to get not only their perception and feedback for the website, but also information about their feelings and attitudes about your company. Unlike surveys, interviews allow you to ask follow-up questions that will produce more in-depth feedback.

Conduct Market Research

A more extended market research is typically managed by conducting focus groups. A focus group is a form of qualitative research where questions are typically asked in an interactive group setting and group members are encouraged to freely speak their minds and share their thoughts and feelings. Focus groups don't necessarily have to include existing customers. In fact, they often include potential customers who meet your demographic requirements but don't know much about your product or service. Focus groups are usually all about testing products and concepts and learning methods to attract new customers. They can be expensive but will provide you with invaluable insight, especially for consumer products and services.

Test Using Personas

Once you have the market information you need, the next step would be to create a persona (sometimes called an avatar) that represents your ideal customer. A persona is a fictional character that represents your website's desired demographic (age, gender, occupation, interests, desires, goals, etc.). You and your web developer should be using personas throughout the project to test all the website's components. Give them names and create short profiles, and then ask yourself, would this message resonate with John? Would Susan like this picture?

Would James be more likely to use our website/product/service versus a competitor's site?

We will talk about customer interviews and personas more in" Chapter 17 - Recommended Website Project Flow: How to Stay on Track and Achieve Results

Use Customer-Centric Messaging

As users visit your website, they will look for interesting information that captures their attention. Customer-centric messaging is all about focusing on the needs and wants of your customers. You tell them what they want to hear, you show them what they want to see, you help solve their problems and you make them feel good in the process. To make your website even more effective, don't sell a product or a service, sell an experience.

Use Slogans & Taglines

One of the best methods to create an experience is by crafting one or two sentence slogans or taglines and prominently featuring them on the homepage and throughout the website. Website visitors today don't read; they scan. Succinct and concise taglines are effective and imperative in delivering your key messages. Make them specific, memorable and consistent throughout the website.

Focus on the Needs of Your Customers

You might think you are the most established company in the industry, you have the most talented team, superior product or service, and you don't understand why anyone would do business with any other company. Most organizations are so passionate about how good they are that they forget one important factor: Your customers don't care about your passion or pride. Your website is not about your company's history, accomplishments or personal egos. This might come as a shock, but most of your customers don't care about any of your "bragging rights." They only do business with you because your products and services are of value to them--not because you're a company with an "established history" or "state-of-the-art" facilities.

Remember this when working on your website. When you lose that focus, and your website becomes more about you and less about your customers, you start losing your customers. The website is built for your customers, so it is important that you focus on the customer's benefits. Your customers want your website to be useful, informative and engaging. If your customers find a value in your website, they will see value in doing business with you.

Have Clear Value Propositions

Most effective taglines are those that contain value proposition. A compelling value proposition focuses on the benefits to your customers and differentiates you from your competitors. It is designed to appeal to your customers and drive them to make a purchasing decision. Ask yourself, who you are? What do you do? How do you help our customers solve their problems? Why should your customers care? What value and proof points do you deliver? Below are examples of some taglines my agency crafted for a few of our projects:

Website For:	Targeted Demographic	Taglines:
Web Design Agency	Companies that want to see results from their website and a return on investment.	*Results On Internet (ROI)*
Business Consultants	Small business consultants with a custom approach and life-changing track record.	*Better Business. Better Life*
Health Insurance	Individuals over 60 years old interested in Medicare supplemental insurance.	*Remember Personal Service? WE DO.*
Social Network	Aspiring artists who want to share their art and be discovered.	*Create. Collaborate. Discover.*
Online Service	Parents of children with special needs looking for babysitters.	*Special Care for Special Children*

Deliver Messages Effectively

Sometimes it is necessary to have more than one important message delivered on the homepage of the website. For example, targeting various audiences or presenting messages that are progressive, sequential or chronological in nature. One of the best methods to do that is a tool called a "carousel". A carousel is a slideshow that changes automatically and allows the display of multiple messages, one at a time. The advantage of this approach is that if one message doesn't resonate with a visitor, another one might do the job. By having multiple messages you are improving your chances that at least one of them will work, and those that do work will strengthen and solidify the other messages in the carousel. By showing one message at a time, you also ensure that they don't compete or distract from the others. I recommend limiting the total number of messages on a carousel to three or four.

Also, consider the use of videos for communicating concepts and presenting ideas that would otherwise take paragraphs to describe. Videos are revolutionizing the web design industry and provide an effective way to engage customers by communicating important messages in a format that requires less time and effort to process. An ideal duration of a video is 30-90 seconds or less. Research shows that most people will not finish watching a video that any longer[9].

Companies pay a high price when their customers lose sight of the value proposition, so be sure that you have effective content on your website. We have discussed it a great deal in "Chapter 7 – Fundamental Principles of Creating a Successful Website". We will also look into the process of producing quality content in more detail in" Chapter 17 - Recommended Website Project Flow: How to Stay on Track and Achieve Results."

Create Effective Calls to Action

An effective Call to Action (CTA) is what ultimately converts your website visitors into customers by urging them to take an immediate

---

[9]   http://thenextweb.com/socialmedia/2014/05/02/optimal-length-video-marketing-content-short-possible/

action, whether buying your product or service online, registering on the website or picking up their phone to call you.

A proper call to action serves as an effective sales tool. The strategy, "If we build it, they will come" simply does not work. Listing your e-mail address or a phone number on your website is not a call to action, and you will lose business to websites that take the extra effort and encourage users to take the next step.

Maximize the Effectiveness of CTA

Effective calls to action lead, urge and entice the website visitor, create urgency and offer rewards. The following are five rules of thumb for creating calls to action that work:

1. Be certain that your call to action works in tandem with your customer-centric taglines and slogans and that it is a logical progression, i.e., the "next step". An effective call to action should always be supported by your value proposition and the visuals. Make it enticing and personal.

2. Strategically position your calls to action and make them stand out. It should be one of the brightest and most visible elements on the page, preferably at the same location throughout the website. One of the best locations is the top right corner or the center of the page that usually draws most attention.

3. This may seem obvious, but tell the user what to do: "Call... click...register" or make it clear to them with the help of the design. This is all about usability. For example, if you have a call to action button linked to your contact form, you don't want the user to have to guess if it is "clickable."

4. Give your users confidence to buy. Think of ways to remove or reduce risks. No-obligation statements work great. In addition, if your service is free or you offer a free trial, make sure to state that also.

5. Encourage your users to respond right away. Create a sense of urgency. Don't give people an option to wait and ponder your offering. You want them to make decision on the spot--impulsively.

CTA Examples

In the previous section, we discussed customer-centric messaging. Let's now look at some of the calls to action that we've used for the same projects:

Website For:	Targeted Demographic	Taglines:
Web Design Agency	Companies that want to see results from their website and a return on investment.	*Start Getting Results*
Business Consultants	Small business consultants with a custom approach and life-changing track record.	*Make Your Business Work for You*
Health Insurance	Individuals over 60 years old interested in Medicare supplemental insurance.	*Ask about FREE in-home Needs Analysis*
Social Network	Aspiring artists who want to share their art and be discovered.	*Register for Free*
Online Service	Parents of children with special needs looking for babysitters.	*Qualified babysitters today. It's free and easy.*

Provide Validation & Support

No matter how great your marketing messages may be, they will not work unless they are believable. If your website visitors don't fully believe in what you say, or it doesn't resonate with them, they will be unlikely to give you their business. It is easy to make bold statements, but how can you back them up to make them authentic and believable?

Create Memorable Experiences

If you want a website that is truly effective, you have to create an experience for your customers. Don't think about your website as an online brochure – a bunch of boring pages filled with text and graphics. Think of your website as a form of Infotainment – a fun and human experience. Unlike traditional service- or product-driven websites, experiences inspire, engage and motivate. They create long lasting impressions. Experiences are the most effective way to convert users into customers.

Apple's Steve Jobs revolutionized consumer technology by, in his own words, "making a dent in the universe." The genius of marketing once said, "Don't sell products, services, or jobs; sell dreams and a vision." Steve Jobs was a master of presentations. One of his most memorable presentations was the iPhone at the Macworld Conference in 2007. Jobs started by introducing "three revolutionary products in their class. The first one is a widescreen iPod with touch controls. The second is a revolutionary mobile phone. The third is a breakthrough Internet communications device[10]." He went on to repeat, "So, three things: a widescreen iPod with touch controls; a revolutionary mobile phone; and a breakthrough Internet communications device. An iPod, a phone, and an Internet communicator. An iPod, a phone … are you getting it? These are not three separate devices, this is one device, and we are calling it an iPhone." The audience exploded in applause.

By building up the drama and then hitting the big note, Jobs created a moment to define the experience. He first stirred up the excitement and then delivered a punch line resulting in a memorable moment.

How do you do that? To create an experience you really have to think outside of the box. You have to look at your products and services not as products and services but as the "dent in the universe" they make. How do they impact the lives of your customers? How do they help overcome customers' problems; make their jobs easier or their lives happier? How can your company's vision help change the world?

---

[10]   Steve Jobs presentation at Macworld Conference and Expo, January 9, 2007

These are big and bold ideas, but this is exactly what makes you stand out. By addressing these points on your website through interactive presentations, videos or real-life case studies, you can present the exciting side of your products and services, something that connects on a more personal level and creates a memorable experience.

Establish Authority & Credibility

No matter what your organization does, people will be more likely to want to conduct business with you when you are perceived as an expert or an authority in the field. No one wants to deal with an organization that is "inexperienced, volatile and amateurish." At the same time, customers are willing to pay more for proven experience and a great track record.

The following are some ideas to project authority and credibility and create a level of confidence in the minds of your website visitors that will capture their attention from the moment they arrive on your website:

- Be sure that your website is designed in a manner that immediately presents an established and professional company. Website visitors often make judgments about the organization by their first impression of the website. Think of your website as silent salesperson. Would you rather buy from a well-versed, sharply dressed salesperson, or a sloppy, poorly dressed one?

- Double-check all the content on the website. Nothing is more unprofessional than having a website with typographical errors, broken links or poor grammar.

- Update your site's content often or at least make sure it doesn't have outdated content, such as a three-year old press release on your homepage or last year's date in the copyright notice.

- Feature case studies, customer testimonials, endorsements and reviews that demonstrate clear and specific results regarding product or service customer delivery. We will cover this more in the next section.

- Write articles, blog posts or whitepapers that provide useful information, guidance and advice for your customers and at the same time position you as the expert in the field.

- Show that there's a real and credible organization behind your site with a physical address and a picture of your office or facility.

- Make it easy to contact you by listing phone numbers and using online forms to contact your company online. I recommend avoiding a list of e-mail addresses, as they will be easily harvested by spammers).

- Have a page on your website that lists your key team members, with their names, pictures, backgrounds and biographies.

- Showcase awards, industry recognitions and any other professional achievements earned by your organization.

- Quote research that supports your claims and list the source, preferably a well-known publication or institution.

- Use data to support your claims. Dress up your numbers with understandable analogies, and incorporate them into the appropriate context.

- Mention professional associations with which your organization is affiliated.

Offer Social Proof through Testimonials

There are few forms of marketing communication that are more effective in establishing credibility, building trust and increasing purchase decision confidence than customer testimonials and reviews. By showcasing satisfied customers' statements on your website, your message becomes more believable. You are really saying, "Don't take our word for it, take theirs."

To demonstrate the power of social proof, Stanley Milgram, a renowned social psychologist, conducted the following experiment[11]: he arranged for a group of people in a middle of a busy intersection to look up at the top of a tall building where nothing was happening. When there was a single person staring upward, only 4% of people passing would stop and look up, but when there were 15 people gathered, a whopping 40% of passersby would stop to join the group. Similar behavior is witnessed (with social proof) where customers observe the actions of others and then make the same choice.

Regardless of what your company sells or does, your prospective customers will seek validation. Recent studies show that nearly 7 out of 10 consumers will check online reviews before buying[12]. Having unbiased and authentic testimonials throughout your website, especially on pages featuring your product line or services, is a great way to reinforce your customers' decision to purchase.

However, customer testimonials can be a double-edged sword. They may actually be hurting your conversion rate if they're not relating to or connecting with your audience. A testimonial from John Doe at ABC Company may not resonate with your audience. Everyone wants to see a recognizable name. This is why companies pay big bucks to get celebrity endorsements. If you don't have big brands as your clients, consider offering your products or services at no charge (or a substantial saving) in exchange for a testimonial.

I also strongly recommend using only authentic testimonials that are written by your legitimate, satisfied customers. Most people will sense fake or insincere testimonials that were written by you with your customers' approvals. Use real testimonials and avoid generic phrases like "best", "satisfied" and "met expectations." Instead, ask your customers to talk about specific results "21% increase in sales," "10% satisfaction rate," "50% in savings," etc. Also, if you cater to multiple verticals, consider tailoring testimonials to different audiences.

---

[11]   http://psycnet.apa.org/journals/psp/13/2/79/
[12]   http://www.ipsos-na.com/news-polls/pressrelease.aspx?id=5929

If you have a consumer product or service, pay close attention to reviews on Yelp and Google+. Make an effort to respond to all reviews, especially negative ones. Responding to a negative review shows that you actually care about the customer experience and are willing to take steps to improve a process or resolve the matter with the customer.

Maximize Conversions by Making it Easy to Buy

Did you know that most sales made on e-commerce websites come from a website search? Did you know that one of the most frequently used tools on manufacturer's website is the dealer locator? Did you know sales can be greatly increased by recommending supplementary products or value-added upgrades? Make it easy to buy and your website's performance will exceed your most ambitious expectations. Below are some recommendations to get started:

Understand Conversions

Remember, a conversion on your website doesn't necessarily mean an immediate monetary transaction. A conversion may also be an expression of interest through a contact form or a registration on your website that would eventually lead to other opportunities. When a website user acts according to your design, we call it a conversion (from a visitor to a customer/lead). A conversion rate is typically measured in percentage of visitors to the website or users who initiate the purchasing process (shopping cart) or demonstrate interest (Contact Us form).

In order to maximize the performance of your website, your goal and the goal of your web developer is to create an easy experience for your customers to buy. Today's customers want to find what they are looking for quickly and effortlessly. Failure to provide accurate information or loading your site with unnecessary distractions will result in lost sales.

Don't Make Visitors Think

In "Chapter 7 – Fundamental Principles of Creating a Successful Website", section "Simpler is Always Better" we talked about the importance of making your website easy to understand and navigate.

Steve Krug's "First law of usability" as described in his renowned book "Don't Make Me Think" is exactly that: don't make your website visitors think.

You website should be intuitive, self-explanatory and precise. There should be no ambiguities or need for guesswork. Your website visitors should be able to glance at a page on your website and see the information they need, and if it's not there, it should be abundantly clear how they can navigate to that information.

If you have to hesitate and ponder what to do next for even a split second, the website is not intuitive. Your website needs to guide the person through all steps of the experience and make it as effortless as possible—from understanding what you offer and why your offer is better than anyone else's, to completing the purchase or expressing interest. If your website visitors can achieve this experience without putting in extra effort or hassles, your website is performing well.

Show the Right Information in the Right Places

We already talked about the importance of customer-centric messaging, calls to action and simplifying navigation, but that is not sufficient. Research shows that in addition to "not requiring your customers to think," you can significantly increase your sales by proactively providing the right information to your customers in the right places and at the right time. Your customers will appreciate the convenience of having readily available to fill their need.

Today's consumers want to see simple checkout or registration process, detailed product or service information, easy product comparisons, unbiased reviews or testimonials and more to help with their purchasing decision. For example, consider placing links to related information, easily accessible contact information throughout the site or quick links to the most often-used functions and high traffic areas of your website.

Streamline the Checkout Process

The checkout process is one of the most important components of any website with e-commerce capabilities. A confusing checkout process that has too many steps guarantees a downturn in sales. Shoppers will simply abandon their carts. An effective checkout process should involve a minimal number of steps, and should guide customers to make the experience straightforward and hassle-free. Your website should also provide a number of payment methods, allow purchasing without registering and provide reassurances on security and privacy.

Don't Waste Customers' Time

During checkout or user registration, you should only ask for the essential information. Don't waste your user's time! Asking for too much information during registration or the checkout process will negatively impact your sales. Distractions are also a deterrent. When a customer is near completion in the checkout process or registration, distractions of unrelated features could make them leave the page or abandon the cart. Once the user is at the final stage of purchase, the objective is to guide them through the payment process or completing their registration. You should never ask a customer to log in or register to complete a purchase. With this in mind you want to have a smooth-running checkout process that is seamlessly integrated within your website rather than sending the customer to a third-party site to complete their purchase.

Make Error Validation User-Friendly

Another consideration during the checkout or registration process is making errors easy to fix. People do make mistakes when completing forms. When a customer encounters an error message, your website needs to facilitate a quick and easy fix and provide clarity on the location and nature of the error. Whether this is a typo in a credit card, an invalid e-mail address or a required field that has no entry, be sure that your website provides clear messages and instructions, visually highlighting fields that clearly show the issue and guides the user through to completion. The fix should not become frustrating or tedious for the user.

Offer Product or Service Customization

Websites that offer product or service customization options (e.g., build your own product or select service components) should make it easy to select, modify and preview available options. This will improve the overall customer experience, maintain their confidence throughout the process and efficiently complete the order that custom-fits their needs and budget.

Use Sales Offers & Incentives

Sometimes you have to sweeten the deal to encourage website visitors to complete a call to action. Providing incentives, such as freebies, special promotions, coupons and discounts, will undoubtedly increase conversion rates.

Utilize Cross-Selling and Up-Selling

Another powerful technique to increase your sales is cross-selling and up-selling. Up-selling is the practice of recommending a more expensive (or more fully-featured) item in the product line that may better serve the customer's needs, where cross-selling is designed to sell additional related products or features. Both approaches are effective in increasing the price of their total order.

Track Abandoned Orders & Conversions

You have worked so hard to get every lead or sale through the website, so the last thing you want is to lose a sale due to a trivial issue. As obvious as it may seem, most website owners don't know that data from incomplete orders or forms can be saved in the database and used by your sales team to follow up with the potential customers.

Beginning the online checkout process or partially completing the form requesting information is not only an indication of interest, but it is a strong purchasing signal. No matter how well designed, intuitive and streamlined your website is, things can happen that can interrupt the order process. People get distracted, experience computer problems or may simply need more information to complete the order. Whatever the reason, if they began the checkout steps, it means they were interested.

Assuming that your website is set up to retain the contact information of a partially completed order (and there are ways to save this data), your sales team can and should follow up. First, you may be able to close the sale. Secondly, you may learn what prevented the visitor from completing the order. Contact with this person may uncover a technical problem or a bigger issue with your product line or services. By tracking and conducting routine follow-up contact on every incomplete order or form, you are on the road to ensuring that no customer is left behind.

Combine & Optimize

As you can see, there is no single proven recipe to maximize your website's conversion, but by adopting all these recommendations, you have a single, seamless experience, that makes it feasible to increase your website's conversion rates. Generally it's not a single feature that sells, but the overall experience your website creates.

Don't Forget International Customers

One common mistake many website owners make is not targeting an international customer base, or not recognizing their international competition. The Internet is global, and a website makes you a global player. If you believe international markets are not for you, your competition may not agree and will be extremely happy to conduct business on your territory. The Internet erases borders between countries and makes entry into new markets easier for a large variety of industries. There are numerous examples where successful Western firms' online dominance was lost to more proactive, global-minded companies from Asia. There are also many examples of U.S.-based websites that happily realized unexpected traction worldwide.

As a company, you should always think big. You should think global. International expansion may not be in your immediate sights, but you may change your focus when you discover opportunities abroad. International business planning can be very challenging, but some basic steps can be taken without investing a lot of time and money.

It's All in Your Head

Many companies set their own boundaries and artificially limit their activities to their immediate geographic markets. This makes sense for some traditional brick and mortar businesses, but where online services are concerned and with boundaries removed, wonderful things may happen. Let me give you an example. Let's say that you are an online service provider based out of the U.S., and your website is in English. If the service you provide could be of use to consumers in Canada, United Kingdom or other English-speaking countries, why limit your company exposure to the U.S.? If you have an existing website in English, you could feasibly tap into additional English-speaking markets with only minor adjustments.

Multi-Lingual Website

If you want to expand into non-English speaking international markets, you should seriously consider translating your website into other languages. Because 70% of the world's population doesn't speak English[13], consider your increased revenues if you took this leap.

A multilingual website means it's been translated in other languages and your users can choose their language preference. In "Chapter 10 - Which Technology is Right for My Website?" Section "Content Management System (CMS)" we talked about multilingual support for your Content Management System. A multilingual CMS allows you to maintain the website in multiple languages and allows your users to select a language of their choice. If your short- or long-term vision for your company's expansion includes translating your website into other languages, you should invest in a multi-lingual CMS when you build your website. You can always translate your website later, but if you don't have multi-lingual support, you will have a content management nightmare when you need the support. It will be more cost-efficient to have all the tools and infrastructure ready from the beginning, as opposed to adding it later.

---

[13] http://en.wikipedia.org/wiki/English_language#Number_of_words_in_ English

Another consideration is getting the content translated. Nothing will turn your customers away faster than poorly translated content. Online translators (like Google Translate - http://translate.google.com/) can be set up to translate your entire website automatically. This might seem like a quick and cost-efficient solution, but the quality of these translations is poor. It will negatively impact the presentation, the user experience and potentially your search engine ranking. Do not consider using one of these services to translate your website, unless you want to be the laughing stock of native speakers. To ensure your site content is translated properly, you should hire a professional translator who speaks and writes the language fluently, and one who understands the context as well as the target market and culture.

Multi-Currency Website

The ability to accept credit cards online makes it easy for you to do business with anyone around the world. You can have customers from Shanghai and Melbourne as easily as customers in Chicago or Los Angeles.

If your website has an e-commerce component, and you have international orders, you should consider adding multi-currency support. With your merchant account, you can already charge foreign credit cards. Credit card companies make it easy for you and the customer by automatically converting currency. However, if you have customers who don't perform transactions in the U.S. dollar on a daily basis, you will need to make it easy for them to shop and compare by showing your prices in their currencies. In fact, this might actually help attract new international customers. Remember, if you make it easy to buy, customers will be more likely to choose you over competition.

There are multiple tools online where you can get daily (and even hourly exchange rates). For example, the European Central Bank features a daily XML feed that can be integrated into your website: http://www.ecb.europa.eu/stats/eurofxref/eurofxref-daily.xml

Multi-Regional Website with Geolocation

You may want to know the difference between a multi-lingual and a multi-regional website. A multilingual website is one that has content in more than one language (e.g., a website in English and French). A multi-regional website specifically targets users in different countries. For example, a version of your website for the US and a version for Canada can offer multilingual support in English and French and currency support for Canadian dollars. Multi-lingual sites often feature same or similar content in multiple languages, where multi-regional websites may feature entirely different experiences, offer country-specific products or services, and use different marketing messaging to target various demographics. Most large international companies have multi-regional websites, and you can see how the experience changes simply by switching to a different country.

Geolocation is the technique of identifying the geographical location of a website user by means of resolving their IP address. Although the IP-based geolocation is not always accurate, it provides insight into the user's origin (including country, region, city, postal/zip code, latitude, longitude and time zone). This information allows you to provide the regional version of your website that corresponds to their geographic location.

If you have a multi-regional website or plan on having one built, you should research and discuss legal, technical and administrative requirements that may be applicable before proceeding with the project.

Foreign Domains

If you have any plans to expand internationally, especially by building multi-regional websites, you should consider registering international domains. Even if it is not in your short-term plans, you should be aware that once someone registers your company's domain name abroad, it could be difficult or impossible to obtain it.

When you think of a domain name, you typically think of ".com", which is the most popular domain. There are others like it that you can register regardless of your location ("net", ".biz", ".info", etc.). These are called generic top-level domains.

There are also country-specific top-level domains (such as "co.uk" in UK or ".ca" in Canada or ".fr" in France). Some of these are fairly straightforward and inexpensive, and you can register them through a mainstream registrar (like GoDaddy - http://www.godaddy.com). Some can be extremely difficult to obtain. Each country has its own rules and some require a company's local presence, registered trustee or trademark requirement before a domain name can be issued. For example, to get an Australian domain name (.au) you must be an Australian registered company or have an Australian Registered Trademark. To have a presence in Brazil (.br), you must be an individual or company with residence in Brazil, etc. Country-specific domains can also be expensive. For example in 2014, Puerto Rico (.pr) top level domain could cost as much as $1,000 per year and Saudi Arabia (.sa) would set you back $400 per year.

Luckily, there are companies like Marcaria (http://www.marcaria.com/) or 101 Domains (http://www.101domain.com) who specialize in foreign domains and can help you sort out all the legal requirements by providing you with trademark and trustee support. For more information on registering domain names, refer to "Chapter 7 – Fundamental Principles of Creating a Successful Website", Section "How You Name a Boat, is How it Will Sail" and "Chapter 16 - Hosting Your Website: What You Need to Know", under "What Hosting Essentials Do I Need?".

Optimize for Repeat Business

At this point, you have optimized your website for conversion and are on track to generate sales. The only question remains: What happens after you close that sale? Is that it? Do you even get to see that customer again, or is this a one-time sale?

Top-performing websites are effective in generating sales, but they are also just as effective in retaining customers and generating residual income. Let's explore how this can be achieved.

Make Reordering Easy

Once a customer makes a purchase from your website, you should make sure it is as easy to return to your site and make more purchases. You can provide this ease by saving the information they have already entered at the time of their initial purchase: contact, shipping and even billing information. By having this information populated in the appropriate fields, customers can realize a repeat order even easier than their initial one.

There may be some reservations on the part of the customer about storing billing information, particularly credit card information. There are, however, safe ways store this data, so you should ask your web developer about best practices in storing billing information, either on your website or with the payment gateway.

In some cases, it may also be beneficial to give your customers the ability to repeat orders with the same product and automatically add these items to their shopping cart. If there are items that need to be reordered on a regular basis, your customers will appreciate having that convenience.

Finally, automatic reordering can be used to reorder at specific time intervals (i.e., products or services delivered every month) or when a customer runs low (i.e., replenish download credits). Such a process ensures that your customers get your service and products in a timely fashion and guarantees residual and ongoing income for your organization.

Implement a Residual Monetization Model

If your website's monetization model primarily relies on one-time purchases, there may be a better strategy to generate ongoing residual income. Some websites rely on hybrid or combination of monetizing methods. Look at "Chapter 14 – Earning Revenue with Your Website: Common Monetization Strategies" to explore some of the popular monetization strategies.

Use Post- Order E-mail Communications

It is a given that you should collect your customers' email addresses with every order. At the very least, this is how you will communicate with them to (1) confirm the order, (2) communicate any issues or concerns with the order, and (3) let the customer know when their order has been processed or shipped. Another reason to contact your customer post-order is that similar to in-cart up-selling and cross-selling. A post-order email (at appropriate intervals of time) is a great way to increase future sales by suggesting related products, or size options, the customer may want to purchase with their next order.

Communication though e-mail is a great way to stay connected with the customer by continuously submitting to them promotional offers of products related to their original order, special offers and discounts, new items or items that they've added to the shopping cart or wish-list but haven't purchased, etc. Sending relevant e-mail communications is clearly a very powerful tool to generate additional sales, but don't overdo it. Flooding mailboxes of your customers will have an adverse effect.

Loyalty & Rewards Programs

Everyone loves getting free stuff or discounts with purchases. A well-designed rewards program built into your website is a sure way to generate repeat business. For example, consider rewarding customers with points for each purchase that can be redeemed with future purchases. This is a great way to build customer loyalty and generate residual income.

Analyze Performance & Continuously Improve

It doesn't matter how effective your website is in converting visitors into customers, there is always room for improvement. You should never rest on your laurels and should continuously seek ways to improve your website's performance. In Part III we will talk about ways to get the most out of your website by measuring its KPI (Key Performance Indicators) and making improvements to driving conversions even further.

Is Your Website Built to Sell?

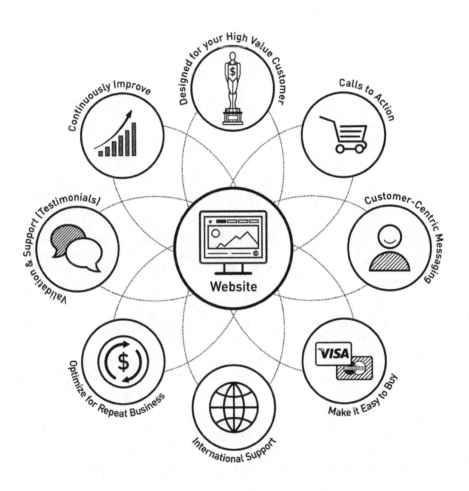

Chapter 13 – How to Accept Payments on Your Website

Online payment processing allows you to get paid on the spot. You've worked hard up to this point to bring the user to the website, capture their attention with customer-centric messaging and engage them to make a purchasing decision with a call to action. If your business model allows it, you should now close the deal by collecting payment directly on your website.

Online payment processing allows your customers to pay for your products or services online, directly on your website and is the resolve of their experience. There are multiple payment methods available, but regardless of the method you choose, you should be certain that your customers never leave your website (for user experience purposes) and that all payment processing methods are integrated into the checkout process as a seamless experience.

Credit Cards Merchant Account

Credit card is the most popular and "traditional" method of online payment. Credit card merchant account is also typically the most cost effective-method for websites with sales of about $10,000 per month or more.

How Does Credit Card Processing Work?

There are several methods of credit card processing available. The most trusted method is the following: The customer submits the credit card information as part of the checkout process. Once the credit card information is provided, the web site validates the credit card number and the expiration date, and then submits it to a payment gateway (electronic clearinghouse) for validation purposes. At this point, the customer's credit card is verified for the availability of funds required to complete the purchase. If the funds are available (authorized), they are reserved by the credit card issuing bank to complete the transaction. In the event the payment gateway does not authorize the transaction, (wrong or expired credit card, insufficient funds, etc.) an error message is displayed to the customer prompting them to check the information they provided or to try a different credit card.

Once the transaction is authorized, the website can capture funds (the actual transfer to your bank account). Capturing funds may be automatic or may require manual review and approval by your personnel (depending on website settings). If there is a significant concern of credit card fraud, it is typically recommended to review all transactions before capturing funds.

At the end of each day all captured funds get "settled" in a batch. This means the bank bundles them for processing. Note that Visa and MasterCard would be bundled together, and transactions from American Express or Discover would be bundled separately. Once a batch is settled (processed), you can expect the funds to be deposited in your bank account within 1-2 days for Visa, MasterCard, and 2-3 days for American Express.

What's Required?

Please note that the implementation of the credit card processing on your website requires having two types of accounts:

1. A merchant account with a bank that gives you the ability to accept credit card payments. There is a separate account that is required for each credit card type you wish to accept: Visa/MasterCard (typically through your bank), American Express (directly through American Express) and Discover (directly through Discover). There are typically credit checks run, when opening a merchant account that may require a personal guarantee from business owners.

2. An account with an online gateway or clearing house (such as Authorize.NET, VeriSign, etc.) to be able to process credit card payments electronically. You can think of an online gateway as a virtual terminal that you can use to process credit card payments without actually swiping the credit card.

Your web developer should guide you through the entire process of opening the required accounts and setting them up to work with your website.

How Much Does it Cost?

There are set-up and monthly fees associated with each merchant account. There also typically setup and monthly fees associated with an online gateway. Note that both are typically negotiable. In any case, you shouldn't expect to pay more than about $20-$30 per account per month.

The more significant expense would be per transaction fees: flat and percentage fees (called discount fees) that you will have to pay for each credit card transaction. Some of these fees are set by the merchant account provider, but the majority of the percentage fees are passed through to the credit card issuing bank. These fees vary depending on card type, your volume and how it was processed. In most cases, you can expect to pay between $0.10 and $0.30 per transaction and 1.5% and 3% off of the purchase amount in credit card discount fees. You should also know that American Express and Discover merchant fees are typically higher than Visa and MasterCard.

Chargebacks

Another issue that you have to be aware of with credit card processing is credit card fraud. Unfortunately, online purchases in the card-not-present environment make it easy for criminals to use stolen credit card numbers.

If you ship products or deliver services based on a fraudulent purchase, you may lose the product or service delivered and the money that paid for the purchase. Once a fraudulent charge is uncovered, the credit card holder typically files a report with their bank, and the bank initiates an investigation. During the investigation, the bank automatically assumes the side of the consumer, and your account is debited for the amount in question plus fees (typically $20-$30 per incident). It is called "chargeback." It then becomes your responsibility to prove that the purchase was legitimate. This may be difficult to achieve in the online environment where you've never seen the purchaser or had access to a physical credit card. To make things worse, if you get several chargebacks, the merchant account may consider your account to be too risky, and they can suspend or terminate your ability to accept credit cards.

Credit card fraud is a growing problem for many online businesses and often results in loss of revenue, decreased productivity, and incurred penalties. To help reduce fraud in the card-not-present environment, there are prevention solutions targeted at protecting your business against fraudulent purchases. Manual review of credit card purchases is one of the best defenses, but also use two proven techniques: Card Verification Value (CVV2) or the additional number on the credit card that validates the card is in possession, and Address Verification System (AVS) that checks that the billing address provided matches the address on file with the bank. There are also advanced measures such as Bank Identification Number (BIN) matching, geographical verification, anonymous proxy detection, velocity filters, purchasing pattern analysis, and others methods you may want to discuss with your web developer.

PayPal

Unlike direct credit card processing that requires setting up a merchant account, a payment gateway and might require a great deal of programming, PayPal was designed as a "plug-and-play" solution that can be easily integrated into any website. This method requires a PayPal account (which can be opened free of charge at http://www.paypal.com) and can be integrated with a website very quickly. You can set up PayPal, and literally accept payments within minutes.

How Does PayPal Work?

Payments through PayPal actually give the purchaser a number of options. For example, they can send money from their PayPal account, use a credit card or automatically draft their bank account. Once the payment is received through PayPal, your PayPal account is debited. You can then transfer the funds into your bank account.

How Much Does PayPal Cost?

While the simplicity of PayPal integration certainly makes it a very lucrative option for smaller websites and start-ups, there are some caveats of which you should be aware. First, PayPal is generally more expensive (currently between 2.2% and 3.9%[14] depending on the type and origin of payment). PayPal also offers merchant accounts, currently at 2.9% + $0.30[15]. Secondly, the "easy" payment integration through PayPal actually transfers the user to PayPal's website, and following a successful payment sends the user back to the website. This is not an ideal method, as the checkout process gets interrupted by transferring the user to a different website.

All this makes PayPal a great payment method for small sites that are starting out, but as your website and your business grows, processing credit cards through a merchant account may be a substantial cost saving.

Google Wallet

Google Checkout was Google's response to PayPal, and it was discontinued in 2013. It was very similar to PayPal but never received as much traction. Google since decided to replace it with a relatively new product called Google Wallet – a virtual online wallet with an app that allows you to turn your phone into a wallet.

How Does Google Wallet Work?

Google Wallet is primarily marketed as a payment method for Android apps and mobile websites. As mobile commerce (M-commerce) is becoming a part of our everyday lives, Google Wallet enables your customers to make purchases easily using a mobile device. According to Google, 97%[16] of mobile shoppers abandon their shopping carts because of all the fields that they have to fill out. With Google Wallet, shoppers can easily pay for their purchases by interfacing with the app on their smartphones.

---

[14]   https://www.paypal.com/us/webapps/mpp/paypal-fees
[15]   https://www.paypal.com/webapps/mpp/merchant-fees
[16]   http://www.google.com/wallet/business/payments/index.html

How Much Does Google Wallet Cost?

Google Wallet is a great tool for accepting mobile payments and requires little integration with the website. Unlike PayPal, it can work with your existing merchant account, so you will not incur any additional charges for payments via Google Wallet, and the only fees Google currently charges is for adding or sending money using credit cards (2.9% fee with $0.30 minimum)[17].

ACH or eCheck

ACH stands for Automatic Clearing House and eCheck stands for Electronic Check, both referring to the same process of taking a check electronically. Electronic check processing is the method of receiving a payment by taking a customer's routing number and account number (the numbers that are printed at the bottom of a paper check) and submitting them for payment electronically.

How Does ACH Work?

You must obtain the permission from your customer to debit their bank account (This is as simple as a checkbox on your checkout screen). Then you collect the information contained on a paper check. You will need to collect the name of the bank, bank routing number, accounting number, and the account type (savings or checking). Once the payment is processed, the customer's account is debited, and your account is credited.

How Much Does ACH Cost?

The main advantage of ACH is that it is the least expensive payment method. You pay a low monthly fee (typically $20-$30) that often includes a certain number of transactions. After that each transaction you typically pay a fixed fee ($0.25 - $01.00) and no discount (percentage fees).

Advantages of ACH

ACH is a great payment method for large amounts since there are no percentage fees and a smaller risk of chargeback. Unlike credit cards that

---

[17]   http://www.google.com/wallet/faq.html#tab=faq-fees

allow chargebacks for a number of reasons (for example, if the customer simply didn't like the product or service) ACH only allows disputes if the amount or date was wrong or the transaction wasn't authorized. All this makes ACH a great alternative for high-ticket payment processing. Setting up an ACH merchant account is similar to getting a credit card merchant account, and typically, the same bank can help you up setting up both.

How To Accept Payments Online

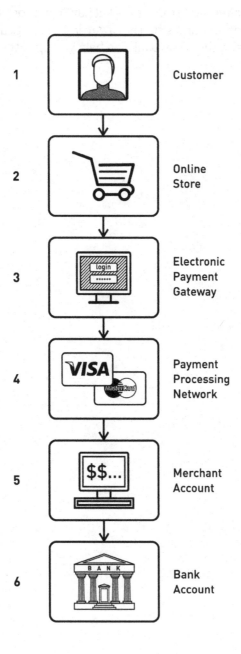

1   Customer

2   Online
Store

3   Electronic
Payment
Gateway

4   Payment
Processing
Network

5   Merchant
Account

6   Bank
Account

Chapter 14 – Earning Revenue with Your Website: Common Monetization Strategies

Not every website is designed to sell products or services directly. Some websites require a solid monetization strategy and a business plan to facilitate profitability. This is especially true for websites that provide an online service or content, social networks, blogs, or service-oriented websites.

To make money with any website, your first priority should be building a loyal base of customers, readers or followers. Without residual traffic to your website, none of the monetization strategies will work. At the same time, if you do have a popular website with a lot of traffic, you can often translate that traffic into revenue. Below are some of the most common ways to earn money with a website:

Selling Advertising

This is probably one of the most popular methods of monetizing a traffic intensive website. Most website owners believe it is a sure way to make guaranteed income. Unfortunately, there is an overabundance of ad inventory on the Web, so prices have gone down. Therefore, so substantial traffic is essential to make any serious revenue through ads on your website. We are talking many thousands of users per month. If your website gets less traffic than that, you probably won't be able to make sufficient revenue through advertising.

Types of Compensation

There are several types of compensation models. Online advertising usually pays in one of three ways:

- CPC (Cost per Click) where you get paid every time someone clicks an ad on your website. It can be a fixed or a variable fee, depending on the ad network you use and the type of advertising you display.

- CPM (Cost per Mille) where advertisers pay for every thousand impressions of their ad on your website (mille is the Latin word for thousand). Impression is the term used for a single ad displayed on your website.

- Fixed Cost where advertisers pay a fixed cost (usually monthly) for the delivery of their ads on your website.

Types of Ads & Delivery Methods

Online Ads come in a variety of type and shapes. Depending on the purpose and the audience of your website, some methods may be more effective in generating income than others. Note that you may need to plan and adjust your website layout to accommodate some ad types. Below are some of the popular ones:

- **Banner Ads** (of varying sizes) are graphical ads displayed within a web page. This remains one of the most popular forms of advertising. Some of the most popular and best performing sizes are: Wide Skyscraper (160x600), Leader board (728x90), Medium Rectangle (300x250), and Rectangle (180x150).

- **Pop-up Ads** are displayed in a new web browser window that opens above a website visitor's initial browser window. These are annoying, and most browsers block them.

- **Overlay** or **Expanding Ads** replaced pop-ups ads, these ads appear superimposed over the website's content (overlay) or expand to show more information when a certain action (a click or mouse-over takes place). These ads typically close or become less obtrusive after a couple of seconds or can be closed by the user.

- **Interstitial Ads** is a type of an ad that shows when a user is waiting for something, most often for their content to load.

- **Text ads** are displayed as links and generally can be embedded by linking individual words or phrases in the context of the website.

Ad Networks

The most popular advertising network is Google AdSense (https://www.google.com/adsense/) – a contextual network that serves ads based on the content of your website, and you are paid per click. It is very easy to get started, but beware that Google AdSense's pay rates are some of the lowest in the industry.

Some of the other pay-per-click (PPC) networks include Media.net (http://www.media.net/) that serves Yahoo and Bing ad networks, Infolinks (http://www.infolinks.com/) and Kontera (http://kontera.com/).

Alternatives include CPM (Cost per Mille) networks that pay per a 1,000 page views: ValueClick (http://www.valueclickmedia.com/), Tribal Fusion (http://www.tribalfusion.com/), and Advertising.com (http://www.advertising.com/).

If you would like to sell advertising directly, look at BuySellAds (http://buysellads.com/)

Managing Ads

Typically, ad networks provide you with code that can be easily plugged into your website. These networks also provide tools to monitor the performance of ads you are running on your website and earned income. They also offer several options from which to choose. This is usually the best way to get started.

However, if you want to work with advertisers directly or run ads from several different advertisers, you may want to run your own ad management system on your website. One of the most popular is OpenX (http://www.openx.org). OpenX is an open source advertising system that lets website owners place their own advertisements on their websites or use advertisements from Ad networks, such as Google AdSense. OpenX works by placing advertisements into predefined "zones" on your website. It lets you upload your own banners and advertisements or use those from ad networks. You position them across the site and track campaigns with varying priorities, payment schedules and quantities of impressions.

Membership-Only Content

Selling premium or membership-only content is a great way to monetize a website. Consider this monetization strategy if you have content that is exclusive and useful. Customers are still willing to pay for online content that is good and offers value. The value may be educational, informative or entertaining. After all, not all content is free. This is why people still buy books, newspapers and magazines.

Typically, websites that offer premium content attract visitors with "free content" as a teaser. Once the user gets a taste of it and wants more, a membership fee is required to access it. A great example is Tuts+ (https://tutsplus.com/) that charges a monthly fee to a huge library of courses and eBooks.

Some websites using this model offer a trial (often 30 days), after which a credit card will be charged monthly until it is canceled. The membership is usually a fixed monthly price. Offering a discount if the membership is paid annually is a great incentive. The customer saves money, and you get the payment up front.

This monetizing model works well because it generates residual income. You have to sell once to continue receiving a subscription fee every month until a customer cancels. In order to keep customers happy, however, you have to supply fresh new content continually.

The type of premium content may vary. Below are some examples of the type of content:

- Educational tools: tutorials, courses, eBooks, guides

- Reports, study or research results and updates

- Members-only forums or blogs

- Members-only features

- Articles, reviews and exclusive commentary

- Whitepapers, professional and technical documentation

- Professional advice: legal, financial, personal

- Personal development: career planning & growth

- Webinars and screen casts

- Videos and images

- Templates and document libraries

The list goes on… The main requirement for this monetization strategy to work effectively is that content is unique and truly useful. A good test is to research whether there is any similar content available anywhere else on the Internet at no charge. If you can easily find similar content that is free, users will not be likely to pay for it. However, if it is unique and not commonly found, there may be a market for it.

Service as a Software or Online Services

A variation on the members-only content strategy is providing members-only tools or services. Similar to premium content, these websites charge a monthly fee for providing convenient access to useful tools or experiences that help solve problems, automate and facilitate tasks or provide other useful services.

Just as with the premium-content, these websites often offer a free trial period, followed by a monthly fee. The monthly fee is usually a fixed monthly fee, and tiered pricing is very popular. A single service may offer multiple account types, where more expensive account types will offer extended access, features and benefits. Prepayment in exchange of discount is also very popular.

A great example of such service is a professional social network—LinkedIn (https://www.linkedin.com/), where you can sign up at no charge but will be quickly encouraged to upgrade to access its best features and services. Another example is LegalZoom (http://www.legalzoom.com/) online legal preparation service that charges for assistance with trademarks, patents, corporations, etc.

Some of other most common websites in this category are those that offer software and tools using an ASP (Application Service Provider) model. This is also known as Software as a Service (SaaS). The concept is that you pay a monthly fee for online software, as opposed to renting it. Examples of such websites are: Salesforce (http://www.salesforce.com/) for sales automation, QuickBooks (http://quickbooks.intuit.com/online) for accounting or Workday (http://www.workday.com/) for HR and Financial management.

Most of these third party solutions are services offered using this model. Below are some of the common examples:

- Job Boards – employers typically pay to post jobs and search resumes (http://www.monster.com/, http://www.careerbuilder.com/)

- Niche or Professional Social Networks – you pay for a membership to a closed community to collaborate and interact (http://www.linkedin.com/, http://www.artistview.com/)

- Consulting services – you pay to get access to personalized consulting service such as legal or financial (http://www.legalzoom.com/)

- Marketplaces – websites that facilitate sale of goods or services for a fee (http://www.ebay.com/, https://www.elance.com/)

- Crowdfunding – websites that assist with raising capital (http://www.kickstarter.com/, http://www.indiegogo.com/)

The list goes on and on. Many online services websites that vary in their offerings, but the idea is similar: you have to provide a unique experience and something that is of great value and quality.

Downloadable Digital Products

Unlike a tangible product, a digital product is something that exists in a digital form and does not have to be shipped to a customer. For example, an eBook, a training course, a picture, a music album or a movie, all can be purchased and downloaded. Selling (or renting) digital product is similar to membership-only content monetization model with one key difference.

A digital product purchase typically signifies a one-time transaction. In other words, customers pay once to download the digital product of their choice as opposed to a monthly fee to access a library of content.

The monthly subscription model is generally a better business model (as it generates residual income), but it may not work for all types of media. For example, if you only have one or two eBooks to sell, you may have a hard time convincing your members to pay a monthly fee, unless you have a new book appearing every month.

In addition, if the service is used infrequently and only on an as-needed basis, customers may be reluctant to pay a monthly fee for access to all content, when they only need access to a portion. This problem can be overcome by selling prepaid credits that in turn can be used to download digital products on an as-needed basis. Stock photography websites have been using this model for years. A block of credits is purchased, and they are used to download photos as needed. This works well, because payments are made in advance. Credits are not used immediately, so when credits are used for the next download, a purchase of more credits will be needed.

Your digital products must represent a value to the end user before anyone is interested in purchasing them. Special attention should be paid to copyrighting, licensing and rights management that would prevent users from sharing your products with the world once they have obtained access. Below are some of the examples of popular digital products frequently sold online:

- Music

- Videos

- Downloadable Software

- Mobile Apps

- eBooks

- Photography & Artwork

Affiliate Marketing

Affiliate marketing involves promoting someone else's products or services and linking to their website where the products or services can be purchased. These links are tracked for every sale (through your website), and you will typically earn a percentage of the sale. This is called an affiliate sales commission.

When done properly, this can generate large revenues, since the payout is much higher than traditional methods of advertising, as long as your website generates sales. You could be making between 5% to 50% (or more) for every sale, depending on the program, the items sold and the volume generated.

Affiliate marketers help companies sell everything from electronics and art to hosting services and eBooks. You may be surprised to learn that all of the biggest online retailers, including Amazon.com and Apple iTunes, offer affiliate programs.

Some of the best performances through affiliate marketing are achieved when your website has the authority and credibility to issue a recommendation for a product or service that is closely associated with the subject matter of your website and is useful to your demographic. For example, if you run an e-commerce store, why not sell products from your affiliates that nicely complement your own products? Alternatively, if you have a website with consumer reviews and testimonials, why not link to the very products that were reviewed?

Below are some of the biggest and well-known affiliate networks:

- Amazon Associates (https://affiliate-program.amazon.com/)

- Commission Junction (http://www.cj.com/)

- Clickbank (http://www.clickbank.com/)

- iTunes (http://www.apple.com/itunes/affiliates/)

Most online retailers have affiliate networks. This information is on their websites, or you can inquire directly. In addition, many tools exist that allow you to run your own affiliate sales-tracking and rewards programs for referrals. If you have e-commerce capabilities on your website, you should inquire with your web developer about adding affiliate functionality, as this could have a great, positive impact on your sales.

Selling Your Website

If your business is your website, selling your website could be the ultimate jackpot. Wouldn't it be nice to get an offer you just can't refuse? But how do you know it's a fair price?

Before we get into the determining factors on your website's worth, let's cover the source of value websites has. There are two reasons why someone would have interest in purchasing your website:

1. They can make a profit of it.

2. They want to get rid of it, because if poses a threat or eats into their market share.

Any serious prospective buyers of your website would be driven solely by their return on investment. Your opinion of your website's worth may not coincide with theirs. After investing all this hard work and money into your website, you may not like to hear this, but it's the reality. Websites are not sold for their potential. They are sold for the revenues they generate. If you are considering selling your website, this is the place to start.

Website buyers typically pay multiples of the annual revenues generated by a website. The factor is usually between 1.5 and 3 times. If your website generates $100,000 annually, you can anticipate between $150,000 and $300,000 as a sale price.

Of course, buyers don't always look at it through this prism. Websites are often sold for substantially less or more, depending on the risks involved, your site's reputation, the state of the website, the underlying technology, comparable sales and how your website ties into the buyer's long-term strategy and planning. In some cases, websites are purchased by competitors to be decommissioned, retaining only the domain name and the customer list or e-mail database.

If you are at a stage where you would like to sell a website, one of the best places to start is Flippa (http://flippa.com/) – a website designed for selling websites in an open auction. Other great resources to announce that your website is for sale are webmaster forums and communities like DigitalPoint (https://forums.digitalpoint.com/) and (http://www.sitepoint.com/).

Website Monetization Strategy

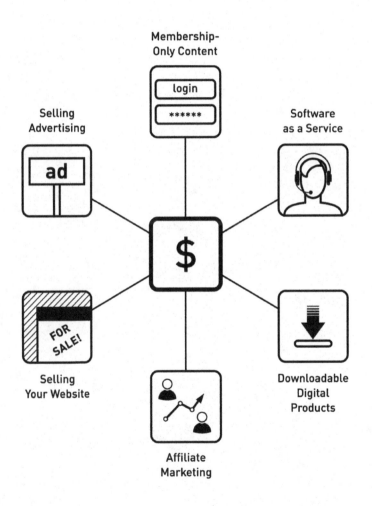

Membership-
Only Content

login

******

Selling
Advertising

ad

Software
as a Service

$

Selling
Your Website

FOR
SALE!

Downloadable
Digital
Products

Affiliate
Marketing

Chapter 15 – Making Your Website Part of Your Business Ecosystem

A sure way to limit the potential of your website is by isolating it from the rest of your business systems and processes. Many companies make this mistake by treating their website as a separate stand-alone tool, missing out on many benefits and opportunities to have their website integrated with the rest of their business value chain.

Web-based Software as a Service (SaaS) solutions allow your organization to be more agile and responsive to constantly changing business conditions and industry trends, optimizing productivity, and improving your bottom line. These tools allow for real-time collaboration and improved productivity among your business units (departments), customers and your vendors or suppliers. Having important business data centralized also allows you to optimize the flow of information, automate various tasks and reduce overheads.

There are many tools available on the market today that can be easily integrated into your website using APIs (Application Programming Interfaces) that allow different software to interact and exchange data. Integrating with an existing solution is often the best plan, as opposed to reinventing the wheel. Most of the best tools require a monthly subscription fee but are often worth the investment.

Let's look at some of the popular ways you can make your website an integral part of your business cycle to achieve the benefits discussed above:

Analytics & Marketing

Do you know who is visiting your website? Do you know what they are doing on your website? Do you know their origin? In order to gauge the performance of your website to ensure that you are aligned to meet your business objectives, you need to monitor your website traffic using an analytics tool.

Google Analytics (http://www.google.com/analytics/) has become the industry standard for measuring website performance. It is a free tool and is easy to use. Additional marketing tools you may want to consider integrating with your website will help you drive traffic to your website and convert it into leads or sales. We will talk more about Google Analytics and additional analytics and marketing tools in Part III of the book.

Sales & Customer Relationship Management

Regardless of the nature of your website, you should have an efficient way to capture leads within the website. Most websites have a Contact Us form that is e-mailed or is ported into a database. It often takes days for these leads to reach the sales team, and many can get lost in the process. There is a better way.

Integrating a CRM (Customer Relationship Management) System within your website can help you manage critical aspects of your sales process by automatically creating and tracking leads from your website with related follow-ups, recording customer interactions, running sales, funnel reports and tracking sales performance. Consider the benefits of having a single customer database used by sales & marketing, account management, customer support, billing, and more.

Some popular CRM systems that are easy to integrate with your website include: Salesforce.com (www.softwareadvice.com), Infusionsoft (www.infusionsoft.com), Act! (www.act.com) and Oncontact (www.oncontact.com) to name a few.

Accounting Automation

Imagine your website automatically issuing and delivering electronic invoices to your customers, processing payments online and applying them to correct invoices, e-mailing payment receipts, paying bills, issuing POs, tracking expenses, and more. All of this can be automated even with your existing accounting systems.

Here are some of the popular accounting systems that allow integration with your website: QuickBooks (www.quickbooks.com), Kashoo (www.

kashoo.com), FreshBooks (www.freshbooks.com), SageOne (www. sageone.com), etc.

Process & Project Management

How do you currently interact with your customers to manage your projects and processes? If you still rely on e-mails, there is a better way.

An online project management environment allows your employees and customers to collaborate, keep track of important milestones and deadlines, assign responsibilities and roles, track individual tasks, manage assets, milestones and costs and monitor the overall progress to ensure timely completion of all projects. As opposed to e-mails, which are hard to track and often get lost, an online project or process management tool can help guide and organize all participants, as well as maintain schedules and budget.

Document & Asset Management

Imagine having a centralized online document repository where all your employees, dealers, representatives, customers or vendors have access to your documents, forms, or marketing materials that need to be regularly shared.

Go paperless! There are online document management systems that have state of the art searching, archiving and cataloging mechanisms to help optimize your workflow. A document repository allows everyone to easily share and exchange assets and collaborate in a secure and centralized location.

Inventory Management

If you are running an in e-commerce website, you should consider integrating your website with a real-time inventory system. An inventory management system allows you to keep track of all assets by conducting automatic inventory counts and guaranteeing real-time and accurate product availability on your website. This allows for efficient reordering when your inventory runs low, processing of backorders and facilitate sales of unique, one-of-a-kind (or custom) items through multiple channels.

Inventory management solutions typically support lot-based inventory management, warehousing, shelving locations, barcode scanning, transactions history, quality assurance, cross-checks, manifests and much more.

Shipping Automation

If you are selling tangible products that require shipping, consider a shipping automation solution. There are tools that directly integrate with UPS, FedEx, USPS and DHL to automate all your shipping needs. You can have your website automate everything: real-time shipping pricing and availability, address verification, package and shipping label creation, pickup calls and even tracking notifications. A shipping solution can also be integrated with inventory management for packing slips, pick tickets, manifests, and automatically handle returns, orders from supplies, Purchase Orders, and a lot more.

Fulfillment & Production Automation

If your online orders are processed by a fulfillment company or by multiple dealers, you can automate the fulfillment of your orders by assigning it to the appropriate party, based on the order type, location and other parameters. Such system can also track fulfillment to ensure timely delivery to the customer.

On-demand production can also be automated. You can automate the planning, production and management of your entire manufacturing process, from the initial order's bill of materials to the final delivery to the customer. This includes work orders, automated thresholds and fulfillment planning, labor/material cost estimates, raw material inventory management, and finished products.

Customer Support

An integrated customer support system can help you handle and resolve customer service requests by tracking and resolving customer issues online. Web-based systems are proven more efficient than systems that are solely reliant on communications through e-mail or telephone, and most systems allow both methods to be fully integrated. Most customer support systems can be customized to handle any kind of requests, from general questions and product returns to billing and quality issues while offering case escalation, automatic reminders and resolution tracking.

Hiring, Recruiting & Training

Continuous recruiting is one of the best ways to help attract new talent to any organization. Why not have a "Careers" section on your website to promote your job openings, receive applications and even collect resumes? You may not need this talent immediately, but imagine the collective resources you can tap into when you need to hire.

There are hiring and recruiting systems that go beyond just publishing job opportunities on your website. There are Applicant Tracking Systems (ATS) that collect and parse resume information, automatically match applicants to appropriate jobs, handle government reports and OFCCP-compliance, and much more. There are also solutions for online employee training, testing, surveying and certification.

Custom Solutions

When existing solutions don't have all the capabilities you need, you may also consider writing one from scratch or customizing an existing one. In most cases, you should approach such projects separately from your main website, and complete all steps covered in this book.

Website EcoSystem

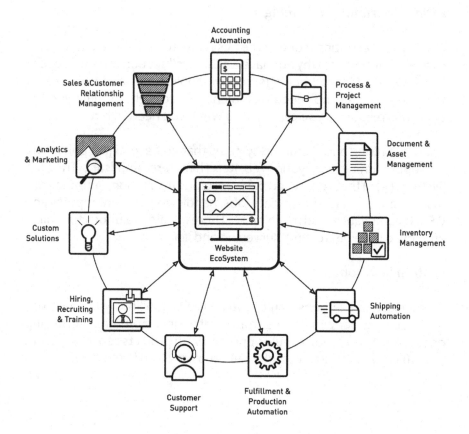

Chapter 16 - Hosting Your Website: What You Need to Know

In order to make the most out of your new website, you need a reliable web hosting partner to ensure that your website is working effectively and without interruption. A web hosting service is a service that allows your website to be accessible via the World Wide Web. Web hosting companies provide space on their servers (owned or leased by clients) located in a data center and you are paying for server space where your website resides. To use an analogy, in the scenario of your website being a mobile phone, your hosting service is your service provider. Without a phone service, your phone will not work.

The scope of web hosting services varies greatly, and there is a great deal of technical detail. The purpose of this chapter is to navigate your through the intricacies and the lingo of hosting service in order to help you make the right choices for your business.

Should I Host with My Web Developer?

At some point during your website project, your web developer will most likely recommend a hosting service for your new website. They may be providing the hosting service as part of their services or recommend a partner web hosting company.

While obtaining hosting though your web developer is usually more expensive, several advantages may make it worth the extra price. Consider the following:

Single Vendor for Your Website

If your web developer manages your hosting, they are solely responsible for all aspects of your website. You have one vendor as a point of contact, and if there are issues, questions or concerns, you have one contact to call – your web developer. You have no concerns regarding technical hosting issues associated with your website, and you can concentrate on your own business issues at hand.

If you choose to select a separate hosting service, be prepared to manage that relationship, from setting up the account to resolving technical issues with the hosting provider's support. If you need to recruit your web developer's assistance in resolving issues with your hosting account, the developer may charge for their time, since the service is provided through an independent third party.

More Responsive Support

The most common dilemma caused by procuring two unrelated vendors for your website development is what I call "finger-pointing." It may be difficult to determine if an issue relates to the website itself or if it lies with the hosting account. This is where you may get the runaround. There is a possibility of the web developer and the hosting company blaming each other, while the problem remains unsolved during all of the finger-pointing sessions. This won't happen in the scenario where one vendor manages all aspects of the website's operation. Most web development companies will assign an Account Executive to your project and will be the single point of contact for the entire process.

Hosting that is Optimized for Your Website

Another advantage of retaining your web developer for hosting services is their hosting service will not only be compatible, but optimized for the websites they build. Web hosting accounts may vary greatly from one company to another, and there is a potential for major compatibility issues with the operating system, database versions, programming language and other specialized software. If hosting is provided by your web developer, you won't have any concerns about the website's operation and compatibility with the hosting account in place. The responsibility falls completely on the developer.

Web developers typically have more control over the hosting accounts they use, allowing them to fine-tune the hosting for compatibility, security, performance and convenience in use. This level of flexibility is not necessarily available through providers of "budget" hosting.

What to Look for in a Hosting Company

Shopping for hosting can be a daunting task. In order to help you choose the right hosting provider, you need to review the following:

Uptime

The availability of a website is measured by the percentage of time in a given time period when a website is publicly accessible on the Internet. Downtime happens with even the best websites. When downtime occurs and your customers can't access your website, you stand the chance of losing business. An inferior hosting company is one that has frequent and unpredictable downtimes with varying reasons. Most companies quote an uptime guarantee. Accept no less than a 99% uptime guarantee.

Support

We've discussed the importance of proper hosting support earlier in the chapter. There will inevitably be issues you will need to address during the life of your website. The methods and timeframes of your hosting company's responses are of paramount importance. Hosting companies who use the preventative management approach and have a solid reputation for quick resolution, are obviously preferred. Carefully review the customer reviews, average response times and satisfaction rates.

Speed

Another important indicator of the quality of hosting service is the speed of their network and hardware's performance. If you find the hosting company's own website slow and sluggish, it is not a good sign. This may indicate a problem with their connection speed, or their network or the type of hardware they use.

Scalability

Will the hosting account be able to accommodate the growth of your website on an as-needed basis? As your website grows, the hosting account must grow with it, giving you everything you need — storage, bandwidth, etc.

Range of Services

Hosting companies typically offer a range of other services including email, domain name registration and SSL certificates (We will discuss these topics later.). It makes things much easier if your hosting company is a one-stop shop for all the essentials you will need.

Rates

As with any other commercial service, you want to make sure that you are being charged a fair price. I recommend comparing prices of several companies, and don't be shy about requesting explanations for higher-than-average rates. However, don't let the price be the sole determining factor. A higher price may be justified if there is substantially more quality in service, support and convenience overall.

Facilities

Your hosting provider's servers are located in a data center. Modern data centers are built specifically for reliability, security and redundancy. They can handle power spikes and outages with the aid of specialized equipment, batteries and power generators. They feature state-of-the-art fire suppression systems, seismic and flood protection, as well as physical security. These additional levels of protection are an important value to consider. Be sure that your provider is hosting your website from a data center that has redundancy and security measures in place.

Network

Network utilized by the hosting provider is another important factor in the quality of their services. Choose providers that are connected to largest Tier 1 bandwidth providers (those who operate their own communication infrastructure as opposed to simply reselling bandwidth), avoiding smaller unreliable providers and networks. Most reputable hosting companies guarantee reliable traffic delivery to all parts of the United States and internationally as well.

What Type of Hosting is Right for My Website?

Hosting services are offered from a wide array of types and flavors depending on the specific needs of your website. You should consult your web developer for the most appropriate and cost-effective hosting service. To assist in your understanding of the different types of accounts, the following are most popular:

Virtual Shared Hosting

This traditional form of hosting will have your website placed on the same server with many other websites (as many as a few to hundreds). All these websites will typically share the resources of the server, such as the processor, memory and storage. The features available with these accounts are typically very basic and not flexible in terms of customization and upgrades (for example you might be out of luck if you need additional storage or specialized software installed). This is often the least expensive hosting option that may be suitable for small businesses; however it is not recommended for enterprise-level websites because of the limiting factors. Consider this analogy: virtual shared hosting is equivalent to renting an apartment in an apartment building as opposed to owning your own single-family home.

Dedicated / Collocated

This traditional form of hosting has the entire physical server dedicated to your website. You have full remote control over the server; however, you typically don't own the hardware (you rent the server). Collocated hosting is similar to the dedicated web hosting service, but you would actually own the hardware. There are managed and unmanaged options, where the hosting company will or will not provide monitoring, management and maintenance of the server. This is a significantly more expensive hosting service, as compared to virtual hosting. The advantage is that you have sole domain over all resources of the physical server. The disadvantage is that you are limited by the very same resources. For example, if you need more storage or memory, it would require installation on the server, resulting in additional cost and maintenance downtime. There are several, flexible hosting options available these days; dedicated/collocated servers are only called for in situations that require specialized setups or physical separation for security and compliance reasons. Using the analogy from the above, having your own server is equivalent to living in a single-family home. There is more room and no "noisy" neighbors, but you are still limited to the physical constraints of the house.

Virtual Private Server

Virtual Private Server or VPS (also known as Virtual Dedicated Server) divides physical servers into virtual servers, where resources can be allocated toward your website on an as-needed basis. You can think of it as a virtual dedicated server without the constraints of a physical server. Because these servers are virtual, they don't require physical setup and are much easier to upgrade. Depending on your websites' growing needs, allocating more memory or storage is done virtually without the need of physically upgrading the hardware. VPS accounts can also come as managed or unmanaged but are typically priced much lower than an equivalent dedicated server. VPS hosting is an excellent choice for large corporate websites because of the scalability and flexibility that it offers. Continuing with the housing analogy, imagine living in a house where you can instantly upsize or downsize your existing space as needed and without having to leave your house while it is under construction. This is the flexibility that VPS hosting offers.

Cloud Hosting

Cloud hosting is a relatively new type of hosting that allows unprecedented, powerful, scalable and reliable hosting. Imagine many servers, often across multiple data centers, combined into a massive pool of resources called a "cloud". Because you're not limited by the hardware capacity of a single server, hosting your website in a cloud is remarkably flexible, giving you the resources you need at the time. As your website grows, cloud hosting can instantly add extra capacity for website expansion or traffic peaks, as it is required.

Also, cloud hosting is often more reliable than alternatives, since other servers in the cloud can compensate when a single piece of hardware goes down. Because cloud hosting is decentralized, it also provides for better redundancy in the event of power failures or natural disasters.

The same lack of centralization may be a disadvantage, as it offers less control on the location data is physically stored, which could be a security or privacy concern.

Cloud hosting companies typically charge only for the resources consumed as opposed to other types of hosting that are billed a flat monthly fee. Cloud hosting is a great alternative to VPS hosting for enterprise-level hosting if data decentralization is not a concern. Imagine hotel living, where you don't reside in a single location, but have access to residences around the world. You use them as you travel and pay only for the locations you occupy. As in VPS, you can upsize or downsize them or use multiple residences at once without constraint.

Custom / Distributed Systems

Websites with huge amounts of traffic and data may require custom setups such as a combination of various hosting types or clustered hosting. Load balancing is used for automatic distribution of incoming traffic across multiple servers in a cluster or clouds. This methodology maximizes reliability, minimizes response time and avoids overloading. All this achieves greater reliability by seamlessly providing the right amount of resources needed in response to the traffic. These types of hosting setups are typically used by popular social networks or online service providers. They can be very expensive depending on your website's specific needs.

What Hosting Essentials Do I Need?

A hosting account consists of multiple features and components. Talk to your web developer to determine what is needed for your website. These features may also affect the cost of your hosting. Below are some of the most common hosting types:

Operating System & Software

In "Chapter 10 - Which Technology is Right for My Website?" Section "Website is A Cake of Many Layers" we talked about various technology "layers" or "web stacks." Most websites fall into two categories: LAMP (Linux-based) or WISA (Windows-based). They respectively rely on a

What Type of Hosting is Right for My Website?

PARAMETER		FLEXIBILITY	SECURITY	SCALABILITY	COST
	Virtual Shared Hosting	●●○○○	●●○○○	●○○○○	●○○○○
	Dedicated/ Collocated	●●○○○	●●●○○	●●○○○	●●●○○
	Virtual Private Server	●●●●○	●●●○○	●●●●○	●●●●○
	Cloud Hosting	●●●●●	●●●○○	●●●●○	●●●●○

choice of an operating system: Linux or Microsoft Windows with the rest of the underlying software — web server software, database engine and programming language. Virtual shared and cloud hosting accounts come preinstalled with all the software that you need, whereas you may need to have someone install and configure it for you for virtual private and dedicated servers.

Note that Windows hosting is typically more expensive than Linux hosting because of licensing fees. If you choose your own hosting, make sure that your website is fully compatible with it by asking your web developer for a complete list of requirements.

Computing Resources (CPU/ Memory)

Your website is literally a computer program that runs on a server. The more people use it, the more processing power and memory the server needs. If it starts to run out of resources, your website may become sluggish or unresponsive and in extreme cases may even crash.

Resources of virtual shared hosting and dedicated servers are limited by the physical hardware on these machines. If your website needs more resources, the hosting company will need to either upgrade the physical hardware (like adding more memory) or move your website to a more powerful server, both of which may result in significant downtime. One advantage of VPS and cloud hosting is that additional resources are allocated to your website instantly and automatically, and you pay only for the resources actually used. This is in contrast to dedicated servers which require rental payment of the actual hardware. Ask your web developer about minimum recommended server requirements for your website.

Storage

Another important resource is storage. While the website itself does not generally take a lot of space, data can. Documents, images and videos can take a substantial amount of space, especially if the data is user-generated (i.e., uploaded by users of your website).

Storage capacity is limited by hard drive space installed on the servers. Similar to virtual shared hosting and dedicated servers, your storage is limited by the hard drives on these servers. VPS and cloud hosting allows you to reserve additional storage on demand from the available pool. Storage is typically billed in gigabytes or terabytes of data stored, unless you rent or own the server (dedicated and collocated), in which case you would pay for the actual hard drives.

Bandwidth

In website hosting bandwidth is the term that refers to the data transfer rate or the amount of data that can be carried from your website to your website's visitors in a given time period. The rule of thumb is that the more users you have on your website, the more bandwidth you will need. Just as with storage, large documents, images or videos (especially HD videos) can use a substantial amount of bandwidth. Think of bandwidth as a pipeline. Only so much water that can flow easily through a pipe. If your website's bandwidth is limited and there is increased traffic, your website will become slower for everyone and at some point may even be unreachable.

Virtual shared accounts typically measure your data transfer every month (how much data is used in gigabytes or terabytes) though accounts advertising unlimited data transfer are becoming increasingly popular. The industry's little trick though, is that with a virtual shared account you are unlikely to generate any significant traffic, as you will run out of server resources much more quickly.

Virtual private servers, cloud and dedicated/collocated hosting sometimes use a different model. As opposed to the actual usage, you pay for the "size of the pipeline" that is measured by the amount of data that can "flow through it" in megabits per second (Mbps).

Setup & Management

In order for your web hosting to operate effectively, both hardware and software have to be managed and maintained on a regular basis. Server hardware regularly breaks and need to be fixed or replaced, and software needs to be upgraded and patched on a routine basis in order to improve security and performance. Furthermore, some types of hosting require setup of physical hardware as well as installation and configuration of software. This can result in additional charges. Let's look at each of the hosting account types separately:

Virtual shared accounts and cloud hosting accounts typically include management services. Because they represent pools of resources shared between multiple customers, the hosting provider manages and maintains everything. You will have no concerns about software or hardware management. With a VPS (Virtual Private Server) hardware setup management is provided (for the same reasons as with a cloud), but the hosting company may charge for software setup and management since it is specific and unique to your needs.

Dedicated and collocated servers typically don't have any kind of management or setup included so there is an associated extra cost. This can become costly, since the hardware would have to be physically assembled and installed and, in the event of collocation, hardware would need to be purchased as well. Also, consider that all upgrades will require physical modification of server's components, so if you outgrow the server you own (or collocate), you are stuck with it. The same holds true with equipment failures. If the equipment you own is in need of repair or replacement, it will be at your cost. Finally, just as with VPS accounts, most hosting companies will charge extra for software setup and management.

Another type of service is monitoring. It is standard with virtual and cloud accounts but may be an optional add-on for collocated or dedicated servers. The idea is that all "vitals" of the hosting account are measured continuously, and engineers keep all hardware and software in top condition, monitoring all functions around the clock. There are tools that will alert them (and you) in the event of an unexpected problem or downtime. Good hosting providers will be able to react and address these problems before you (or your customers) will ever realize an occurrence. Modern hardware can even notify technicians if there is an anticipated failure, allowing preventive maintenance to take place.

Most hosting providers also offer hands-on-deck service that you can use on an as-needed basis: from rebooting the server to assisting with installation of required software. These services are typically billed on an hourly basis.

Backup & Disaster Recovery

Backup is functionality that you hope you will never need, but when you do, you will be glad it is there. There are many situations where it is possible to lose your data: from hard drive failures and human error to malicious hacking and natural disasters. While in most cases the website can be restored by your web developer, it always takes time. If your website has evolved or it has substantial accumulated data (like orders in an online store), or a social network (where users upload content), this data can be lost forever without proper disaster recovery plans.

Most hosting providers have several layers of redundancy built into the equipment. If you lease (dedicated) or buy (collocated) servers, make sure you have the same level of redundancy. Two server components that fail most often are hard drives (where data is stored) and power supplies (units that power the entire server). Both have internal moving parts, so this is why they are likely to fail over time. The best plan is two have at least two of each. For example, data is mirrored across multiple hard drives, and the server is powered through two outlets. In case one component fails, the other one is concurrently operational, allowing maintenance personnel to replace the failed part without even turning off the server.

Regardless of hosting account type used or the purpose of the website, have reliable, routine and automated backups of all your data. Typically, virtual shared accounts and cloud hosting include backup, but on virtual private servers and dedicated/collocated servers, this may be an additional service.

The most common type of backup is "daily incremental" with a 30-day rotation. This means your data is backed up daily, but the backup only contains the changes since the last backup. The 30-day rotation means your hosting provider will keep the snapshot of your data for the past 30 days. This will allow you to restore your website to any point within the last 30 days.

Most of the time, hosting companies back up only the website and its data (excluding other vital server software) to save on storage and cost. With virtual private servers and dedicated/collocated servers, back up everything, including your operating system and settings that it can be easily restored – this is called "mirroring" or a "server snapshot". In case of a server failure you will be able to get a "copy" of the entire server up and running without the need to install and configure everything from scratch.

Also, consider backups into remote secure locations. In case of an event of catastrophic proportions (natural disaster or a terrorist attack), the entire data center could be off the grid. In this case, a backup that is in the same data center will do you no good. You will not be able to access it. "Over the wire" or "off-site" backups to a remote location provide you with an additional level of protection and peace of mind.

Backups are typically billed monthly based on the amount of data you need to back up (measured in gigabytes or terabytes). Remote backups are naturally more expensive since they also take up bandwidth on a daily basis. If your data is highly sensitive, backups can be scheduled more frequently. Note that unless it is a fault of their own, most hosting providers will also bill you for backup retrieval and restoration. Keep in mind that backup retrieval takes time and does not always work out as planned, so count on it only as a last resort.

Security

One of the jobs of your web developer and the hosting provider is to maintain the security of your website. You have a role in your website's security as well. Below are some basic common-sense recommendations to prevent security-related incidents from taking place:

Your web developer will provide you with access information (username and password) to manage your Content Management System (administrative console) and website. Your hosting provider should also provide you with access to the hosting account's control panel, where various features of your hosting account are managed.

This login information is required to access administrative functions of your hosting account or website, but in the wrong hands, it can potentially cause irreversible damage. It is your responsibility to keep this login information safe and secure. Writing it on a sticky note on your monitor is neither safe nor secure. Choose strong passwords (ideally over 8 characters long and containing lower and upper case characters, numbers and special characters). Change the password regularly (at least once a year) and do not share your password with anyone. All team members should have unique passwords. Make sure to deactivate access for any employee who leaves the company. Make sure that all employees subscribe to the same security policy.

If you believe that a security breach has taken place, notify your web developer and your hosting company immediately. Ask them to research and thoroughly explain the circumstances of this breach, and insist on taking steps to ensure it does not happen again.

Signs of a security breach may be unauthorized changes to your website (where the content is defaced or removed), your domain routing to a different website, your bandwidth, and server load or storage consumption unexplainably goes through the roof or you cannot log in or access your website. Most attacks have to do with compromising your website's security by uploading malicious code or trying to exploit vulnerability. Some attacks (like data theft) can be very difficult to detect. Unfortunately, there are attacks that are difficult to defend against, like a coordinated DoS (Denial of Service) attack that overloads your web server with bogus requests rendering your web server slow or unresponsive. Even some of the biggest and most protected websites often suffer from these attacks.

If your website becomes compromised, you may wonder who was responsible for this action. It is extremely difficult to tell for sure. Your hosting provider may be able to track the IP address of the attacker, but in most cases, it is a dead end. Attackers often use proxy servers to avoid detection. An attack could be relatively harmless where a teenager tests a hacking tool from the Web, or devastating by corporate espionage or sabotage performed by your competition, organized crime or even foreign governments.

In order to minimize exposure, avoid storing any kind of sensitive information as part of your website. This may include identity information (names, e-mails, addresses or phone numbers), passwords, social security numbers, bank accounts or credit card numbers. If you do need to store this information, make sure it is properly protected and encrypted using the best methods the industry has to offer. Talk you your web developer about any concerns that you might have.

Control Panel

As previously mentioned, as part of your hosting account, you will be provided access to a Control Panel (a common one known as cPanel) that allows you to oversee and manage various functions of your hosting account. This may include managing your website files, e-mail accounts, domains or databases, as well as accessing statistics and other information.

Some of these functions may be extremely technical that you may want to avoid, and some may be useful, like creating a new e-mail account or resetting a password. Have your web developer or hosting provider explain the functions of the control panel. Also, make sure that you keep this information even if you decide opt out initially. If you decide to change your web development company or hosting provider, they will likely need access to the control panel to update or move the website. In most cases, you get an e-mail with this information when your hosting account is set up. Save the e-mail and again, make sure that you protect this information. If the wrong person gets access, you have lost control of your entire website.

Domain Names

Probably one of the most important assets of your website is your domain name. A domain name (e.g., yourbusiness.com) is your website's public "address" on the Internet. We discussed it in detail in Chapter 7 – Fundamental Principles of Creating a Successful Website, section How You Name a Boat, is How it Will Sail so you may want to refresh your memory if you do not recall the details.

Without the domain, name people will not be able to navigate to your website. Your e-mails will stop, and your entire company's web presence will cease to exist. This is why it is critical that you remain in control of your domain name at all times. Do not let anyone "take care of it for you." If your domain name does not get renewed on time, it may be disabled (preventing users from accessing your website or you proper routing of your incoming e-mail), or worse, someone can take over your domain name. I have seen this happen on many occasions, and believe me—you don't want this to happen to you.

To avoid losing your domain name, make sure you understand where the domain name was registered, make sure it is paid for in advance and renews on time. Have the login information handy and safeguarded. If you are not sure about it, ask your web developer or hosting provider immediately.

In order for your domain name to point to your website, you need several components. First, make sure that your domain name is pointing to your hosting provider's name servers. You will need to have access to your domain name to change it or provide your hosting company with access to do it for you. Second, the hosting company needs to know the domain information, so they are able to point it to your website. Keep in mind that domain name changes are not instant and can take up to 48 hours to propagate the Internet.

Another point to consider is getting additional domain names (as many as you want) for your website if appropriate. These domain names can be different extensions (like .org, .net or .us) or international domains (like .ca, .co.uk, .de, .fr, .au, etc.) You may point them to the same website or sections/versions of your website (important for multilingual websites).

Also, you need to be aware of sub-domains. A sub-domain precedes your domain. For example, if your top-level domain is "yourbusiness. com", a sub-domain would be "subdomain.yourbusiness.com". Unlike top-level domains they don't have to be purchased and registered, and you can easily create as many as you want. In fact, it may be useful to create short user-friendly addresses and many hosting control panels, allowing you to manage sub-domains. For example, you can create a sub-domain "blog.yourbusiness.com" that points to your company blog or "store.yourbusiness.com" that goes to your company's online store.

SSL Certificate

What is an SSL certificate, and why would you need one? If you have an e-commerce website or transmit any kind of sensitive information, you definitely need an SSL (Secure Socket Layer) certificate. It provides a method of encrypting data as it travels across the Internet to ensure the information cannot be intercepted for malicious purposes. You should have an SSL certificate installed and connection encrypted if any of the following are true:

1. Your website has user authentication (passwords and logins) to allow access to restricted information.

2. Your website processes financial information (online orders, credit card numbers, bank accounts, etc.).

3. You transfer or store sensitive data: social security numbers, IDs, birth dates, license numbers, etc.

4. Your website works with any kind of medical or legal information.

5. Your website contains any kind of restricted proprietary or confidential information, legal documents, contracts, client lists, etc.

You can tell if your connection is secure by making sure that the URL in your address bar begins with HTTPS, not HTTP. That extra "s" stands for "secure." Most browsers will also show a "Lock" icon indicating that the connection is encrypted.

Your hosting provider should be able to assist you in obtaining an SSL certificate. First, you need to purchase the certificate from a trusted vendor. Your web developer or hosting provider can order it for you, or they can refer you to a source. Typically, there is an annual fee to obtain a certificate, and the SSL-issuing authority may have to verify your identity (or the identity of your business) before issuing the certificate.

Once issued, the SSL certificate will need to be installed on your server in order for the secure (HTTPS) connection to work. This is done by your hosting company. Typically, if you get the SSL through your hosting provider, they will take care of it. Finally, your web development company needs to configure your website in a way to make use of the secure connections when necessary (for example, when logging in or completing a purchase in your online store).

E-mail

E-mail is another service that is often included with your hosting account. While some organizations prefer to keep their e-mail separate, many host their website and their e-mail with the same hosting provider. Domain name settings (MX record) tell mail servers on the Internet where to route your e-mail. This is another reason to keep a close grip on your domain name.

You may have e-mail management through your hosting account's control panel. This is where you can set up and manage your organization's e-mail boxes (just as with e-mail accounts), aliases (automatic e-mail forwarders) or autoresponders (messages you want returned to the sender, like an "out of office" message). Some control panels may even have e-mail spam filters, virus protection settings and more. Having access to these functions will allow you to manage all of your e-mail needs in house without having to go to your hosting provider each time you need to create an e-mail box or reset a password.

There are many different types of mail servers available to you, but most will require you to know the name of the server, as well as the user name (typically your e-mail account) and a password in order to receive and send e-mails. You can use this information to send and receive e-mails on your office and home computers, laptop, tablets, smart phones and more. Some security settings require you to check e-mail before sending or connect to the mail server in a certain way. If you have any issues, contact your hosting provider for more information.

By default, all e-mail you receive resides on the server indefinitely unless your mail client (like Microsoft Outlook) or device (like a smartphone) downloads the message and deletes it from the server. All these e-mails (especially the attachments they may contain) may accumulate over time using considerable storage space. The best way to prevent this huge accumulation of data is to download your e-mail and delete it from the server. You can do this automatically in the settings of your e-mail client or device. Another setting allows you to keep e-mail on the server for a specific number of days.

An administrative e-mail account that receives all e-mails that undeliverable to a recipient. This is called a "catch-all" account. You may want to check it on a regular basis to make sure there are no important messages missed. Most often, this is a catch-all for spam.

Finally, I would like to share a few very simple techniques to reduce the amount of spam received through your company's mailbox:

1. Keep business e-mail separate from personal. Don't use your business e-mail for registrations on websites that are questionable. Removing spam on your Gmail or Yahoo account is easier, and it is less likely that you will miss or accidentally delete an important e-mail.

2. Don't post your organization's e-mail addresses on your website (or anywhere else for that matter). Use online contact forms instead. Spammers automatically harvest e-mail addresses they find online, so if you publicly post your e-mail address, you can be sure it will be picked up by spammers.

3. Beware of "unsubscribes". You may think you are unsubscribing from an e-mail, but in reality, you are telling the spammer that your e-mail is active and legitimate. While this is unlawful in the United States, there are known cases of international spammers engaging in this practice. If certain spam gets out of control, talk to your hosting provider about ways to reduce it.

FTP

As you know, e-mail is not a very effective method of sending or receiving large files. File Transfer Protocol (FTP) is a better method used to transfer large files or multiple files at a time and is also the primary method used by your web developer to upload files to your website (for the purposes of updating it).

In order to use FTP to transfer files, you need software called an FTP client. This is the same idea as managing files on your computer, but it allows their transfer to and from a remote server over the Internet.

Almost all hosting accounts include FTP support and most will give you control over FTP accounts via the hosting accounts' control panel. This panel can be used to establish FTP accounts in the same way you set up e-mail accounts. In order to connect to an FTP server you need to know the server's address, as well as a name and a password.

In the days of DropBox and Google Drive, use of FTP for file transferring and sharing is becoming obsolete. However, if you ever need to upload multiple large files directly to your website, this may be the only reliable way to achieve it.

How Much Should I Pay for Hosting?

Hosting prices vary greatly based on the type of the account that you need. It is therefore important to understand differences among types of hosting accounts, how they are billed and the options that are available. You should also note that hosting prices have been dropping rapidly. Most hosting companies will give you discounts in exchange for prepayment. This may be tempting, but remember that by doing so, you lock yourself into a relationship with the hosting provider for years.

Virtual Shared Hosting

Virtual or shared hosting are the least expensive hosting accounts and are typically billed at a flat monthly fee. Most hosting providers offer unlimited disk space and bandwidth with your virtual shared accounts. While this may sound very appealing, keep in mind that these types of accounts are only good for small websites with little traffic, and will not be able to accommodate a large website with a lot of visitors. They are also quite limiting in the type of access offered and what you can do with this type of hosting. Because of this fact, you can't compare it to VPS, Cloud or dedicated hosting types in terms of flexibility.

Dedicated / Collocated

The pricing components of a dedicated (leased) server are usually hardware, bandwidth and management. Because you are leasing the equipment, prices will vary depending on the server specifications. A more powerful server (faster processor, more memory and storage) would cost more than an entry level server. Remember that with collocation you have to purchase the equipment separately, so there are upfront hardware costs.

Another pricing component is bandwidth (see Bandwidth below) and server management can either be included with the dedicated server or priced separately. See the Setup & Management under What Hosting Essentials Do I Need? for more information about server management.

Virtual Private Server

VPS hosting prices could vary greatly, depending on the resources allocated (CPU, memory and storage). Even though these servers are virtual, the pricing structure and components are similar to dedicated servers but you can expect to pay significantly less because there is no physical hardware to set up and maintain specifically for your account. Just like with dedicated servers, with VPS hosting you pay for bandwidth you use (see Bandwidth below) and the account or may not include management services with the standard package.

Cloud Hosting

Because cloud hosting is so flexible and there are no specific resources assigned to your account (rather you get them on demand) you would typically be paying for the actual usage. This is where it gets weird. There are no fixed monthly prices and most hosting providers would bill you for cloud hosting on or per-hour basis (usually in minute increments). Yes, you got it right, you would be paying per hour of computing time. This can generate significant savings over time, as you are only paying for the resources you are actually using.

Estimating cloud hosting monthly fees could actually be quite difficult. It would also depend on a number of factors, such is incoming vs. outgoing traffic, the origin of traffic, various add-ons, etc. Luckily, most companies have online calculators where you can plug in the numbers to estimate the monthly cost.

Custom / Distributed Hosting

Custom setups for distributed hosting / load balancing can be priced from several hundred dollars to thousands or even tens of thousands of dollars per month. It all depends on the setup and the infrastructure required by your organization and is usually needed only for very large and complex websites.

Bandwidth

We talked about bandwidth in the section What Hosting Essentials Do I Need? and the amount of bandwidth you need will affect your overall hosting prices. Bandwidth is sold either in the "throughput of the pipeline" (measured in Megabits per second) or in overall data transferred (measured in gigabytes or terabytes per month).

Different companies may measure it differently but you can easily convert between the two: 1 Mbps equals roughly 320 gigabytes per month. The best model for your situation depends on the traffic situation. If your traffic is steady and uniform, you might be better off using the traditional model paying for data transferred, where if your traffic is unpredictable and you may have unexpected spikes, you might want to pay using the throughput model (in Mbps).

Most providers won't (reasonably) limit you on the bandwidth throughput but as your pipeline "expands" due to flow of traffic, you will be paying for the entire "size of that pipe". It is called "burstable billing" which is a method of measuring bandwidth usage based on peak use. Most hosting providers use the "95th percentile method" which means that as long as 95% of the time your bandwidth was within the current size of the pipeline, you would only be billed for that. This method allows you to have a short (5% overflow) burst in traffic without overage charges.

Bandwidth price goes down significantly as your demand goes up due to volume discounts. In other words, pricing for 1 Mbps could be double that of the per Mbps price of 100Mbps.

Storage

Data on your website (databases, images, videos, etc.) may take up a lot of room. Additional storage can be easily allocated on demand with most of hosting types, with an exception of dedicated servers, where additional hard drives would need to be physically installed. Some hosting providers may require you to upgrade to a more expensive account, while others will offer additional storage at extra fees as part of your current hosting accounts. Just like with bandwidth, you should know that you should be getting volume discounts as your storage requirement increase.

There are also multiple services where storage can be "virtualized" meaning that your website could be in one place, but its data can be stored somewhere else. There are cloud storages and CDNs (Content Delivery Networks) that are specifically designed and optimized to host and deliver large amounts of data. These services typically work better and are more cost effective than traditional "everything under one roof" setups.

Domain Names

Domains registration and renewal is inexpensive and typically the least expensive is the .COM domain. The cost is nominal, and significant discounts are offered when pre-paying for several years. I highly recommend doing so, as we've previously discussed the dangers of losing your domain name due to forgetting the renewal date until it is too late. This is why I recommend registering or renewing your domain names for five or even ten years at a time.

Please note that this quoted pricing covers new registration or existing domain name renewal. If you want to purchase someone else's domain, they are free to charge whatever they want to transfer the ownership to you. This can be hundreds or thousands of dollars depending on the value and the popularity of the domain name. The most expensive domain name ever purchased was "VacationRentals.com" purchased for $35 million in 2007[18].

There are additional top-level domain name extensions, such as .net, .org, .biz and more that have varying prices. Finally, registering international domains can be fairly expensive and difficult. Some domains in Africa and the Middle East may price out at $200-$400 annually[19].

---

[18] http://thenextweb.com/shareables/2013/08/13/15-of-the-most-expensive-domains-of-all-time/
[19] http://www.marcaria.com/

SSL Certificates

SSL certificates are sold similarly to domain names. You pay annually and pre-paying for two or more years will most often afford you a discount. SSL certificates come in a wide array of types and flavors: from basic SSL starting at about $50/year to EV (Extended Validation) requiring extensive verification and starting at about $200-300/year (at the time of the writing of the book). There are even some more expensive variations, such as Wildcard SSL certificates covering your entire domain or certificates with higher encryption strength. SSL Certificates can have many different bells and whistles at additional cost, so beware of unnecessary add-ons.

Changing a Hosting Provider: What You Need to Know

So you are thinking about switching hosting to a different provider. Either you want to save money or you are not happy with your current level of service. Changing your hosting provider may not be as straightforward as you would assume. Although you plan carefully, many details can unexpectedly go wrong resulting in your website's downtime and frustration. In order to avoid downtime, you should be properly prepared, have the switchover thoroughly planned and be aware of possible problems.

What Will You Need?

1. First, you will need to have full access to your current (or former) hosting account. This may include access to the hosting account's control panel, FTP, SSL or Remote Access.

2. Secondly, you will need to have the same type of access to the new hosting account.

3. Finally, you will need to have access in order to modify your domain name record.

How to Make the Transfer Seamless?

If you are transferring your current website, all of the website's files and data (database) have to be transferred initially to the new account. Then you want to make sure that the website is fully operational on the new hosting account. Since the domain name is still pointing to your old hosting account, normally you can access the new account using the IP (numeric) address. You can get this information from your new hosting provider so you can fully review and test your website.

If you are restructuring your website, it may not be necessary to transfer the old website (even though you should archive it), and you can simply upload the new website to your new hosting account. As a rule of thumb, you should conduct a complete back up from the old hosting account.

After your new website is ready to launch with your new hosting account, it is time to point the domain name to the new hosting provider. This is where you will need to access your domain name and change the "name servers" that point your domain name to a hosting provider. There is generally a primary and a secondary server, and they look something like this: "ns1.yourhostname.com" and "ns2.yourhostname.com." You will need to change them to the name servers supplied by your new hosting provider.

As soon as you save this information, your hosting has officially "moved." It is as simple as re-pointing your domain name from the old hosting provider to the new one.

Note, however, that due to how the Internet works, it normally takes anywhere between 24 to 48 hours for this change to propagate the Internet. This means that during this transition time users may still be accessing the old website via the former provider's location, but after 48 hours, everyone will be directed to the new hosting account. Because of this delay, one of the best times to make the transition is Friday evening. This guarantees that by Monday morning everyone will be accessing the new account.

Who Will Transfer the Website?

It is common courtesy for the new hosting company to assist you with the website's transfer. Ideally, they should take care of all the details for you with your minimal oversight. Alternatively, you may ask your web developer to help transfer the website, but they may charge for their time.

Is New Hosting Compatible with the Website?

You and your web developer (or hosting provider) should check compatibility issues prior to beginning the move. Keep in mind that your website requires a specific environment and may rely on specific software and even exact versions to operate (see Chapter 10 - Which Technology is Right for My Website? section Website is A Cake of Many Layers). If your new hosting account is not fully prepared, your website may not function properly or operate at all. It is best to have your web developer ensure the compatibility of hosting with the website, since they are the experts.

Don't Forget About Your E-mail!

Your new hosting provider may also offer email services that are including with the hosting of your website. If so, you have even more preparation. Neglecting proper transfer of your e-mail accounts may result in losing your e-mails for days, or worse, permanently.

The best course of action is to open the exact e-mail accounts on the new hosting server so when the domain name is switched, the e-mails are directed to your new provider's servers. This will ensure that no e-mails are lost. If you are able to transfer all the accounts and settings (including passwords) exactly, this will make the transition seamless for everyone using your company's e-mail domain. If any settings (like the mail server or passwords) will change, it will require all users to update settings on their e-mail clients and devices so they can send/receive email. Also, note that if you storing any of the e-mails on your current server, you may want to download and archive it, as it will no longer be accessible after the switch.

Common Hosting Mistakes to Avoid

Hosting is more than just a server somewhere in a data center. Hosting is a home for your website. Making poor choices about your hosting can impact your business and affect the performance of the website and cause major frustration.

Let's look at some of the common mistakes often made with hosting:

Hosting Your Website Internally

Unless your company owns a data center, hosting your website internally is one of the worst decisions you can make for your website. In What to Look for in a Hosting Company we talked about all the aspects that comprise a good hosting company. In order to ensure uninterrupted and reliable presence of your website on the Internet, you want it hosted in a data center that is built specifically for reliability, security, and redundancy and one that is staffed around the clock.

Now compare this to your facilities. Most companies have a server room with some redundancy in place. However, are you prepared for a power loss, fire, flood or other natural disaster? Are you prepared for a server breakdown at 2:00 AM on Sunday?

The reality is that, unless your company owns and operates a multi-million dollar data center, there is no way to achieve the same level of redundancy and reliability hosting your website from your facilities. It doesn't matter how state-of-the-art and powerful your servers are or how talented your IT team is, the first power or network outage will bring down your website and render them useless.

Another consideration is connectivity. Hosting providers are typically connected to Tier 1 bandwidth providers, avoiding smaller and unreliable providers and networks, where your office probably uses consumer-grade Internet connectivity, which is designed for in-office Internet use but not for hosting websites. Without separate redundant bandwidth, users on your company's network and visitors to your website will be using the same bandwidth, slowing the connection for everyone. Finally, how often have you experienced a slow connection or lost your connection completely in the past? These factors would affect your website as well.

You should have a hosting provider host your website for the same reason you hired a web developer to create your website. It is feasible to have this service in-house, but you chose a professional to take care of this for you.

Not Understanding Hosting Options or Services

If you do not have a basic understanding of the various components of your website and how it is constructed, it is very likely you either are overpaying for the service or you are not getting the necessary level of protection and redundancy your website requires.

When it comes to hosting, ignorance is not bliss; it is a curse. If your website is not properly backed up, you lose all your data, or the sensitive information gets stolen, because it is not encrypted. This may result in a huge liability.

A measure of excellence in hosting services is seen when no issues are present, and it operates smoothly. The problem is that when it doesn't operate well, it is too late. It is ultimately your responsibility to make sure that your hosting setup is ideal. Talk to both your web developer and the hosting provider to ensure your website is backed up, secure and hosted in the most reliable way.

Don't just settle for your hosting account without reviewing it thoroughly at least once a year. The hosting industry changes every day. Prices are steadily decreasing, and new technology appears frequently that allows more economical and reliable hosting services. To offer an example, we have recently replaced eight five year-old servers for a client with just one new server that actually consumes a fraction of the power used by the old servers. This is a prime example of how technology can save money and provide better service. If you are still running that old, dusty server, this might be a good opportunity to consider switching to a VPS or hosting in a cloud.

Losing Control of Your Domain Name

Where it pertains to your company's web presence, the domain name is your most important asset. Without it, there is no website, no e-mail and your entire company's web presence ceases to exist.

This is why you should protect and restrict access to your domain name's record. You need to properly renew it in a timely fashion, and be keenly aware of its expiration date. Don't ever let your domain name expire!

Make sure you know where the domain name was registered, make sure it is paid in full, renew it on time, and have all the login information conveniently accessible, but safeguarded. See "Chapter 7 – Fundamental Principles of Creating a Successful Website" for more information.

Losing Your Hosting Information

Losing access to your hosting account means that you are not in control of your website. Furthermore, losing or misplacing this information is irresponsible and dangerous. No matter how secure the website is, anyone with access to your hosting account can gain control of the entire website and all its data. Hosting access information in the wrong hands can give criminals or your competition the ability to deface your website, upload malicious software/viruses or steal your company's information. Without hosting information, you won't be able to transfer your website to a different provider or even have your web developer make any changes to it. This is why it important to keep the hosting access information handy, but safeguarded at all times.

Chapter 17 - Recommended Website Project Flow: How to Stay on Track and Achieve Results

At this point, you are ready to get started on your new website project. You have reviewed your project goals, agreed on the project management methodology and learned several potential obstacles to avoid. The purpose of this chapter is to familiarize you with the trajectory of the project phases from project initiation to closing. You can think of it as a road map to the completion of your website. Make sure you review it and discuss it with your web developer before embarking on the project.

Every website is different, so it makes sense that the components of the website project flow will differ as well. Various web developers have their own steps and flow that may or may not follow the one presented in this chapter. The project flow you find in this chapter is standard, so you are likely to be presented with something very similar.

Most project management approaches segment the project into four consecutive stages (Phase I-IV) and one throughout the project (Monitoring & Closing):

- Phase I - Initiation

- Phase II - Planning

- Phase III - Execution

- Phase IV - Closing

- Monitoring & Controlling

Recommended Website Project Flow

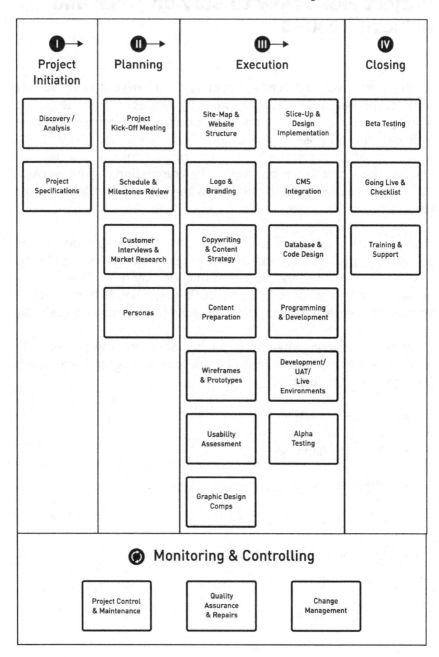

Let's look at each of the stages in more detail:

Phase I - Project Initiation

The Project Initiation phase is all about defining the project and setting goals. During this phase, you should set and revisit the website's objectives. The best way to accomplish this is by answering the simple question: (Finish this sentence.) "The website will be successful if..." I recommend using the S.M.A.R.T. model for setting the goals for your project. (See Part I of the book).

Frequently, most project initiation activities are done during the sales process. After all, in order to plan and price out a project, one needs to fully understand the requirements and the scope of the website project. If you have already secured the services of a web development company, chances are you have already been through these steps. It is, however, still a good idea to revisit them and understand how they apply to the overall process.

Discovery / Analysis

During this stage, it is common for web developers to ask you to complete a questionnaire or website worksheet to define business objectives and determine strategy. In addition, many web developers would prefer to interview stakeholders (team members on your site with interest in the project) to incorporate their vision, identify requirements and gain in-depth insight. Finally, it is a good idea to study the completive landscape, for design, functionality and positioning to identify various strengths, weaknesses and opportunities posed by your competitors' websites.

Project Specifications

Would you build a house without architectural blueprints? You could, but you probably wouldn't want to live in the house. A website is no different. A website is a complex system that requires careful technical planning. It must be precisely engineered and designed in order to be a success. It simply cannot be done well without a proper blueprint.

A blueprint for a website is called project specifications document. It is generally put together by the web developer's technical team and may be part of the proposal or prepared in a separate document.

Unlike the requirements document, which tells everyone WHAT to build, the specification document concentrates on HOW to build it.

A well-written specification document offers precise solutions and outlines all work to be delivered, describing the details of the project, including its features and functions. This detailed document is required to evaluate the scope of work, in order to estimate the cost and resources required for the completion of the project accurately. No website development should even be attempted without such a document.

Phase II - Planning

The Planning phase is the most important time for your project. Before any work is started on the project, make sure that enough time and resources are allocated for proper planning and analysis. This includes conducting a kick-off meeting, setting up tools and laying the foundation for your website project.

Project Kick-Off Meeting

A kick-off meeting is usually a very pleasant event. All the stakeholders and management are in the same room for the first time. The project is starting and everyone is optimistic about what is to come. The energy in the room should feel like the sky is the limit.

A productive kick-off meeting should be more than just an introduction of team members and handshakes. The kick-off meeting is the best time to make sure that everyone is in agreement regarding the requirements of the project's scope, deliverables, risks, schedule, milestones, and the terminology. It is a great opportunity to establish communication channels and roles, define and schedule stakeholder involvement, including meetings, reviews of proposed methodology, agreement on the format and review process of deliverables.

At this point, you should feel like the web developer is in control of the project flow. The developers should conduct the meeting while demonstrating ownership of the project.

Schedule & Milestones Review

As part of the kick-off meeting, you should determine and set project milestones. It is a good idea to create a project schedule based on the project start date, dependencies and the finalized scope of work. The kick-off meeting would be the perfect time and place to review the project schedule.

Big plans are hard to follow and may not be always realistic. The best approach is to divide the project into several major phases and starting with the larger units, you can work your way down to individual roles and tasks. Don't try to assign a set-in-stone completion date to every detailed aspect of the project. It will probably be impossible to maintain.

Understand the major milestones and what comprise the milestones. At this point, a projected completion date can be established. As far as individual smaller tasks, you can schedule activities (and update the schedule) throughout the project. This will give you the most flexibility, if you need more time or want a goal completed sooner than originally scheduled (as long as the overall projected launch date is maintained).

Customer Interviews & Market Research

Proper market research is all about getting inside your customers' heads. Depending on the specifics of your project, you may choose to interview your existing customers to get their perspective and feedback, not only for the website's sake, but also to reaffirm their relationship with your company. This information will be invaluable in creating the new website, because it addresses the needs of your current client base, and helps to attract new clients.

Another form of customer interviews is focus groups. A focus group is a form of qualitative research in which a group of existing (or potential) customers is asked about their opinions, perceptions and attitudes toward your company's product or service and the way it is represented by your website. Questions are typically asked in an interactive group setting where group members are encouraged to speak openly. Conducting focus groups can be a costly and time-consuming endeavor, but it will provide invaluable insight.

The kick-off meeting is a great opportunity to determine the feasibility of conducting a focus group, and then prepare a list of customers and interview questions.

Personas

Personas are great tools for focusing on and targeting specific market segments for your site. Personas are fictional characters that represent your website demographic (age, gender, occupation, interests, desires, goals, etc.). We typically recommend creating about five different personas and testing user experience against these personas with your website.

Phase III - Execution

Project Execution phase is the third phase in the project life cycle where your website finally starts taking shape. This is the phase of the project where the physical website is built. It is typically the longest phase of the project and usually consumes the most energy and resources.

Define steps as covered in Chapter 9 - Managing Your Website Project the Right Way, Section "Define Steps and Project Components." Also, depending on the chosen project methodology (see Understand the Project Management Methodology), some of these steps may overlap, while others may require a completion and a sign-off on previous phases.

Below are the most common steps and components of a website project that often take place in the sequential order:

Sitemap & Website Structure

Most web developers would say that your website starts with the sitemap. The sitemap isn't a part of your new website – it IS your new

Target Audience / High Value Customer

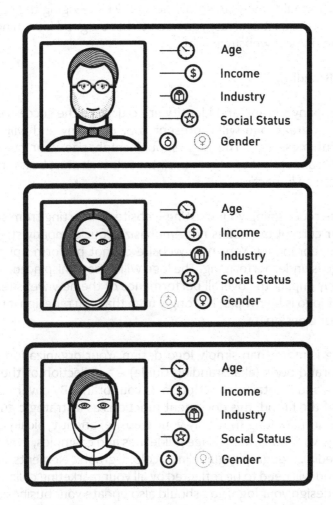

website. Before beginning work on your website, plan how to organize the flow of content on your new website in the most effective way.

Start by creating an inventory of your current website and reorganize the content in the most user-centric manner. Remember, your typical website visitor may not be familiar with the structure of your organization, your product or service offerings or industry's jargon and terminology. It is important to structure your website in the most intuitive way so your customers can navigate to it easily and effortlessly.

While you should always maintain flexibility in changing the structure of the website as it evolves, you need to have a good launching point as you begin your website project.

Logo & Branding

Your company's brand and identity are crucial to the success of your website. A great logo will represent your company and will convey important messages. The logo should emphasize your company's strengths, and reflect your core business values. It must be memorable and create an impact.

If you are redesigning your existing website, or starting from scratch, and your current logo does not emphasize your company strengths, consider rebranding. Your new website cannot perform optimally if your logo is underperforming. The logo will appear misplaced, and will negatively impact the overall performance of the new website. If you feel your logo is below par, I strongly urge that you redesign it prior to the website design.

Branding is more than simply logo design. Your organization should have a brand book (aka Branding Guide) – a collection of the brand elements and a detailed description of your brand. By covering every aspect of the brand, this document functions as a strategic guideline for all your marketing (not only your website) and it typically covers: logo, logo variations, logo usage guidelines and examples, avatars (for social media), typography guidelines, colors, graphic elements, etc. The new brand will need to be reflected by all your marketing collateral, so if you redesign your logo, you should also update your business cards, letterheads, signage, etc. to achieve consistency with all public-facing materials.

Your web developer may offer you rebranding services, or you may hire a company specializing in logo design and branding. My advice is to hire a company that has sufficient experience in the field of logo and brand design and one that can demonstrate a solid portfolio of completed works.

Copywriting & Content Strategy

The execution of your website project should follow proper market research (see Phase I - Project Initiation andPhase II - Planning). The first step is *copywriting* direction and taglines.

We have discussed copywriting in the "Chapter 7 – Fundamental Principles of Creating a Successful Website". *Copywriting* is the process of writing content for marketing purposes, not to be confused with *copyrighting*, which is the process of obtaining a copyright or legal protection for your unique content.

As covered in "Effective Design Strengthens Your Message" in "Chapter 7 – Fundamental Principles of Creating a Successful Website", unleashing your website's marketing potential starts with the main taglines, messages, and calls to actions. Everything else on the website (visuals, designs elements, etc.) is there for the purpose of strengthening and solidifying your main messages.

If you don't have effective taglines or calls to action for your website, consider hiring a professional copywriter to craft them. It will be an asset well worth the investment. As we've previously discussed, taglines and slogans that focus on the needs and wants of the customer (customer-centric) are essential to capture the attention of your potential customers. Professional copywriters can write taglines that will deliver a memorable and clear value proposition into the hearts and minds of your customers, and it will reinforce their buying decisions. For more tips on effective copywriting, please refer to "Chapter 7 – Fundamental Principles of Creating a Successful Website".

Your web developer can help you determine if sufficient attention is dedicated to copywriting. If your developer does not offer this service, consider hiring a marketing professional who specializes in taglines. You may also ask them to draft the rest of the text for the homepage, your mission statement and the overall content direction.

It is recommended that you discuss this part of the stage of the project with your web developer, and determine who will work on writing, editing and uploading content for your website. Most web developers probably spend more time creating templates than writing content. Templates are blank pages on the website where the content will eventually reside. Think of a template as letterhead that contains your company's logo, contact information, and other design elements (that will remain consistent throughout the website), and all you have to do is populate the content specific to that page. Once templates are created, it is essential to agree whether the web developer will be populating the content or your team will do it internally.

Content Preparation

Cover all content on your website; establish who will manage this project and the time frame. An adequate amount of time needs to be allocated for content preparation. Do not wait until the site is done to work on content. You may be surprised by the time and effort it takes to produce quality content. Content is the primary reason for website project delays. People tend to be over-confident in their abilities to write content for new websites, so proper planning of content preparation will help keep your website project on track.

If you are planning on doing content writing in house, consider hiring a professional editor. You don't want improper grammar or poorly worded language on your website. A professional editor can make your website's content shine. Copywriters and editors are different individuals with different skill sets: *copywriters* write the content and provide direction based on the marketing objectives, where *editors* proofread and edit existing content (usually provided by your company) for grammar and language.

Knowledgeable copywriters that understand your business and can target your demographic generally charge a premium price. I suggest that you have *copywriters* produce main messages, taglines and the overall direction, and have *editors* polish the rest of your content. Most content (even in the roughest form) should come from within your organization. No one knows your business and your clients better than you do. Copywriters and editors can take your words and massage them so they flow better, but in my experience, some of the best ideas can originate from within your company. Either way, you should work closely with both copywriters and editors until you are entirely satisfied with the result and it passes the test with personas.

Finally, another element is content entry or content migration at the end of the project. When the content is ready, who will enter it into your website? Consult your web developer about content migration. Since most websites are equipped with Content Management Systems (CMS), many web developers expect the customer to enter their own content.

You may enter finished content into the website yourself, unless the amount is excessive, or you have already determined it is the role of your web developer. This is a great opportunity to practice using your content management system, as well as to test it before the website is live, and you are on your own. The web developer should obviously provide you with enough training and guidance, but this is a great practice exercise for you. The website must be nearly completed before the content can actually be entered, but it is a good idea to have an early start at content preparation.

Wireframes & Prototypes

Most customers don't fully understand wireframes and their necessity. They are also somewhat controversial in the industry. Many successful web development companies skip this step completely because they feel it is time-consuming and unnecessary. I believe that wireframes are critical to the proper flow and the overall success of your website. Therefore, what are they, and why should you care?

Website wireframes are also known as a page schematics or screen blueprints and are sometimes referred to as prototypes. A wireframe is a visual guide that represents the skeletal framework of a website page. It shows the location and layout of various elements, including content and navigation, as well as the interactive and functional elements.

Wireframes typically do not include actual design and typography, and are often prepared in black-and-white. Their purpose lies in the user experience. In other words, wireframes focus on a website's content and information flow as opposed to its appearance.

So why should you and your web developer spend time on wireframes as opposed to proceeding directly to the design? The rationale is very simple. Design can be subjective and is often a matter of personal taste. We are influenced by our first impressions and by whether visuals stimulate our senses and excite us. This is why it is easy to overlook and miss important factors in the first design draft. Wireframes allow us to focus solely on the user experience and functionality without the distraction of visual design. They allow us to decide what information to display, which information is more important or takes precedence, how the website will interact, how the information will flow, and finally, show how various scenarios can play out and even create interactive environments. You can see all that and experience your new website for the first time before even seeing the first design comprehensive (or "comp").

Wireframes can be changed and revised more easily than design comps. They provide a setting to review and discuss concepts before producing designs and making critical changes prior to the design stage. The results in much better design comps and fewer iterations as the project progresses.

There are many ways to construct wireframes. Some companies create low fidelity (less detailed) sketches on paper that are quick and easy to produce. This may be sufficient for some simpler websites. For more complex websites, such as social networks or websites with a lot of interactivity, high fidelity, detailed and sometimes event-interactive wireframes are preferred. These types of wireframes are often used for documenting the website project because they incorporate a level of detail that more closely matches the experience of the website user and the final design, and therefore they take longer to create. Development teams may also use such interactive wireframes later as a reference during design implementation and programming; for example, what happens when you press a certain button, or take a certain action.

When reviewing wireframes, the important thing to remember is that they are just schematics. Don't assume that that the visual design of the page will just be a colored version of what you are seeing. Have your web developer walk you through the wireframes and explain everything on the screen. They should be able to provide justifications for all elements, why they are positioned where they are and why this layout and flow is optimal.

Wireframes typically start with a single page (usually the homepage) to establish a direction and then focus on the rest of the website as dictated by your site map. Note that you technically don't need a wireframe for every single page of your website, just for those pages that are unique or different from the others.

Usability Assessment

Most websites have usability problems. Most of these problems prevent users from coming back and can result in unpleasant and sometimes frustrating user experiences. Such problems can be avoided easily by designing high fidelity, interactive wireframes and reviewing them for usability issues early in the project.

A renowned web usability consultant and author, Steve Krug, offers a very simple test for usability: "Don't make me think."[20] People don't like to puzzle over how things work. Another test from Steve is "Don't waste my time." It is frustrating when excessive time is spent searching for information. Most people will just move on. If your website's use is not intuitive and information is difficult to find, you and your web developer should go back to the drawing board.

For a true usability assessment, it is important to have someone with a fresh perspective, someone who is not familiar with the website. This individual will provide a better perspective (like a typical website user), and their feedback will be invaluable.

For more information and tips on making your website user friendly, please refer to "Chapter 7 – Fundamental Principles of Creating a Successful Website" and specifically section "Simpler is Always Better."

---

[20] Don't Make Me Think: A Common Sense Approach to Web Usability, Steve Krug

Wireframes & Prototypes

LOGO   Products Services About Contact   SEARCH

◁ CUSTOMER CENTRIC VALUE PROPOSITION

CALL TO ACTION ▷

SERVICES

⊠ ⊠

NEWS

⊠

⊠

⊠

ABOUT US

⊠

Products Services About Contact   SOCIAL MEDIA ⊠ ⊠ ⊠

© ALL RIGHTS RESERVED

FOOTER

Graphic Design Comps

Graphic design is probably one of the most exciting steps of a website project. This is where you get to actually see your new website for the first time. This is also where all the previous elements--taglines and copy, wireframes, branding and other components come together supported by the visual elements, such as style, colors, images, photography, typography and other design elements.

Your web developer may refer to the static screens or images of the website's appearance as "design comps" layout. You can think of them as "screenshots" of the website. Usually they are provided to you in the format of JPEG or PNG files. Some companies may have online collaboration tools that allow you to view the design comps and various revisions, as well as to provide space to insert comments and feedback. It is a normal practice for your web developer to walk you through the designs. This is a great opportunity for you to learn their rationale and arguments, express your opinions and ask questions.

Just like wireframes, design comps typically start with a single page (usually the homepage) to establish the design direction and then focus on the rest of the website, following your wireframes and the sitemap. Similar to wireframes, you don't need to review the design for each page of the website. There will inevitably be pages that are similar, so the focus should be on the unique pages.

While working with design is usually engaging and exciting, nothing is more frustrating than disagreements over design with your web developer. Experienced web designers will concur that this is typically the area of website projects where most disagreements take place. While you may have excellent ideas for the design of your website, remember that you hired an expert to create successful website design. Trust their judgment and when all fails, ask for an independent review. If you haven't read "Chapter 8 - Things That Drive Everyone Crazy in Website Projects and How to Avoid the Stress", and specifically sections "Micromanaging and Doing your Web Developer's Work" and "Designing for You or Your Boss", please do so now. This will save you a lot of time and frustration.

Another common problem to avoid is described in the same Chapter, section "Changing Your Mind and Getting Hung Up on Details". This may also result in a serious loss of productivity and time, potentially costing more money. Whenever you are uncertain, give your web developer the benefit of the doubt. After all, you hired them for their expertise.

We often get asked "How many design comps will you provide?" Some organizations go as far as to insist: "We would like to see three to five versions [of the same page]." This is a bad idea. Here is why. At this point, your web developer should have done all the work (market research, interviews, branding, copywriting, wireframes, usability assessment, etc.) in order to produce ONE excellent design comp. If all of these prior steps were performed correctly, consistently and consecutively, there should be very little deviation in design for what is right for your website. You should focus all your efforts on producing THE BEST POSSIBLE design that meets the objectives. If you follow the steps outlined in this book, there should be only one coherent visual representation of what you have already agreed--just one, not more. Using the same logic, all other alternative versions would be inferior. Why would you spend the time on them? You may think that by looking at multiple designs you would be able to pull some ideas from several sources. In reality, you will create a "Frankenstein" of a website that will drive your web designer crazy in the process.

By the same token, your web developer shouldn't impose a maximum number of revisions. Many companies do just that. I believe this is the incorrect approach. Let's say you have a maximum of three revisions and the design still doesn't meet the requirements. Should you have to pay for another revision?

Make an effort to understand what comprises an effective web design. It can actually be productive and helpful to view the design comps from the points described in "Chapter 7 – Fundamental Principles of Creating a Successful Website", and specifically section "Effective Design Strengthens Your Message". This will allow you to provide your web developer with valuable and objective feedback, as opposed to subjectively relying on the aesthetic qualities of the design. Also, don't forget to test the designs for the personas you've created, as well as checking your designs against the "Don't Make Me Think" principle.

Another consideration for your website is Responsive and Adaptive Design. If you want to get the most out of your new website, you should understand how mobile support affects the design of your website. For more information on this topic, please refer to "Chapter 11 – Why Mobile is no Longer Just an Option".

Finally, you should know that the graphic designers have the source files they used to create these designs. They are typically PSD files (Adobe Photoshop™), which is a popular vector format for graphic designers. Vector means that it allows for modification (change, move, add or delete) content as necessary. You may request these files for your archives in the event you want to make significant design changes to your website with a different web developer down the road.

Slice-Up & Design Implementation

A client once asked me, "What are you going to slice? What are you going to do to my website?" I realized then the term "slice-up" (web design jargon) is unfamiliar to most people.

In the previous step of Graphic Design, the outcome is a series of static images representing your website. However, websites are not static images. You can interact with them. In order to make this work, the PSD files have to be converted into HTML/CSS/JavaScript. Please read "Chapter 10 - Which Technology is Right for My Website?" specifically, section "Client-Side Coding" (for the technologies illustrating the functionality).

"Slice-up" or "slicing" is the process of dividing a single picture file into multiple image files displayed as part of the web page. In the early years of web design, sliced images were held together using tables, and a web page was literally "sliced up" into pieces. Modern interactive page layout includes extensive use of Cascading Style Sheets (CSS) and works differently, but the term stuck and remains an important step in web design.

This step marks the stage where your website starts to take shape, design is converted into HTML/CSS/JavaScript, page templates are constructed (and possibly integrated with a Content Management

System), usability testing is performed, and HTML/CSS are tested for cross-browser/cross-platform/resolutions compatibly.

What does all this mean? It is actually very simple. At this stage, you are able to open various parts of the website as a website for the first time. In other words, you are looking at your website not as a series of mockups but as web pages that you can open in your browser (Internet Explorer, Google Chrome, Firefox or Safari). In fact as part of this phase, your web developer should confirm that the website works in various environments. Specifically, the following should be checked:

1. Website compatibility with different "mainstream" browsers, such as Internet Explorer, Google Chrome, Firefox or Safari. There are additional browsers, and "old" versions of the above-mentioned browsers that may not be fully supported, but they typically represent a small percentage of Internet traffic, so there is typically no concern.

2. Website compatibility with browsers in certain Operating Systems (OS), specifically Apple OS and Microsoft Windows. You may be surprised that these two particular operating systems display colors differently, and browsers may work differently on each OS.

3. Website behavior on various resolutions. Every monitor and screen size is different, so the website will also behave in a unique manner. Modern websites should "resize" automatically and should look good on screens of all sizes from a mobile device's screen to that huge monitor you always wanted. Ideally, important elements must not be cut off visually (or require scrolling on small screens), and by the same token, visible "edges" of the website must be perfectly fit to large screens.

4. Website compatibility with mobile devices, specifically horizontal and vertical orientation on mainstream tablets and smartphones (see "Chapter 11 – Why Mobile is no Longer Just an Option" for details).

5. It is a good practice to ensure that certain coding practices are maintained when building your website, and there are tools to check (validate) the code. These tools' functions are to validate the components of your website (HTML: http://validator.w3.org/, CSS: http://jigsaw.w3.org/css-validator/) to ensure compliance with industry standards. Validated code reduces compatibility problems with various browsers and devices. However, please don't obsess over achieving 100% validation. At times, it is impossible to fully validate the code, and there may be no need for it. Many mainstream websites (like Google) don't fully validate, but this doesn't pose a problem. The important objective is to catch only the detail that may cause serious problems.

CMS Integration

In the Section "Content Management System (CMS)" of "Chapter 10 - Which Technology is Right for My Website?" we talk about selecting the appropriate Content Management System for your website. This is an important decision that your web partner should help you make. You should read about different types of Content Management Systems and understand the impact that each choice can have on your project.

During this phase of your project, your web developer will be installing the CMS you collectively decided on using and integrating the slice-up (converted designs) with the CMS. It is important for you to remain integrally involved throughout this phase; after all, you are going to be using the CMS later. It needs to work well for you. You can achieve this by asking your web developer to show you the CMS before the rest of the site is completed to see that it meets your expectations. You should also have a training schedule in place. You should have at least two or three individuals trained in the Content Management System, so if one of your team is unavailable, your website can be updated and managed with back-up resources.

Managing a website through the CMS is an art in itself. A good CMS should give you a sufficient degree of control but must also be easy to use. Don't settle for a CMS that doesn't offer ease of use. It must be straightforward in its design, so it doesn't require a web developer to operate and manage your website. This defeats the purpose of having a CMS in the first place. Read "Chapter 10 - Which Technology is Right for My Website?" if you are still not sure that the proposed CMS is the best choice for your specific website.

While you want to have control of your website, too much control is not a good thing. Imagine members of your team each "doing their thing" on different pages of the site assigned to them. I have seen this too many times: entire websites built within the website— mismatched styles, wild fonts and colors. Not only is such a website an unorganized mess, it is also incredibly difficult to clean up and maintain over time. Consistency is the key. A well-done website should have predetermined design and stylistic parameters: from use of proper fonts and colors to text alignment and placement of images. A well-implemented CMS should have predefined styles: plain text, main heading, subheadings (of several levels), links, bulleted lists, numbered lists, etc. With these style guidelines in place, your team will not have to make these choices randomly. You and your web developer should also discuss the proper use of styles. The developer should offer examples, templates and checklists to follow. This should not be perceived as a constraint, because you hired professionals to design and develop your website. Make the most of your investment and have them implement the proper style guidelines for you. Applying these guidelines consistently will produce a clean, uniform, professional and polished look, exactly the way the designers envisioned it.

Transferring content from your existing website or pasting it from Microsoft Word can be problematic. When you copy text from another CMS from your website into your browser, your e-mail or Microsoft Word, you are actually copying/pasting all the formatting and styles from that source as well. You do not see it, but it is there. This "hidden" code, not easily visible to you, may produce undesirable results when transferring content and may even potentially break the layout of your new website. While some CMS have "clean-up" tools for pasting, they are not 100% reliable in my experience. The single method that has been proven over the years is to copy/paste text into Notepad (under Accessories in Windows) first and then copy/paste it from Notepad into your CMS.

Notepad is a plain text editor that guarantees all styles and formatting will be stripped out, and you have plain content. You may then have to apply the predefined styles that come with your CMS (headings, links, bulleted and numbered lists, etc.) to create the desired structure.

Talk to your web developer about all these topics, and ask them to provide you with thorough training and guidelines. We have found it very useful to record screen casts (screens with narrated videos that can be a great benefit during training). These screen casts can be used on an ongoing basis for refresher classes and new team training. Don't be afraid to ask questions well before the completion of the project. Depending on the flow of your project, your CMS may be ready in advance of other phases of the project, and may actually get ahead of the curve by preparing and entering the content. Note that insufficient content and CMS deficiencies discovered at the end of the project are two of the most common reasons for website launch delays. By addressing issues and resolving them at this point, you may avoid major frustration later on.

Database & Code Design

Charles Mingus, a highly influential American jazz composer, once said: "Making the simple complicated is commonplace; making the complicated simple, awesomely simple, that's creativity."[21] This is also true in web development. The very websites that are you are using daily: Facebook, Twitter or Google are so efficient and easy to use that most don't even know these websites are marvels of engineering. They are incredibly complex systems that took some of the best minds in the world years to build and perfect. What makes them so easy to use is the incredible technology behind it.

All modern websites are complex and intertwined systems that require a great degree of technical planning before breaking ground on writing a single line of code. This phase is very technical: database and data flow diagrams are drawn, code classes and objects are outlined, APIs documentation is carefully studied for third-party integrations. All this is done to ensure that the website will operate and function in accordance with the specifications and business

---

[21]   http://en.wikiquote.org/wiki/Charles_Mingus

requirements. Proper architecture is the key to the website's flexibility, scalability, performance and security. Careful planning and documentation along the way is imperative before any programming begins.

You may not want to take part in this phase because frankly, you have to be a web developer or a programmer to make sense of it, but you may want your IT resources to get involved to ensure that proper planning takes place. It may also be helpful to request some of these diagrams and outlines for your archives. You may think of them as architectural or engineering blueprints for your website. These materials will later be used to build the website so they may also be used as references tools to better understand the website's structure if there is a need for it in the future (for example, if your IT person or another team would need to make changes to the website).

Programming & Development

The programming (sometimes referred to as development) stage of the project is where all components finally start working together. Programming will breathe life into your website. Your website becomes a responsive, interactive experience versus a static, dull, online brochure. Programming is required to make the business logic work. Features, like user registration, log-ins, shopping carts, credit card processing, or even integration with a Content Management System, all require programming.

In "Chapter 10 - Which Technology is Right for My Website?" we talk about various technologies and programming languages that are often used in web development. It can get technical, but the most important aspect is the implication of the technology you select on the future of your website—control and cost of ownership. Regardless of the chosen technology, your company must have unrestricted access to all of the website's source code, and you must ensure that this technology is common and universal, so it can be supported by other web development companies. If your web developer uses a proprietary, closed-source CMS system, you will likely be tied to your web developer for the life of your website.

Prior to this stage, your web developer should set up a development environment (see Section Development / UAT / Live Environments), a code repository and a versioning system. Code repositories are used by more experienced web developers and allow them to track changes to the code, revert to earlier versions—all in a controlled, structured environment.

Programming can follow a number of project management methodologies. In Chapter 9 - Managing Your Website Project the Right Way), Section "Understand the Project Management Methodology" we talk about various project management methodologies and specifically, Waterfall vs. Agile approach. It is important that you understand the difference between the two and how your choice of methodology will affect the flow of your project.

For large projects, development is done by many programmers concurrently. You may ask how they coordinate their efforts and guard against overwriting each other's work. This is where proper tools (the code repository, for example) and management come into play. There is typically a Technical or Development Manager who coordinates the work of multiple programmers and ensures that all aspects are synchronized. The work is often split into subprojects (sometimes referred to as sprints). These sprints are further split into individual tasks and assigned to programmers.

At early stages of this project phase, your web developer may show you segments of the website that are functional. This is done so you can review, test and provide your feedback while they are simultaneously working on other segments of the website. Be sure to read "Monitoring & Controlling" and "Quality Assurance & Repairs" further in this chapter, which covers the importance of the review and testing process being as efficient as possible.

This stage of the project is also a great opportunity for a "reality check." Remember that the projects started with a proposal and a requirements document, which represented a "vision" for the project. At some point, it is very likely that something will go wrong: a technical problem will be too difficult to solve, or the resulting solution will be different from the outcome you originally envisioned. It is not the end of the world, so don't be quick to blame the web developer. In fact, there are many situations where such unexpected changes are easily solved, and it is better to address them prior to launch as opposed to patching and fixing things later. We will cover this further in the chapter, in the sections "Quality Assurance & Repairs" and "Change Management".

Development / UAT / Live Environments

At some point before your website goes live you should take time to review and understand the environment setup for your website. Typically, your web developer will provide you with two or three "copies" of the website running simultaneously in different "places". This is done to separate untested website additions or changes and outright experimentation from your live website. As the time of launch approaches, you should be provided with access to the following environments:

- The development (sometimes called Sandbox) environment is a server usually at your web developer's end, where the website was originally built and where new additions and changes are applied and tested before rolling out to the live website. Chances are you already have access to it. This is where the new website is temporarily parked. This is a restricted, password-protected copy of your website (presented to you during the course of the project). It is also common to retain this environment after the site goes live so you and your web developer can separate the live website from changes, additions and fixes until they are fully reviewed and tested. Note that while the development website should have the exact functionality as the live website, the content and data on the live website may differ in content over time (since they are completely separated).

- UAT (sometimes also called Staging) environment refers to User Acceptance Testing. This is another restricted area where you may be shown the website changes or additions to obtain your approval. This may be combined with the Development server (where your developer works) or

228

be completely separate from it (where you review). This typically depends on the complexity of the project and the set-up of your web developer. In order to get the UAT copy of your website as close as possible to the live site, there are often tools designed to synchronize the content (and the databases) in order to create the most realistic environment for your testing and review.

- Live (also called Production) environment is where your public website resides (www.website.com). The live website should be completely separated from the Development and UAT environments. Clients often get confused by the fact that there is more than one copy of the site, and when making changes on UAT/Development, they expect to see those changes on the live website. These changes will not take effect on the live website until your web developer copies them over. That's the whole point – to keep the live website separate from testing or experimentation. You and your web developer should review and test any changes, additions or fixes on the Development or UAT environment before making the change to the live website.

- Talk to your web developer about these environments, and determine how they will be used. Save all the URLs and logins that the web developer provides, and pay attention to which website version you are working on! We have often looked at the development copy of the website, thinking it was live or vice versa. This can be dangerous (especially when editing the live website in error), so always pay particular attention to the URL (address) of your website, and never run experiments on the live website. This is the exclusive purpose of the other environments.

Alpha Testing

You may have heard the terms "Alpha Testing" and "Beta Testing" but are unsure about their exact meaning. Named after the first two letters of Greek alphabet, these are two stages of testing before a website is considered successfully completed and ready to go live.

Alpha testing is the first stage of testing after development. Beta testing is done after the website passes alpha testing. Alpha Testing will be a test among your team and your web developer's team to confirm that your website works and is ready to go live. At this point, you have probably been looking at and testing parts of the website. Now you get to test it in its entirety.

Your web developer should be running a series of tests, such as user acceptance testing, user experience testing, browser, platform and device compatibility testing, regression testing, penetration and security testing, performance and load testing, among others. We talked about various forms of testing in Chapter 9 - Managing Your Website Project the Right Way, Section "Address Quality Assurance".

Your role in Alpha testing will not be technical. That is the responsibility of your developer. Your objective should be to view your website from the perspective of your customers and determine whether the finished website meets all the objectives and requirements you set at the beginning of the project. The purpose is to measure real users' abilities to use and navigate the website before it goes live. Refer to Section "Monitoring & Controlling" and specifically "Quality Assurance & Repairs" for additional tips on testing.

The website needs to pass Alpha testing, in order to move on to Beta testing. If the website fails any testing, the web developer should make fixes, and the website should be retested until it passes. Make sure that you allow enough time for proper testing before launching the website live. We will talk about the dangers of rushing through this process later in the chapter.

Phase IV – Closing

The Closing phase includes all the activities necessary for finishing the website development project, signing off on it and launching the website live. It is signified by your formal acceptance of the website and by officially transferring the control of the website to your organization.

You and your web developer have worked hard on the website for months. Everything that you've been doing has been leading up to this moment. This phase marks the end of the website project and the unveiling of your website to the rest of the world.

It is finally the time to put your new website to the test. Before you do that, familiarize yourself with the following important steps as part of the Closing phase of the project:

Beta Testing

When your website is ready, or at least when you and your web developer think it is ready, it is now time to put it through additional testing. We have discussed alpha testing in the previous section. Beta testing is done after the website passes alpha testing and prior to going live. Beta testing is the last stage of testing, and typically involves showing the website to users outside your team and your web developer's team. You may think of it as a trial run for your website.

At this point, the anticipation of the new website builds, and you might think that all this testing is unnecessary. After all you and the web developer already tested everything. Right? Wrong! You might recall the infamous debacle of the launch of HealthCare.gov in 2013, the $300+ million website built for online insurance exchanges for the "Obamacare" (Affordable Care Act). To refresh your memory, the website went live on October 1, 2013. Serious technology problems stalled the launch of the website, rendering it inaccessible to millions of Americans. Weeks later, CGI Federal, the primary contractor for the website, testified before Congress that they warned administration officials the website faced problems before the October 1 launch. They warned that the time allotted for testing was "not adequate to complete full functional, system, and integration testing activities." The administration decided to proceed with the website launch despite the warnings, resulting in a complete fiasco upon the website's launch.

Don't make the same mistake with your website! The whole idea behind beta testing is to show the website to individuals who have never seen it before—selected customers, colleagues not involved on the project, family members and/or friends. At this point, you and the web developer have worked on the project so long that you have developed "tunnel vision." When that happens, even obvious issues can remain unnoticed.

This is the value of beta testers. They will have a fresh new perspective and may notice issues or errors that have slipped by your discerning eye.

The best beta testing is most effective when it is done with your target demographic. If you can show the website to a sampling of your customers or potential users, you will get feedback that is valuable and relevant. Beta testing is usually less focused on finding and fixing bugs, though you will most likely find some. It is more focused on user experience and ensuring that the website will work for the target audience and will achieve the business objectives that you defined in the beginning of the project.

The best way to do website beta testing is in a structured and controlled environment. This means being in control of who actually sees your website's content and when they see it. You will then collect the testers' findings in way that will allow you to find and fix problems. Since your new website is not live yet (and may still be password protected), you may have to request that your web developer provide temporary access of the website to your beta testers. In order to make testing the most effective, it may be a good idea to assemble a checklist of components of the website you want tested and reviewed. This checklist will give the testers guidelines and focus. Some of the common issues to focus on are:

- How effective is the website in communicating the value of your company's offering? Do messages and visuals resonate with the visitors?

- How effective are calls to action? Does the website make visitors want to make a purchasing decision?

- Is it is easy to navigate? Are visitors able to find information effortlessly?

- How does the website look and work on their computer, browser, and mobile device? Are there any complaints?

- What emotions are evoked from the design of the website? How does the website make them feel?

- What's wrong with the new website? Is there anything that can be improved?

You may want to request your beta testers to watch for errors, glitches, typos, etc. that they notice. Another good idea is to provide your beta testers with instructions on how to properly record and report bugs and issues so your web developer can resolve them efficiently and effectively. Please see the "Quality Assurance & Repairs" section later in this chapter for tips.

Training & Support

In Chapter 9 - Managing Your Website Project the Right Way, section "Agree on Training & Support" we talked about various ways to structure the training and support for your website project. As previously suggested, you may want to have multiple team members trained on your side in case any of them leave the company or are unavailable to assist or train others. Make sure to take plenty of notes. I also recommend screencasts. They are very easy to create, and you should ask your web developer to record one for you during the training session. There is special software like Camtasia (www.camtasia.com) that lets you record on-screen activity (anything you see on the screen) along with the voice of the presenter. If your training session is done over remote presentation tools (like GoToMeeting), most of them also have the functionality to record the session. The resulting videos may come in handy when you need to refresh your memory or train a new employee on the website.

Another suggestion from Chapter 9 - Managing Your Website Project the Right Way, was to discuss how the website would be supported after the launch. Your website is like a car – it requires ongoing maintenance and fine-tuning. It doesn't matter how good your car is; if you fail to change your oil on a regular basis, it will start losing performance and eventually the engine will stall. Don't let this happen to your website! Have a discussion with your web developer about the support process and protocol. It is just a matter of time before issues surface, so you should have an understanding on the support process and costs associated with it.

Your web developer will most likely offer you a support package at some point of the project. Some companies will offer an ongoing service and will charge a monthly fee; others will offer you to purchase a block of hours that can be used for support and further improvements to the website. Make sure that the proposed plans factor in your needs, budget and internal capabilities. I strongly recommend that you have a support plan where your web developer takes a proactive approach on managing, supporting and continuously improving your website.

Going Live & Checklist

After all the hard work you and your web developer have invested, it is finally time to take your website live. At this point, you are probably very eager to see your website live. While this is probably the most exciting time in the project, lack of proper planning may spell out disaster. When a website is launched, little details can often be forgotten or overlooked. This can result in a botched website launch that will ruin your new website's unveiling and will cost unnecessary frustration and expense. This can be avoided by proper planning and preparation.

You should realize that going live isn't really a matter of "flipping the switch," or at least you shouldn't look at it that way. Going live should be a carefully coordinated ballet of activities that will ensure a smooth-running, problem-free and well-choreographed launch of the website.

The following five steps will help you properly prepare for your website's launch:

1. **Is your website's hosting account prepared?**
    Is the environment ready? Do you have all the log-ins ready? If you haven't done so, please read "Chapter 16 - Hosting Your Website: What You Need to Know".

2. **Did you back up the old website?**
    If you have an existing website, have a backup in the event that you have to roll back to it. You may also appreciate access to the old website as a reference tool.

3. **Did you fully complete alpha and beta testing?**
   Be sure to read sections "Alpha Testing" and "Beta Testing" to ensure that the website was thoroughly tested.

4. **Did you set a "go live" date and time?**
   Be sure that you and your web developer agree on the specific date and time of the website's launch. You also want to be certain that you are available during this time to oversee the launch. I don't recommend launching the new website in the evening or on Friday. In case there any critical issues, you and your web developer team need to be available to address them. The best time to launch is early in the day and at the beginning of the week.

5. **Did your web developer successfully complete their prelaunch checklist?**
   Any reputable web development company should have a checklist used to ensure that nothing is missing or that a detail has been overlooked. It is recommended that your web developer submit the completed checklist to you showing all the items are complete.

✻ *Download:* *You may download the following sample prelaunch checklist for your project:* www.ResultsOnInternet.com

If all the answers to these five steps are "Yes," then congratulations, you are indeed ready to go live! If one answer is "No" or there is any uncertainty, I strongly recommend postponing the launch until you are confident that all issues have been fully resolved. This will save you time, money and headaches.

When you are finally ready to go live, I recommend doing what's called a "soft launch". A soft launch is the release of a website, to a limited audience without publicly stating your new website is live. I recommend that you have your new website up and running for several weeks to a month before doing any kind of announcements, press releases, invitations, marketing or advertising campaigns to drive traffic to the new website. Why? The reason is very simple. If there are any serious issues, you will limit the exposure. This is a safer approach that allows you to further test the viability of the website and fine-tune it as necessary before "the crowds come." If any serious problem is uncovered, it is better to find it and fix it before you have all your customers see the new website. This may save you from an embarrassing situation. It may also save marketing dollars on a website that will not effectively deliver on those marketing efforts.

Lessons Learned

Now that your website is live and you are happy with the outcome of the project, it is a good time to reflect on the project. Some web development firms will ask you to complete a satisfaction survey or participate in a post-launch interview. It is important that lessons learned during the project are captured and analyzed. Look and both positive and negative experiences: was the website completed on budget and on time? How were problems and obstacles handled? What should have been done differently?

If your web developer doesn't initiate this conversation, bring it up. Be sure to share both positive and negative experiences. In my experience, every vendor would be open to such a conversation. Honest, straightforward discussion of what worked and what didn't is beneficial to both parties.

Finally, don't forget to thank your web developer! I can't tell you how often this little gesture is overlooked. Remember, the success of your website depends on many hard-working individuals who spent long hours planning, designing and programming your website. Many of them were putting in extra effort just to see your website succeed. It's always recommended that these professionals be recognized. They had a major role in making the project happen!

What's Next?

You may think that with the launch of your website the project is done. In reality, it is only the beginning. If you want to get the most out of your website, and to fully meet and exceed your business objectives, you and your web developer should closely monitor and continue improving the website. This includes measuring its performance, collecting customer feedback and analyzing competition for continuous tweaks, adjustments and further improvements to the website.

The entire next section of the book will focus on your actions after your new website is launched. Please don't stop reading here, and don't reduce your efforts. This will mean the difference between an "OK" website and a world-class, results-driven website that will exceed your wildest expectations.

Monitoring & Controlling

Even the website projects that are carefully planned, fully resourced and thoroughly executed will face challenges and difficulties that you and your web developer will need to overcome. This is why the phase monitoring and controlling is present in your project. Unlike other phases, the activities in this phase are intended to occur continually throughout the project.

The objective of these activities is to ensure that the project is on time, on budget, and completed with minimal risk. The process involves comparing actual performance with planned performance and taking corrective steps if necessary.

Project Control & Maintenance

The best way to monitor the project's progress is to have regular review meetings and/or phone calls with your web developer. In Section "Schedule & Milestones Review" we discussed setting milestones for your project. Timely and quality completion of these milestones will ensure that the project is on track. However, you should not depend on your web developer to update you with progress. Staying proactive and informed throughout the entire project is critical to ensuring optimal positive outcome of the project.

As a stakeholder in the project, you want to be involved with the following:

- Have a solid understanding of where you are on the project and whether it is on budget and progressing in a timely fashion.

- Identify potential issues or problems, and work with the web developer to find solutions.

- Ensure that all project activities are on schedule.

- Measure the completed work against the objectives and expectations you set.

- Make ongoing decisions about resources: human, financial or material.

- Maintain clear and continuous communication between your team and the web developer's team.

Quality Assurance & Repairs

Your website is built by humans, and humans make mistakes. There will be unavoidable problems that need to be corrected. Regardless of experience level of your web developer, and how much time and effort you collectively spend on testing, there will always be technical issues, logic gaps, typos, programming bugs, broken links, browser compatibly issues and many other unforeseen problems. It's all about finding these problems and fixing them. We've talked about it in Chapter 9 - Managing Your Website Project the Right Way" Section "Address Quality Assurance" so let's talk about your role in this process.

The QA process covers everything from the initial design concepts including functionality and business logic, right down to each line of code that makes the website work. Most of the QA will be performed by your web developer but you should also participate by reviewing and testing all aspects of your website. Your market understanding and non-technical perspective gives you an advantage to see things from your customer's vantage point, allowing you to discover issues that are missed by your web developer.

It is important to understand that not all issues and problems you face are going to be obvious. In fact, some issues are extremely difficult to uncover, as they will only reveal themselves under certain circumstances. Below are some of the common problems you may want to watch for when testing your website:

- Functionality problems – Does everything work the way you and the web developer intended? Does the website accomplish its mission? Do all functions work correctly with no visible errors?

- Logical gaps / business logic – Are there any features that are clearly missing or don't make sense? Is the user experience consistent with your expectations, and is it logical?

- Usability problems – do other people understand how to use the website and its functions? Is it easy and intuitive for them to use and find the desired information?

- Compatibility problems – does the website work consistently on all screen sizes, operating systems, browsers and devices? Are there any visible differences regarding responsive design?

- Content problems – Are there any typos, spelling or grammatical errors? Do all links work, do all videos play and do all documents open?

It is important that you and your web developer have a protocol in place for reporting and resolving issues during the project and after the website's launch. You should always have open and responsive lines of communication with your web developer.

When you uncover a problem, it is very important to report it to the web developer promptly and with as many details as possible. Telling them "something doesn't work" is not going to get the issue resolved quickly. Remember, if the web developer cannot recreate the problem, they won't be able to fix it. They wouldn't even know where to look. Don't make them guess. This will simply waste valuable time, and you will lengthen this frustrating call to get to the source of the problem. Make it easy for them to recreate the problem at their end by pinpointing it and providing detailed information.

The rule of thumb is if you can recreate the problem by tracing these steps and using the information you provided, so can the web developer. This means, they will be able to track the problem and resolve it

Here are some tips for error reporting:

1. Explain in detail what happened and where you noticed the issue. Write down all error messages. If possible, attach a screenshot (print screen).

2. If the problem requires certain conditions (for example, you have to be logged or add a product to a shopping cart), make sure to give step-by-step instructions so they can recreate the exact issue. Walk them through the steps methodically and carefully, so they can recreate it on their end. Be very specific, to the point of telling them, for instance, the user who logged in or the product you added to the shopping cart.

3. If there are other external elements involved (information you were entering, files you were uploading, etc.) be sure to include that information as well.

4. Finally, tell your web developer which web browser (Internet Explorer, Google Chrome, Mozilla Firefox or Apple's Safari) with the version number you are using, and what device was being used at the time (iPhone, Android tablet, desktop computer, etc.).

Change Management

Change management refers to the process for implementing additions, changes or updates to a website in a timely and non-disruptive manner. As we discussed in Chapter 9 - Managing Your Website Project the Right Way" Section "Discuss Project Changes," changes are not necessarily negative. At some point, you may realize that there are alternatives or better ways to achieve your project goals through these changes. It is also possible that something may go wrong in the course of the project (for example, a technical problem will be too difficult and costly to solve).

Even though changes may incur greater cost and take more time, they are at times worth the investment. In some cases, when properly structured, changes can actually save time and money. For example, during the course of the project you may uncover a way to automate or streamline certain processes that will save your team or a lot of time in the long run.

You shouldn't be afraid of changes, but beware of feature creep (see "Chapter 8 - Things That Drive Everyone Crazy in Website Projects and How to Avoid the Stress", Section "Allowing Feature-Creep") and the impact new features or changes may have on your website project.

Always keep in mind the following three rules of thumb when deciding on whether to proceed with a change:

- How much is it going to cost, and is it worth the benefit realized from the change?

- How long will it take, and is the delay worth the wait?

- How will this change affect the rest of the project?

Problems to Look for:

Functionality Problems

Logical Gaps

Usability Problems

Compatibility Problems

Content Problems

Error Report Checklist

☑	AB ···+	Explain in details what happened and where you noticed the issue. Take a screenshot.
☑	1 2 3 o-o-o→	If the problem requires certain conditions, give step-by-step instructions so the issue can be recreated.
☑	↗	Be sure to attach any external elements (information you were uploading etc.)
☑	🌐 🦊 e ⊙ ○ ○	Specify which browser and version number you were using.

Summary of Part II

Understanding the components and characteristics of a successful website, making educated choices about technology and following the recommended project flow are all essential to the successful outcome of your project. It is your responsibility to plan the project in tandem with your web developer as well as to remain an active, informed and educated participant throughout the entire process.

The following key points will help you stay focused on what matters throughout the website project:

1. Understand the fundamental principles of creating a successful website. Ensure that all components are accounted for in your website project.

2. Avoid mistakes common to website projects. This will save a great deal of time and money as well as eliminate unnecessary stress for you and your web developer.

3. Define the project methodology, steps and milestones of your website project. Discuss roles and responsibilities and set up effective lines of communication. Review and agree on deliverables, change requests, warranty limitations as well as training and support included with the project.

4. Review and discuss the choice of technology: the web stack (LAMP or WISA) and the Content Management System (CMS) used. Understand the consequences of these choices including licensing, cost of ownership and support.

5. Ensure that your website is built with mobile support and is designed to work across all devices: desktops, laptops, tablets and smartphones.

6. Know your High Value Customers (HVC) and work with your web developer to create an experience designed to convert visitors into customers. Utilize best practices starting with

customer-centric messaging, effective Calls to Action (CTA) and conversion optimization.

7. If needed, have a solid monetization strategy for your website and understand methods of accepting payments online.

8. Make your website an integrated part of your business ecosystem. Discuss opportunities for integrating your website with your other business systems for reducing operating costs and improving workflow.

9. Choose a reliable hosting provider; understand hosting types, essentials and the process of switching hosting providers. Avoid common mistakes and never let your domain name expire.

10. Understand all steps of the recommended website project flow: Initiation, Planning, Execution, Closing, Monitoring and Controlling. Ensure that your project includes all the necessary steps from customer interviews and market research to copywriting and quality assurance.

Part III
The Website is Live – Now What?

Congratulations on your new website! It looks great, works great, and you are getting a lot of praise for all your hard work. That means you are done, right? Well, not quite.

In reality, your work is just beginning. Your website is a living and breathing organism that requires continual attention. If you want to get the most from your investment, you need to continue monitoring, marketing, improving and fine-tuning your website. Without this ongoing attention, your website will slowly and inevitably diminish in its performance and competitive edge, and you will be back to square one.

This part of the book will focus on the post-launch phase of projects for you and your web developer, so your website will stay on track and exceed your business objectives.

> *"Success is not final, failure is not fatal: it is the courage to continue that counts"*
>
> *Winston Churchill*

Chapter 18 – How Well is Your Website Really Doing?

Now that your website is live, ask yourself, how is it doing? It is remarkable that most organizations cannot answer this question. Many months, sometimes even years, pass after launch, and it is still unclear if the organization is better off with the new website. The truth is, they simply don't know. They don't know, because they don't measure.

Remember the S.M.A.R.T. objectives you set for your website in the beginning? The "M" in S.M.A.R.T stands for "Measurable". The discipline is to measure the website's performance so you are assured that you are on track. If you are not, you can take corrective action.

This chapter will teach you how to measure, not only the successes of your website, but also the failures so you can continually improve and work toward reaching your business objectives.

How to Measure Your Website's Performance

Measuring your website's performance is tricky. In order to get the most from the process, you have to understand what specifically you are measuring, why you are measuring it and what you can learn from the metrics to *improve* the website's performance. Remember, you can improve by measuring failures, not just successes.

Most people rely on default information they obtain from website traffic reports. They look at the number of visitors to the website or the number of leads or sales the website has generated. If the numbers are growing, the site owner is happy and believes: "Our website is doing really well!"

What do these figures really tell us? The number of visitors shows how effective your marketing efforts are in bringing traffic to the website. Typically, more traffic leads to more sales and leads your website will generate. The problem is that none of these metrics reveals the effectiveness of your website in converting website visitors to customers.

If your website objective is to increase leads, you obviously want to know the number of leads your website generated; however, that number only works in the context of the number of visitors to the website and only for a specific duration of time. A much better indicator of the website's performance is the conversion rate (i.e., the percentage of website visitors that actually transitioned to leads or customers). This percentage represents the website's true ability to convert. The higher the conversion rate, the better the website performs; and conversely, the lower the percentage, the worse the performance. If you make changes to the website, changes to the conversion rate will tell you if it is performing in conjunction with your expectations.

This is just one example, of a metric that most websites should measure. Let's dive in to explore the others.

How to Measure the Immeasurable

Sometimes customers say, "Our website objectives can't be measured." I always reply, "All business objectives can be measured; we are only limited by our thinking." If you are willing to think outside the box, you can creatively find a way to measure ANY website objective. Let's look at some examples:

If your website's objective is to increase the number of leads through the contact form or sales through an e-commerce store, that's easy. You can easily track these numbers, so let's look at some more complex examples.

What if your website's main objective is to motivate prospects to pick up a phone and call you? You can measure this by setting up a separate phone number for leads coming to the website. By routing calls through a dedicated number, you can track the website's performance. Another option is to offer a special promotion on your website, which entices the visitor to take advantage of it by picking up the phone and mentioning this promotion during their call.

What if your website is designed to generate foot traffic to your brick and mortar store? You can measure this too. By offering unique coupons or discounts on the website, you will be able to measure business the website generated.

If your website's objective is customer satisfaction, you can survey your customers. If the objective is brand recognition, you can measure changes in social media chatter. If the objective is to improve workflow, you can track the amount of time users spend on certain tasks. True, some of these methods may not provide perfect accuracy, but they will do the job of establishing benchmarks that will in turn give you the ability to analyze your website's performance.

You don't even need that level of creativity. You can simply ask customers how they learned about your company or organization, and if they visited your website. The bottom line is every S.M.A.R.T. business objective is measurable; you just have to find the most analytical and informative methods and tools.

KPIs Are your Best Friends

Companies and organizations have been using Key Performance Indicators (KPIs) for years to evaluate and measure their projects' successes. While any given organization typically has access to great amount of data, the "Key" in Key Performance Indicators references the most important to the organization—the data that provides analysis of the big picture.

Most professionals in the industry refer to website statistics as metrics or dimensions, but for the reasons mentioned above, I prefer to focus on KPIs – metrics that matter. With modern website reporting and analytics tools, we are often confused with the wide variety of reports offered. While it may be interesting to learn all the characteristics about your website's visitors, this wealth of information may be irrelevant. By immersing yourself in dozens of unimportant reports, you will lose focus on the key factors. It's like doing a brain MRI of a patient with a broken leg—it is irrelevant.

To continue with the medical analogy, think of KPIs as the vitals of your website. It's the pulse, temperature and blood pressure that will help determine if your website is "healthy" or needs medical attention quickly. If you measure the right vitals and perform the right tests, you will quickly become aware that your project is progressing according to plan. The key is to look at the appropriate KPIs.

Another way to look at your website's KPIs is as milestones or contributing components to the overall effectiveness of the website. Just as an irregular blood pressure reading may be an indication of a heart problem, a low conversion rate may be an indicator (or forewarning) that your website will not reach its sales objectives.

More factors than conversion rate may affect your sales. You have to analyze the average order value, shopping card abandonment rate, percentage of repeat orders and the overall volumes, to name a few. All these KPIs will directly correlate to the sales your website generates.

While all this information can be initially overwhelming and intimidating, the key is to focus on 5-10 KPIs that make the greatest difference. We will select the KPIs that are important for your website objectives later in the chapter.

Measuring KPIs with Google Analytics

The web analytics space is crowded, with dozens of products competing to analyze your website's traffic. There is one tool, however, that stands out: Google Analytics.

Why Google Analytics?

For one, it is free. It is also easy to use, and it is remarkably full-featured. Google has been continually improving Google Analytics, and it has become an industry standard, currently used by more than 50% of the top 10,000 websites in the world[22]. Even websites that use other analytics tools often rely on Google Analytics as a backup tool or for comparison purposes.

Getting Started

Another reason for Google Analytics' popularity is the ease of setup. If you already have a Google account, setting up an analytics account is a breeze. You simply open an Analytics account under your main Google Account, verify the ownership of the website, and insert the tracking

---

[22] http://en.wikipedia.org/wiki/Google_Analytics#Popularity

code into your website. This literally takes minutes, and if you need assistance, your web developer will be there for you. Google Analytics will start collecting data immediately, and when it simmers for a few days, you can start reviewing reports.

Dimensions vs. Metrics

Before we dig in, it is important to have an understanding of some basic terminology you will find in Google Analytics. In particular, there are two building blocks that are important--dimensions and metrics.

Dimensions describe data. For example, a geographic location can be described by coordinates, zip code, city or country. All these are dimensions. A value for a city dimension could be *Chicago, Los Angeles* or *New York*. Dimensions appear throughout reports and can be added or applied to organize, segment and analyze your data. Some examples of dimensions in Google Analytics include geographic locations, demographics, traffic sources, landing pages and more.

Metrics measure data. They are individual elements of a dimension that are measured by a sum or a ratio. For example, a *city* dimension could be associated with a *population* metric that measures the sum of all residents in a given city. In other words, for a *Chicago* dimension, population of 2.8 million would be its metric. Some examples of metrics in Google Analytics include number of visits, pages per visit, conversion rate, bounce rate, etc.

All reports in Google Analytics maintain default dimensions and metrics. However, in order to get the most from your reports and to achieve more in-depth analyses, you often need to apply additional dimensions and metrics.

What Reports Should I Be Looking at?

As previously stated, your primary focus should be on the KPIs that are vital to reaching your website's overall objective. When you use Google Analytics or any other analytics tool, you will see dozens of reports showing various data. How do you know which KPIs are important for your website?

251

Dimension vs. Metrics

Dimension

City: Chicago

Metric

Population: 2,714,856

City: LA

Population: 3,904,657

City: New York

Population: 8,405,837

A good starting point is your website's S.M.A.R.T. objectives. Review your objectives and methods to reach these objectives, and then work in reverse—from the result, backward. For example, if your website's overall objective is to increase the number of leads, you should focus on your website's effectiveness in converting visitors to quality leads in addition to the amount of traffic your website gets.

Let's look at some of the most common KPIs and how they are used to measure your website's progress toward various objectives. We will use Google Analytics as an example, referencing Google Analytics Reports. Similar reports and terminology are available in other analytics programs as well.

Acquisition-Behavior-Conversion (ABC)

Google Analytics recently rolled out a new report format that clusters data and reports based on ABC's: Acquisition (amount of traffic to your website), Behavior (level of engagement your website has) and Conversions (effectiveness of your website in converting visitors to customers or leads).

You will identify this Acquisition-Behavior-Conversion (ABC) breakdown in many reports throughout Google Analytics. You will also notice that Google Analytics reports are organized by Acquisition, Behavior and Conversions. Audience is also a component of Google Analytics, but AABCs doesn't make as much sense, so we will focus on ABC's: Acquisition, Behavior and Conversions:

Why ABC's Are the Most Important KPIs?

We described the importance of measuring the KPIs that are vital in achieving your website's S.M.A.R.T. business objectives. Regardless of your website's specific objectives, measuring the Acquisition-Behavior-Conversion (ABC) cycle will be crucial to reaching them, and here is why:

- **Acquisition** measures traffic to your website and tells you how your website acquires visitors.

- **Behavior** tells you how effective the website is in engaging visitors; it also tells what areas they view and actions they take on the website.

- **Conversion** tracks the effectiveness of the website in converting website visitors into customers or leads.

"Conversion" is typically the metric that shows whether your website is on track in meeting your S.M.A.R.T. business objectives. Conversions usually refer to sales (checkouts), leads (in the form of completed Contact Us forms), user registrations, and other actions users take that measure your website's effectiveness of converting website visitors to customers or leads.

While conversions are one of the most important metrics to measure, you should also focus appropriately on Acquisition and Behavior. After all, if there is no traffic to your website, or your website (Acquisition) fails to engage (Behavior), there will be nothing to convert. Think of ABCs as the customer lifecycle on your website. All three are vital to your website's success, so let's look at individual KPIs:

Acquisition-Behavior-Conversion (ABC)

A	B	C
Acquisition KPIs	**Behavior KPIs**	**Conversions KPIs**
Visitors	Bounce Rate	Goal Conversion Rate
Percentage of New Visitors	Pages per Visit	Goal Completions
		sales leads contacts
Number of New Visitors	Average Visit Duration	Goal Value
		$ $$$ $$

Acquisition KPIs

Without traffic, your website is dead weight in the digital space. Regardless of the level of effectiveness your website has, it will not fulfill its mission, if there are no visitors. This is why you must track the following Acquisition KPIs:

- *Visits* –the number of people visiting your website. This shows how effective your marketing is in generating traffic and bringing people to the website. You want the traffic to your website to be steadily consistent and increase over time. Quality traffic can always be converted into leads, sales or other forms of revenue. However, it is also about quality of traffic, not quantity. We will focus on this later in the book.

- *New Visits (%)* – the estimate of the percentage of first-time visits. It is the ratio of unique visitors to returning visitors, or a percentage from the total number of users. You have to look at this number in the context of what is happening and what you are trying to accomplish. A high percentage of new users may be a good sign that your new marketing campaign is producing results. However, if there are no new marketing efforts, a high percentage may also represent a subtle sign that you have a substantial base of one-time visitors, and you are not building a loyal following or generating residual traffic to your website.

- *New Visits* –the number of first-time visits (people who had never visited your site before).

Behavior KPIs

Behaviors are best thought of as a path toward a goal. Behavior KPIs inform you of users' behaviors on your website. This insight is crucial to ensuring optimal user experience and improving it over time in order to maximize conversions. Following are basic behavior KPIs you should track:

- *Bounce Rate* – This metric shows the percentage of single-page visits (i.e., people who leave the website quickly after visiting the first page). These users didn't proceed anywhere from the landing page. This number needs to remain low. If you have a high bounce rate, it usually means one of two things:

    1. Your website is ineffective in capturing and engaging visitors, and it is not user-centric or user-friendly. It can also mean there's a "turnoff" that causes a visitor to lose interest.

    2. Your website is attracting the wrong audience. Your visitors may be seeking something else and they abandon your site when they realize it is not exactly what they want.

- *Pages per Visit* – This metric shows the average number of pages people viewed during their visit. Usually, the higher this number, the more effective your website is in promoting the view of additional pages on your site during their session.

- *Average Visit Duration* – This metric reveals the visit duration—average amount of time visitors spend on your site per visit. This also provides a level of engagement indicator. However, there is a flip side to this metric and the Pages per Visit metric. A high number may represent a problem. For example, if your website visitors hit several pages or spend an inordinate amount of time on the website, it may mean they can't easily find what they are seeking. It is imperative that you analyze this metric in the context of your website and discern what it actually means. Is it good that more pages are visited and more time is spent on the website? It depends on the pages. For example, if visitors spend a lot of time reading multiple articles on your blog, that's great. Your website is performing well. However, if you are observing the same behavior in the checkout process of your e-commerce component, this may be an area of concern. Perhaps the checkout process is laborious and unnecessarily complicated.

Conversions KPIs

Conversion KPIs measure business outcomes. This is the measurement of the true effectiveness of your website's performance and confirms that you are on track to reach your website's business objectives.

The first step is to determine the action that defines a "conversion" on your website. The conversion must align with website visitors' actions you want them to take. A conversion may be a purchase, an information request, subscription, an online registration or any other desired action taken by a user.

Google Analytics uses *goals* to track conversions. When a goal is complete, a conversion is logged. The method Google Analytics employs to measure goals is primarily through *destination* pages. For example, if a user ends up on the "Thank you for your order!" page, this tells Google Analytics that the user ordered a product or service; this is the only way the user would arrive on that page.

You should request that your web developer assist in establishing goals to track conversions on your website. Without goals, not only will you be unable to take full advantage of Google Analytics, but also you will not be able to measure your website's level of performance.

Once goals are set, let's look at some basic conversions KPIs you will see across reports:

- *Goal Conversion Rate* – this metric shows the percentage of visits that resulted in a conversion to the goal. If we were to single out one KPI for measuring the effectiveness of your website, this would be it. There is no better indicator to gauge your website's effectiveness than its conversion rate. All the steps taken from this point on should be focused on maximizing the conversion rate. Simply put, if the conversion rate is high, and you bring more quality traffic, your sales will go through the roof. On the other hand, if the conversion rate is low, it doesn't matter how much traffic you bring - you will be wasting time and money bringing traffic through an ineffective website. You want this number to be as high as possible and increase over time, resulting from ongoing website improvements and marketing efforts.

- *Goal Completions* –this metric shows the number of conversions. Where the *conversion rate* measures effectiveness, the *number of conversions* measures the impact on your business. As the traffic to the website grows, a healthy conversion rate will result in sales, leads, subscriptions, registrations or any other action you consider a conversion. Another example of a possible conversion indicator for your website could be liking or sharing a post on social media or watching an embedded video. This measures the action and not the loading of a specific page. Goals in Google Analytics can also be used to track: visit duration (i.e., at least 10 minutes of interaction), number of pages per visit (reading at least five articles) or events (videos, plays or social recommendations). Google Analytics allows the set-up of up to 20 goals, so you can assign goals to anything with a measurable impact.

- *Goal Value* – this metric shows the monetary value of conversions. You can assign goals a monetary value, so you can actually see the worth of each conversion to your business (i.e., you can see your total sales numbers). Have your website developer pass the order information to Google Analytics so it can capture the exact value of each order. You can also track actions like average order values, total amounts sold, purchasing trends, most popular categories or top selling items.

You can also assign arbitrary numbers to goals ($1 for subscribing to a mailing list and $5 for completing a Contact Us form). By giving each goal a dollar value, you can prioritize. For example, if you believe that leads that originate from LinkedIn are twice as valuable as those from Facebook, set the dollar amounts accordingly.

Audience Analysis

Audience Reports by Google Analytics give you an at-a-glance view of your website visitors. They tell you not only how many people come to your website, but also who they are, what their interests are, their geographical location, and whether they are a first-time or returning visitor. This collective information will allow you capture a profile of the visitors on your website and compare it to the personas that you established earlier in the project. Remember, you don't want just any visitors to your website; you want the right visitors who represent your HVC (high value customers).

Audience Overview

When looking at audience reports, most people don't go past what's called vanity metrics (default reports containing numbers of visits, page views, unique visitors, etc. These metrics are easy to understand but don't provide feedback on your website's performance. We already covered Visits and New Visits under "Acquisition KPIs", so let's review some of the other common vanity KPIs:

- *Pageviews* – unlike a visit, which represents a single session of a visitor browsing your website, a pageview is recorded for every page visited. In other words, if someone visited your website and browsed five pages, it will show one visit and five pageviews. This metric is most useful when you are selling advertising and want to maximize ad impressions.

- *Unique Visitors & Returning Visitors* – differentiates the number of people who visit your website for the first time as opposed to being a returning visitor. A better way to look at these numbers is the ratio of unique visitors to returning visitors or as a percentage of the total number of users. If you website's business model relies on bringing visitors back to the site, the percentage of returning users will clearly show the website's effectiveness in generating residual traffic to your website. If your goal is to retain visitors (like a subscription model), you want to see this number steadily increase.

Demographics

One of the benefits of Google Analytics is that Google knows substantially more about your website visitors than other tools. Most Internet users have Google accounts, and when visitors browse your website, Google can compile demographic information about your users, such as their age or gender. This information is invaluable to ensure that you are bringing the appropriate traffic to your website. For example, if your company sells large manufacturing equipment but for some reason teenage girls make up a large share of your website's traffic, you are not bringing the right visitors to your website, and no matter how effective your website is, it will not convert because it was designed for a different demographic.

- *Demographic Match* – measure the percentage of your traffic that matches the demographic you defined for your website.

Interests

Are your website's visitors actually interested in purchasing your products or services? Similar to demographic information, Interests reports allow you to learn more about your website's visitors to ensure that they represent your high value customers (HVC). These reports provide you with a psychographic breakdown that can help to determine personalities, values, attitudes, interests and lifestyles of your website's visitors. Affinity categories will show you that visitors in these segments are more likely to be interested in learning about the specified category of products or services. Similarly, in-market segments will give you a breakdown of users who are more likely to purchase products or services in the specified category. These reports are crucial to understanding your audience needs, wants and desires.

- *Interest / Psychographic Match* – similar to demographic, measures the percentage of traffic that matches the psychographic profile of the personas you created for your website.

Geo

Geo reports tell the language and location of your website visitors. You can drill down, not only by country, but also by state and city. If you market products or services to local customers, this information is vital to your success. For example, if you are a retail chain in Chicago, you want to see that most of your traffic originates from the Chicago area. This website is unlikely to benefit from traffic from Karachi, Pakistan. Language preference is also very important, for example if you discover that a big portion of your website visitors have Spanish as their first language, and you cater to Spanish-speaking customers, it might be time to do a Spanish version of your website.

- *Geographic Match* – measure the percentage of your website visitors that match the geographic region(s) your organization is targeting.

Behavior

Behavior reports give you a more in-depth breakdown of new versus returning users, frequency and the recency of visits (number of pages per visit) as well as the correlation between time spent on the site and the number of pages visited.

Technology

Technology reports are probably more useful to your web developer. They show which browsers and versions are used to access your website—Operating Systems (OS) and Internet Service Providers (ISPs). You and your web developer should focus on the Browsers report. You should test and review your website periodically in the most popular browsers you see in this report. You will then have the confidence that your website is working optimally for your diverse audience. For example, if you find that there are many people accessing your website using old browsers, check that your website works correctly in these older browser versions.

Mobile

Similar to technology reports, Mobile reports will show the number of people who have been accessing your website with a desktop or laptop versus a tablet or mobile device. The breakdown by devices allows you to see which mobile devices are used most often. You should test your website on these mobile devices to ensure that it offers the optimal user experience.

Visitors Flow

The Visitors Flow report is a graphical representation of the paths navigated by visitors to arrive on your website. This report provides great insight into the visitor's interaction--which pages are touched and the location within your site where most drop-offs occur. More importantly, you can segment and filter this report by any other metric.

Acquisition Analysis

Acquisition is all about acquiring traffic or driving visitors to your website. Google Analytics' Acquisition reports provide a window on your visitors' Acquisition-Behavior-Conversion (ABC) cycle.

We will talk about how to multiply traffic to your website in "Chapter 20 – How to Grow Traffic and Market Your Website" For now, let's focus on measuring how visitors are acquired.

Acquisition Overview

The Acquisition Overview report allows you to measure the performance of various traffic sources (channels) through behavior and conversion analysis. This report obtains a clear picture of the channels that are most effective. The report shows the Acquisition-Behavior-Conversion (ABC) cycle: how the website acquires users, their behavior on your website and the path to conversion.

In order to make the most sense of this report, let's dive into what this collective data reveals.

Channels

Before we talk about channels, it is important to understand the difference between sources and mediums. A *source* is the place that was last visited before reaching your website (e.g., a website or a search engine), and *medium* is the method a visitor used to arrive at that source (by clicking on an ad or a link in an e-mail).

Channels determine the medium website visitors used to get to your website. It is important to know how much traffic each channel generates (in comparison with other channels), but it is also important that you determine the quality of that traffic. In other words, which channel performs better and holds the highest conversion rate? Knowing the most effective specific channel allows you to focus your marketing efforts on bringing more traffic through that channel. Let's go over some of the common channels (mediums):

- *Organic Search* – this includes traffic that search engines (Google, Yahoo and Bing) send to your website from search results. Organic means that a search engine includes your website in search results "organically" (or because it is a good match for the user's search), and not because you paid for it.

- *Paid Search* – unlike organic search, paid search is exactly that – you pay search engines' ad networks like Google Adwords or Bing Ads to send traffic to your website.

- *Other Advertising* – traffic generated from any other form of paid advertising that Google Analytics recognizes.

- *Direct* – usually means that someone accessed your website directly, either through typing in your website's URL or a bookmark.

- *Referral* – visits through any websites that link to your website or "refer" traffic to you would count as a referral.

- *Social* – traffic generated through social networks like Facebook, Twitter, Google+ or LinkedIn.

- *E-mail* – visits through links in emails (for example, Gmail or Yahoo Mail).

All Traffic

This expanded report shows the top sources of traffic to your website without factoring in the medium. This report will allow you to identify which sources generate most traffic and understand their association with the medium. For example, Google (organic search) or Twitter (social).

All Referrals

The Referrals report lets you see what websites (and pages within the websites) link to your website and actively refer traffic. You can see the amount of traffic referred and the extent to which the referred visitors interact with your website.

If your traffic-building plan relies on driving traffic from other websites, this report will tell you exactly how well this strategy is working.

Campaigns

While the Referrals report already shows you the origin of traffic, custom campaigns will help you break it down further. Google Analytics allows you to add campaign-specific parameters to any URLs that allow it to collect more information about your referral traffic. For example, if you distribute a monthly newsletter, you can measure how many people clicked on links from each newsletter and track the Acquisition-Behavior-Conversion (ABC) cycle for each newsletter separately.

Keywords

The Google Analytics' keywords report used to be a fantastic resource to see which keywords bring the most and best traffic to your website. Unfortunately, Google has recently changed the way its searches are conducted by encrypting search queries of logged-in users. This means that you will no longer have easy access to the keywords that were used to find and navigate to your website. Instead, expect to see the infamous "not provided" where Google formerly displayed keywords.

Google's official position is that this change was instituted to protect users' privacy. There are many industry professionals, however, who believe that Google has ulterior motives since the "not-provided" is only an issue for organic search queries, and paid search is not affected.

Some keywords information is available under the "Search Engine Optimization" section. We will discuss alternative solutions to measuring what keywords generate more traffic in "Chapter 20 – How to Grow Traffic and Market Your Website" In the meantime, the two Keywords reports that Google offers are:

- *Paid* – keywords that brings your traffic through search engines' ad networks like Google Adwords or Bing Ads.

- *Organic* – keywords that generate traffic from search results in search engines like Google, Yahoo and Bing. Organic means that your website appeared in the search results because it was a good match, and not because you paid for it. Expect to see fewer keywords in this report as time passes because of Google's restrictions.

Cost Analysis

Cost Analytics is a great new addition to Google Analytics that was still in the Beta stage when this book was written. I do expect this tool to remain accessible because of the value it provides.

When spending money on paid marketing campaigns, how do you know which campaigns are most effective? The Cost Analytics report can be used to analyze visits, cost, and revenue performance of all your paid marketing channels, such as AdWords, paid listings, etc. This report compares the cost of each campaign with the revenue it generated, allowing you to see how differing marketing initiatives perform. You can also run comparisons for channels, keywords and campaigns.

Please note that Cost Analytics is part of Universal Analytics and may require an upgrade to the tracking code. Universal Analytics is Google's program, which is designed to improve the way data is collected and processed in Google Analytics.

AdWords

If you are running PPC (Pay-Per-Click) campaigns, you should explore the number of AdWords reports that Google Analytics offers in order to optimize your spending.

Google Analytics' AdWords reports give you post-click performance metrics for your paid traffic through AdWords. These reports help you track campaigns, bid adjustments, individual keywords' performance, placement and keywords' positions and more. By reviewing Acquisition-Behavior-Conversion (ABC) cycles, you can see users' behaviors when they click on your ads, as well as conversions and measures of ROI (return on investment) and RPC (revenue per click).

Social

Social is becoming an increasingly important marketing channel. Measuring the performance of your social initiatives is important to the overall success of your marketing. The following Google Analytics Social reports can help you to determine what works and what does not:

- *Social Overview* – this report provides a quick overview of visits and conversions generated from various social channels, including a breakdown by social networks. The Social Value graph compares the number and value of all completed goals to the ones that resulted from all other channels.

- *Network Referrals* – this provides a breakdown by social networks and shows how visitors from social sources interact with your site.

- *Data Hub Activity* – this report provides an analysis of how users engage with your site content on various social networks. The information comes from the Social Data Hub - a platform that social networks use to integrate their social data with Google Analytics.

- *Landing Pages* – when content is shared or discussed on social networks, it is important to know what content is shared and where it is shared. This is the nature of the Landing Pages report.

- *Trackbacks* – this report tells you which social networking websites are linking to your content and in what context, so you can replicate the successful content on social media.

- *Conversions* – this report shows conversion numbers' monetary value for the social networks that generate traffic to your website.

- *Social Plugins* – social plugins (for example, Facebook "like" or Twitters "tweet" buttons) allow visitors to share your content on social networks. This report shows what content is being shared and where.

- *Visitors Flow* – this report is a graphical representation of the visitor's navigation through your website.

Search Engine Optimization

The Search Engine Optimization (SEO) reports in Google Analytics provide an overview of your website's performance in Google Search. Note that this data is from Google Search only and is provided through Google's Webmaster Tools. Unlike the previously available keywords data, this data has limitations: Google rounds this data making it less accurate; it is provided with a 2-3 day lag and is limited to 2,000 keywords. Despite the report's name, these facts make Search Engine Optimization a little more difficult.

These reports are only available if you added and verified your website with Webmaster Tools. If you haven't done so, ask your web developer to assist. Please note that the following data will not begin collection until the Webmaster Tools account is set up:

- *Queries* – this report shows the queries (keywords) users typed into Google to reach your site. The report shows the number of impressions of your website in search results, the number of clicks on these results, the CTR (Click Through Ratio) as well as the average position of your website for the keyword.

- *Landing Pages* – this lists your website's pages visitors landed on when clicking on search results in Google in addition to impressions, clicks, average positions and CTR.

- *Geographical Summary* – finally, this report provides the general view of impressions, clicks, and CTR by country. You can also switch the primary dimension to Google property that allows you to see same metrics for different types of content search, such as images, text, video, etc.

Behavior Analysis

I previously described your website user's behavior as the path to conversion. The following Behavior reports provided by Google Analytics are designed to help you improve the visitor's experience to meet their needs and guide them toward conversion:

Behavior Overview

The Behavior Overview report focuses on individual pages of your website, as opposed to the entire site. It gives you an overview of pageviews, unique pageviews, average time spent on each page, bounce rate and exit rate. You can also review how the content is performing by page URLs, titles, search terms or events.

Behavior Flow

Similar to other flow reports that Google Analytics offers, the Behavior Flow report lets you visualize the path visitors traveled from one page to the next. This report allows you to discover what content is most engaging. It shows how people arrive at the website (landing page) and where they go from there (interactions) as well as exit (drop-off) points. Note that the Behavior report can be used to visualize pages and events (video plays, for example).

Site Content

Site Content reports focus on just that – your website content. They show what content is more engaging and effective. Based on this information, you can understand how well your content really addresses the objectives of your site:

- *All Pages* – this report shows the effectiveness of individual pages with a breakdown by pageviews (number of times that a page was loaded), unique pageviews (from first-time visitors), average time spent per page, number of entrances per that page, page's bounce rate and exit percentage (how often people exit the website from that page) as well as page value (transaction revenue + total goal value)/unique pageviews.

- *Content Drilldown* – this report is similar to All Pages but instead of showing a list of all pages on the entire site, it groups them by parent sections. In other words you can see structurally, which top sections of the website are more important (i.e., Products, Services, About Us) and then drill down to individual pages within these sections.

- *Landing Pages* – Landing pages are the first-entry pages that visitors access when they arrive on your website. In addition to the same metrics, as in the other Site Content reports, this report focuses on the ABC model and includes conversion data that shows the effectiveness of these entry points relating to conversion. Note that in many cases most active landing pages are not your website homepage. In fact, many times users will be entering your website through search engine results, and at times individual pages can outperform the homepage (for example, if you are conducting content marketing and have an effective article or a popular promotion). If your landing pages have a high bounce rate, or visitors spend only a few seconds on these pages, it is most likely an indicator that these pages do not meet visitors' expectations or that they are not effective in engaging and retaining the visitor's attention.

- *Exit Pages* – similar to Landing pages, exit pages are the last pages that visitors see when exiting your website. This report will tell you which pages are the main drop-off points for your website. If they also happen to be your most effective landing pages, perhaps they are ineffective in engaging visitors. On the other hand, if many visitors leave your website from pages that conclude transactions (like a "thank you" page following a purchase or an information request), that is an indicator your website works as it was intended.

Site Speed

Your website's speed plays a critical role in the website's ability to convert. Today's website visitors are impatient, and if your website is slow, they will move on. Research shows that your website can lose traffic at the average rate of 7% per second of wait time while your page loads[23]. The statistic for users on mobile devices is even a higher percentage.

Google announced that website speed has an impact on search ranking in the search giant's results. The faster your website is, the better positions you will achieve in search results.

Website speed optimization is extremely technical, so you should ask your web developer to review reports for improvement. The following reports will help you and your web developer optimize your website for speed:

- *Overview* – The overview shows your page load times broken down by components and across different dimensions (i.e.,

---

[23]   http://blog.kissmetrics.com/loading-time/

in different browsers and in different countries). These numbers will reveal what components of your website are slower and how the demographic is affected.

- *Page Timings* – this report provides a breakdown of the pages that are the slowest to load, so your web developer can optimize them for better performance.

- *Speed Suggestions* – provides speed recommendations for the pages that load slowly with help from Webmaster Tools. This report should be studied by your web developer.

- *User Timings* – allows the website owner to measure timing of specific events or user interactions. This report requires additional set-up that must be completed by your web developer.

Site Search

Today's customers want to find what they are looking for quickly and effortlessly, and failure to provide the specific information they seek will result in lost visitors and conversions.

If your website has a search box, analyze the entries to learn the commonalities among the searched keywords. This gives excellent insight into the needs of prospective customers.

Google Analytics needs to be configured prior to tracking search queries. Ask your web developer to help you with this step, and then take a closer look at the following reports:

- *Overview* – the search overview tells how many of your visitors search your site, the search terms your visitors use and how your visitors subsequently engage with your site.

- *Usage* – this report gives the ABC breakdown between visits that included an internal site search and those that did not. This gives you a great overview of the search feature's effectiveness.

- *Search Terms* – this report gives the breakdown of the popular search terms your visitors use, as well as other parameters, such as the number of times they viewed search results, exits from your site following search, time spent on the site resulting from search, etc. This data tells you the specifics of your visitors' expectations of your website. The fact that they search for it means they have an interest, but it additionally informs you that they have not been able to find it on their own. This can potentially mean there is room for improvement in website navigation and usability.

- *Pages* – Similar to search terms, this report shows the breakdown of specific pages that visitors searched on your website. This data may reveal deficiencies where website users weren't able to find what they wanted on a particular page and then proceeded to using search.

Events

Events are user interactions with your website that don't require loading a page, for example, playing a video, printing a page, downloading a file, liking a page on Facebook, etc. Since most data in Google Analytics comes from page loads (i.e., when a link is clicked and the user is taken to another page on your website), setting up *events* allows you to track *actions within* these pages.

Events can be a valuable tool that measures the user's behavior as it leads to a conversion. For example, let's say that you have a video embedded in your site's homepage. You want the visitors to watch the video that is designed to engage them and, coupled with calls to action, drive them to conversion. How can you measure interactions of your users with this video? This can be achieved by making use of events.

Setting up events requires additional technical set-up that should be completed by your web developer. First, you should decide which events you want to track. You can set up multiple events in different categories (Video, for example), as well as various actions, e.g., Play, Pause or Label (any additional information, such as the title of the video). The more granular information you provide, the easier it will be to track. For example, you can track *Plays* of the *Video* with the label *Main*, or better yet, see how many of these Plays lead to a conversion.

- *Overview* – the Overview report lets you see the big picture of events throughout your website, including the breakdown by category, action and label. Similar to goals, you can assign arbitrary event values to measure their importance or impact. For example, a video play can be a value of one, and if the user viewed the entire video, it would rank a ten.

- *Top Events* – shows you the ranking of events by the number of occurrences, total event value, average value, etc.

- *Pages* – this report gives a breakdown of pages where events took place with the number of occurrences, total event value, average value, etc.

- *Events Flow* – the Event Flow report lets you visualize the steps visitors took prior to an event.

AdSense

If you serve ads on your website using Google AdSense (see "Selling Advertising" in "Chapter 14 – Earning Revenue with Your Website: Common Monetization Strategies"), these reports will help you review performance of the ads that you serve (e.g., eCPM, Unit Impressions). This requires linking your AdSense account to your Analytics account (consult your web developer for help with that).

Experiments

We will elaborate more on experiments (also called A/B & MV Testing) in the section "Fine-Tune Your Website for Better Results" of "Chapter 19 – How to Get the Most from Your Website".

Experiments are primarily conducted to improve goal conversion and allow testing to determine what page design is most effective in converting your visitors. Google Analytics has a built-in tool for setting up and running experiments on your website. A web page variation is selected and tested for performance. Google Analytics is able to test up to five variations of a page and run up to twelve experiments concurrently.

In-Page Analytics

In-Page Analytics allows you to make a visual assessment of visitors' interaction with your website. The data is displayed as visually overlaying your website. This tool allows you to assess the following: did the visitors focus on the content you wanted them to see, did they get positive results from their search and did they click on the calls to action that you wanted.

We will go into more detail about additional tools under "Chapter 19 – How to Get the Most from Your Website" For now, let's focus on what Google Analytics has to offer:

- *Control Bar* – When you open this report, Analytics displays your website with various metrics visually overlaid on your website. The control bar across the top of the report lets you select the metrics to show and hide the color scale for bubbles and to turn the browser-size visualization on and off.

- *Show Bubbles* – bubbles indicate the links website visitors clicked. The numbers inside bubbles represent the metric you chose in the control bar (clicks on these links, for example).

- *Show Color* – Color feature applies different colors to bubbles of different values (similar to Heatmaps, see "Heatmaps & Scrollmaps" under "Chapter 19 – How to Get the Most from Your Website"

- *Browser Size* – This neat feature lets you see the portion of your website that is visible to the selected percentage of users without scrolling. For example, if you selected 80% in the control bar, the Analytics will show you the portion of the webpage that at least 80% of users can see without vertical or horizontal scrolling.

Conversion Analysis

A conversion is the completion of an activity on your website that is important to your business' success. As previously described, tracking conversions ultimately measures your website's overall business performance. You can gauge if your website is on track to reach its S.M.A.R.T. business objectives. If it is not, you can make necessary adjustments. We will detail this in "Chapter 19 – How to Get the Most from Your Website"

Let's see what Google Analytics offers for conversion reporting:

Goals

If you haven't done this yet, the first priority should be defining *goals* you want to measure and having your web developer configure Google Analytics to track these goals. You must define goals in Google Analytics in order to track conversions. If the goals are not set up properly, the conversions report will show no data.

To determine what goals are worth tracking, you have to be clear on your objective for your website's purpose in the first place. Ask yourself what the website needs to do so it reaches the S.M.A.R.T. business objectives you defined for it. Then work in reverse. An example of a goal would be a purchase, an information request, subscription or an online registration or any other action that gets you closer to your website's S.M.A.R.T. business objectives.

Note: although you can set multiple goals, don't go overboard. Track only those goals that are directly beneficial to your business. Irrelevant goals can distort the real picture, will lead to wrong marketing decisions and will cost very real dollars.

- *Overview* – the overview report gives you a big-picture look at how your website is doing in conversions, including the total number of goals completed, goal value, goal conversion rate, abandonment rate and the breakdown of completed goals.

- *Goal URLs* – this report shows you the pages of your website that generated the most goal conversions.

- *Reverse Goal Path* – shows the path visitors took by listing URL of pages of one-, two- and three-step points prior to the goal completion location.

- *Funnel Visualization* – goals can have funnels – an established flow of pages users must follow to reach their goal. Each step tells you how many people (and percentages of those people) proceeded to the next step versus abandoning the process altogether.

The funnel report is an invaluable tool you want to use to continually tweak you website to optimize conversions. For example, a funnel is able to track users through steps of your checkout process. A high drop-off percentage at one of the steps may mean that your customers are intimidated, lead off or distracted.

There are many ways you can apply this concept. You can even have funnels for simpler goals, like a "Contact Us" form. You may wonder: where is the funnel? There is only one form: either users fill it out or they don't. How about measuring how many people arrive at the Contact Us page (shows intent) versus actually completing the form? This statistic is useful to measure the performance of the form itself. How many people actually completed the form as opposed to those who opened and abandoned it?

- *Goal Flow* – The Goal Flow report gives you a visual representation of the path your visitors took through your website toward a goal. This report will shed light on your website visitors' behaviors and will tell you if they are navigating your website toward the goal in an expected way.

E-commerce

If you sell products or services directly on your website, it is imperative that you have your web developer set up e-commerce tracking. E-commerce tracking will let Analytics collect and measure transactional data like product performance, purchase amounts, billing locations and more. These reports will give you an understanding of how your business is doing, and it gives you a measure on the return of your marketing dollars.

- *Overview* – the e-commerce overview report gives you an analysis of your website sales: the conversion rate, number of purchases, revenue, average order amount and quantity purchased, as well as the top revenue sources and your best sellers.

- *Product Performance* – this report tells you exactly which products your customers buy, quantities purchased, and revenue generated by those products.

- *Sales Performance* – provides a breakdown of sales performance by date so you can review the best- and worst-performing days.

- *Transactions* – shows the breakdown by order total, tax, shipping and quantity information for each transaction.

- *Time to Purchase* – this report gives you a great insight into the average number of days and number of visits it takes your customers to make a purchase (counting from the moment they arrived at the website initially to the moment of purchase).

Multi-Channel Funnels

The Multi-Channel Funnels is probably the most under-used and the least understood feature of Google Analytics, yet one of the most powerful. The reason most people don't even look at these reports is because they lack the basic understanding of the value of this data.

What is a multi-channel funnel? In the reports we have reviewed so far the goal conversions are credited to the last source (channel) that brought the visitor to the website. But, what role did other websites and social media referrals search or ads play in that conversion? Multi-Channel Funnels show how all channels of traffic to the website work in harmony to convert your visitors to customers.

- *Overview* – the Overview report gives a bird's-eye view of conversions and assisted conversions (those associated with more than one channel) and allows selection of a maximum of four channels to visualize the overlap between them (where one, two, three or all four channels played a role).

  Note: In this report and all other Multi-Channel Funnels reports, you can adjust the Look Back Window (a period of between 1 and 90 days prior to each conversion).

- *Assisted Conversions* – An assist for a conversion is a channel (a source or a medium) that appears anywhere on a conversion path (except the final interaction). For example, let's say that a visitor originally found your website in Google (Organic Search), then saw a mention on Facebook (Social), then bookmarked your website and returned through the bookmark (Direct) to complete the purchase. In this case, both Facebook and Google assisted in the conversion. Using the example above, the Assisted Conversions report shows the contribution of each channel in the conversion: Last Click ("Direct" in the example) is the number of conversions and revenue the channel closed (i.e., the final interaction). First Click ("Organic Search" in the example) is the number of conversions and revenue that the channel initiated (i.e., the first interaction). Assisted/Last Click or Direct Conversions summarizes each channel's overall role in conversions: a value close to zero means that the channel produced more conversions than assists; where a value close to one means that the channel generated more assists than direct conversions.

Multi-Channel Funnels

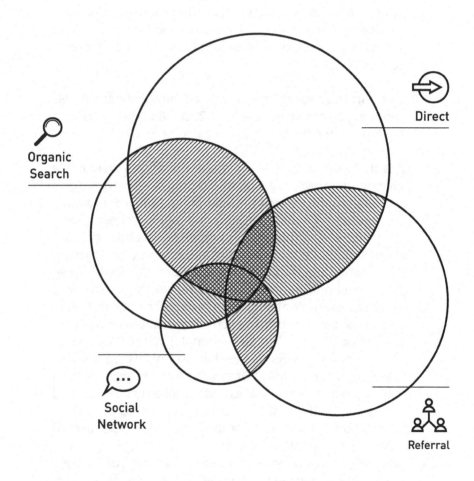

Direct

Organic
Search

Social
Network

Referral

- *Top Conversion Paths* – this report shows the most common Multi-Channel Funnels (MCF) paths visitors took toward the goal. For example, if your top-performing MCF is "Organic Search > Direct," this means that most users find your website in search engines, bookmark it and then return to the website to complete the purchase. You can change the dimension in this report to source/medium, source, path and others to have a good picture of the various routes your users take to return and complete a purchase.

- *Time Lag* – Similar to Time to Purchase report, this report gives you the number of days it takes visitors to make a purchasing decision. You can see the breakdown by the number of days that occur between the first visit and the conversion. By doing so, you will learn a great deal about the sales cycle of your website.

- *Path Length* – this report shows the number of interactions (between 1 and 12+) it took visitors to become customers.

Attribution Modeling

Of all Analytics reports, Attribution models are probably the most complex. They require a very deep understanding of your business model and how different channels work in harmony to generate conversions. It requires scrupulous and precise set-up, so be prepared to spend sufficient time learning to the full use of this tool. Otherwise, avoid it completely. Hasty decisions made on reports that are improperly configured or analyzed can send you in the wrong direction.

So what is Attribution modeling? It is the process of understanding each channel's involvement in conversion and assigning the proper credit for its contribution to the conversion. With the help of Multi-Channel Funnels, we've already learned that there are multiple channels contributing to conversions, but are they equal in their contribution? Not quite.

As every business is different, and every business' sales cycle is different, attribution modeling helps you understand the buying behaviors of your website visitors as they apply to your scenario. This helps determine the most effective marketing channels for your marketing dollars.

Google Analytics is equipped with several baseline attribution models that define how credit is distributed to interactions in a conversion path. There is no model that fits a business' needs exactly, so the best model depends on your specific business and your advertising objectives:

- *Last Interaction* – assigns 100% credit to the last interaction. It is useful in campaigns that are designed to attract visitors at the time of purchase and sales cycles that have little or no consideration phase. This model is also referred to as Last Touch and is great for fast-moving consumer goods.

- *Last Non-Direct Click* – ignores direct visits and assigns 100% credit to the last channel. Google Analytics applies this model by default to Multi-Channel Funnels. It is also used for other reports, so this model is a good benchmark. If your traffic shows that visits from other channels always preceded direct visits, this model will filter out direct visits.

- *First Interaction* – (aka First Touch) assigns 100% credit to the first channel with which the user interacted. It is useful for campaigns that are designed to create initial awareness of a brand and attract customers who were not previously exposed to it. If you are a new player in your niche market, and your brand is not known, this may be a good model.

- *Linear* – gives equal credit to each interaction in a conversion path. It is particularly useful if your campaigns are designed to maintain constant contact with the customers and if all touch points in your sales cycle are equally important. An example is a customer support oriented service.

- *Time Decay* –assigns more credit to the interactions that occurred closest to the time of conversion. The time decay model is useful for short promotional campaigns (one or two days); where you want to give more credit to interactions that occur during the promotion.

- *Position Based* – factors in the order of interactions and assigns 40% credit to the first interaction, 20% credit to the next interaction and 40% credit to the last interaction. It is useful for campaigns that have initial touch points to introduce the customer to the brand and final touch points that result in sales.

- *Last AdWords Click* – use this model if you advertise through Google AdWords. This model will assign 100% credit for conversions to the last Google AdWords click in a conversion path.

- *Custom Models* – you can also edit attribution models or even create your own by selecting a baseline model and tweaking parameters.

  After you select the model or models that are a good fit for your business, it is important to understand the metrics they illustrate:

  - *CPA – Cost Per Acquisition shows the cost to generate a single conversion (on average) under a particular model.*

  - *ROAS – Return On Advertising Spend is calculated by dividing the conversion value (total sold) by the total dollar amount spent on a particular channel.*

By selecting an appropriate attribution model, you can see the performance and the ROI on each of the channels. Note: you may have to upload your non-Google cost data sets (for example, if advertising is purchased in search engines other than Google) so the cost information is available in the Google Analytics reports. Ask your web developer for assistance with this step.

Real-Time Analysis

As the name suggests, the Real-Time reports show visitor activity in real time on your website. These reports are updated continuously. As you browse these reports, you can actually see numbers increase (in green) or decrease (in red). Analytics even highlights the information as it changes in real time.

Users are considered "real-time" if they have been active on your website within the past 5 minutes. Standard reports' sessions are defined by 30-minute time frames. Real-Time reports are very useful in monitoring time-sensitive campaigns and promotions, as well as changes on busy websites, where it is important to know how your users interact with your website in real time. All real-time reports show the number of people on your website at a given point in time, as well as their page views per minute and per second.

Real-Time Overview

This report provides a birds-eye view of what's happening on your website in real time, such as the breakdown of new versus returning users, top sources of incoming traffic (referrals, social, keywords) as well as top active pages and users' geographic origins.

Locations

This report is similar to Audience Analysis > Geo, with the only exception being the display of geographic locations of active users.

Traffic Sources

Real-time Traffic Sources report is similar to Acquisition Analysis> Channels, but it also shows the channels and media that have generated traffic to your website in the past 5 minutes.

Content

Just as the name suggests, real-time Content report shows the specific pages your users are viewing presently, including the breakdown of desktop versus mobile users. This report is similar to Behavior Analysis> Site Content.

Events

Real-time Events report allows you to see how your visitors interact with your website in real time: video plays, file downloads, prints, etc. It is similar to Behavior Analysis> Events, only in real time.

Conversions

Similar to Conversion Analysis > Goals, real time conversions show completion of goals (as defined for your website) in real time.

Intelligence Events

At this point, you may be wondering: who in the world has the time to review all these reports? Wouldn't it be nice to have a professional analyst review your reports on a regular basis and provide you with the bottom-line and revealing data in a concise manner? This is the exact function of Google Analytics Intelligence.

The service continuously monitors your website's traffic, and as soon as it detects significant changes, it alerts you. Even more impressive is that Analytics Intelligence explains *why* a particular variable has changed. For example, it will provide analysis as to why you have more traffic to your website or why your sales went down unexpectedly. Now, how amazing is that!

Google Analytics is a very useful tool that can save a substantial amount of time conducting your analysis. However, beware...the tool is not perfect. You will most likely find some analyses unreliable and inconclusive. However, it is an amazing tool that will save countless hours drilling down to what matters.

There are two kinds of Intelligence alerts that are available for you to review:

Automatic Alerts

Analytics automatically detects any abnormalities in your traffic and presents you with daily, weekly and monthly alerts, all based on data from the same time frames. You can see all alerts sorted by the level of importance in the Overview tab, or you can focus strictly on Daily, Weekly or Monthly reports. All reports allow customization to shift the importance as well as to drill down into a detailed report when you want to explore the details further.

Custom Alerts

Using Analytics Intelligence, you can also create custom alerts in several scenarios. You can instruct the tool to flag specific data. For example, let's say you purchased a billboard space in Chicago. You can set Analytics Intelligence to alert you when website visits from Chicago increase by 20% over the previous month's activity. You can opt to receive alerts via e-mail or text messages.

How to Get the Most from of Google Analytics

As you've learned, Google Analytics is a powerful tool, and by now, you are most likely overwhelmed by what it can reveal about your website's performance. You may be wondering how to wrap your mind around all these reports and how to extract data that is useful and relevant in reaching your business objectives.

To help you get started, let's look at 10 easy steps you can take to get the most from Google Analytics:

Never Lose Focus of What You Are Measuring and Why

The most common mistake made with Google Analytics is getting excited about the reports that may be fun to review but are meaningless where it relates to business: "Oh, look, we have visitors from 127 countries." Now ask yourself, how does all this information help in achieving my business objectives?

Everyone makes this mistake. In fact, most people only view "vanity metrics" focusing solely on number of visits to their website. If the traffic to the website is growing, they are happy. But, is it enough?

At this point, you know that it is not. It is imperative to know: Are these the right visitors? Do they buy our products or services? If yes, where can we get more of them?

The key is to focus on 5-10 KPIs that are important in achieving your website or business objectives. Forget about everything else (or at least spend a minimum amount of time in reviewing this irrelevant data); make time to review the reports that are of paramount importance.

Measure Conversions with Goals

As previously outlined, the first step is to define and set goals. Just as your website needs to have S.M.A.R.T. business objectives, your Google Analytics account should be configured to measure conversions using goals. Conversions will confirm that you are on track to reach your business objectives. Your conversion rate is the most important KPI, regardless of the objective and the purpose of your website.

If you have more than one goal, you should also assign arbitrary monetary value to each goal, even if the value doesn't relate to a transaction's purchase value. This allows the measurement of the overall performance in regard to goals that have a bigger impact and get you closer to your business objectives.

For more information on goals, and their set-up and configuration, please refer to "Conversions KPIs" under "Acquisition-Behavior-Conversion (ABC)" as well as "Conversion Analysis"

Properly Configure Google Analytics

Proper configuration of your Google Analytics account is not only key to the accuracy of your data, it also provides several additional instruments and tools to better analyze your traffic. These instruments are not available with an "out of the box" application of Analytics. The following checklist of 10 items will help ensure your Analytics is set up properly:

1. Set up and track events; see "Events"" under "Behavior Analysis"

2. Track campaigns; see "Campaigns" under "Acquisition Analysis"

3. Set up Analytics for e-commerce; see "E-commerce" under "Conversion Analysis."

4. Set up tracking for search on your website; see "Site Search" under "Behavior Analysis"

5. Enable Demographics and Interest reports; see "Demographics" and "Interests" under "Audience Analysis"

6. Connect Webmaster Tools to track keywords and site speed; see "Search Engine Optimization" under "Acquisition Analysis" and "Site Speed" under "Behavior Analysis"

7. Use experiments to measure improvements; see "Experiments" under "Behavior Analysis."

8. Learn multi-channel funnels, and apply attribution modeling; see "Multi-Channel Funnels" and "Attribution Modeling" under "Conversion Analysis."

9. If you use AdWords, be sure to tie the account; see "AdWords" under "Acquisition Analysis"

10. If you use AdSense, be sure to tie the account; see "AdSense" under "Behavior Analysis".

Create Custom Dashboards & Reports

As you know by now, Analytics offers lots of data, and it is easy to spend many hours retrieving the data that is most meaningful to you. Luckily, Google Analytics allows you to create custom dashboards so you can quickly access the most valuable data.

After you've identified the most important KPIs, spend time creating a dashboard or two that focus exclusively on the metrics that are pertinent to your business goals. Even though you can create up to 20 dashboards, I would recommend strict focus on only what's important—the 5-10 KPIs you identified.

Google Analytics also offers a Solutions Gallery of pre-made dashboard templates that have been submitted by other users. Some of these dashboard templates are very effective. In fact, I created and shared one called "10 ROI KPIs" in the Conversion category that focuses on the most common KPIs we measure at my company.

✴ **Download:** *You may access this dashboard from* www.ResultsOnInternet. com

Google Analytics also allows you to create custom reports. It's a feature that most users ignore, but it is a great way to create a perfect report specifically designed for your needs. For example, one of my favorite custom reports shows the referring URL combined with the destination URL on a website. This allows me to track visits from any of my articles published on the web to specific pages on my website. While there are other ways to trace data, this custom report allows quick access to the data.

Review Reports Regularly

No matter how well you design your custom reports, they are useless if you don't review them regularly. You simply won't know the effectiveness of your website or what improvements need to be implemented unless you monitor your website's KPIs on a regular basis.

Review your main KPIs weekly and conduct a thorough review of reports once a month. You may want to monitor your KPI's traffic-intensive or e-commerce websites on a daily basis. Also, review the performance of your website immediately following any major updates to check that the performance is not affected negatively or that it has been improved.

Compare to Past Performance

Google Analytics reports display results from the past 30 days by default. You are probably aware that you can select any date range, from a shorter range (like a week) to a longer range (a year, for example).

Another powerful feature is the "Compare To" checkbox that allows you to compare your current results to any date range in the past. When reviewing reports, you always want to compare them to historic data. Specifically, you want to see positive changes over time in areas that matter. Google Analytics shows changes in nominal values (i.e., 10 more conversions) and percentages (i.e., 10% more conversions).

KPIs won't reveal much without this comparison. For example, let's say that last month your website had 100 conversions and a 1% conversion rate. Is that good or bad? Well, it depends how this month compares to previous months. If last month you had only 50 conversions, 100 is certainly an improvement. However, what if last month your website had only half the traffic you have this month? If that is the case, you conversion rate dropped to 0.5%. This is not good. Maybe there were changes on the website that affected conversions, or perhaps you are sending the wrong type of traffic to the website. Either way, at first glance you may believe the website performs better, where it actually performs worse.

The perspective changes everything, doesn't it? Comparing your website's current performance to the past provides a benchmark or a point of reference. You should routinely conduct comparative KPI reviews so you have the confidence of knowing that you are moving in the right direction. It is especially important when implementing improvements. After all, the only way to measure what works and what doesn't is by comparing results before and after any modifications.

Use Primary & Secondary Dimensions

Most Google Analytics reports allow change to the primary dimensions of the report. This allows you to further drill down to get more detailed information. For example, in Location reports, you can view visitor statistics by the following dimensions Country, Territory, City, and Continent, depending on the amount of detail you want. In some cases additional dimensions give you access to a lot more information. For example, under Audience Analysis> Technology, the default Browser report gives you a breakdown of browsers used to access your website, but other dimensions give you access to see much more information about your visitors: Operating System, Screen Resolution, Screen colors, Flash versions, etc.

Some reports allow the application of secondary dimensions to provide more information in the same table. For example, let's say you are looking at Behavior Analysis> Site Content, the All Pages report gives you a breakdown of the most popular pages on the website. Adding Source as the secondary dimension allows a visual of the Source from the traffic's origin.

Applying secondary dimensions allows you to customize your reports to the point where you can cross-reference your data with different data points.

Alternative to dashboards, you can also save shortcuts to any customized reports. Once on the report, you can click on "Shortcut" to add a link to the current configuration of this report on your Home tab. All report customizations, including advanced segments, secondary dimensions, sorting, etc. will be automatically applied when you access the report with this shortcut.

Create & Apply Advanced Segments

Segments allow you to "segment out" traffic based on specific criteria and compare performance of that "segment" to the performance of the entire website. Segments can be applied to any reports throughout Google Analytics. You can create segments based on dimensions, metrics, visit date, etc. This powerful tool allows you to create reports within reports. Here are some examples of segmenting uses:

- Classify visitors and viewing reports on users who converted (purchased something, expressed interest, etc.) so you may study their behaviors on the website more closely. You can even create "classes" for users based on the revenue they create.

- Identify high-value customers (HVC) by using the Recency-Frequency-Monetary Value (RFM) segment. For example, customers who purchased recently, visited frequently or engaged in most conversions, are more likely to purchase again.

- Focus only on specific sections of your website (for example "Products" or "Services") and analyzing the performance of these money makers without the "noise" from the rest of the website.

- Narrow down the visits that resulted in a conversion from a specific keyword, source or medium, so you understand the effectiveness of various marketing channels.

- Focus on new visitors who arrived on the website during the time frame of a specific campaign to measure the performance of your marketing campaigns.

- Focus on non-converters (users who don't make a purchase, etc.) to study their behavior and understand why they do not convert, and then devise a plan to target them more aggressively and precisely.

- Study conversion rate analysis to better understand and segment your audience. For example, how does your male audience compare to female audience when it comes to conversion rates.

- The list goes on. As you can see, segment is an extremely powerful tool that allows you to analyze reports with real business applications. Segments can become advanced so you may need your web developer's help in the set-up. Once set, you can apply them to any reports in Google Analytics.

Clean Up Your Reports with Filters

As part of the project, you and your web developer frequently visit your website. This traffic accumulates. While it may be negligible for traffic-intensive websites, these frequent visits can be somewhat misleading for smaller websites with less traffic.

You can configure Google Analytics to exclude the traffic from your office IPs, your web developers' IPs and even your home IPs to ensure that only the real and clean traffic gets recorded. These settings are in Analytics administration.

If you have other sections or systems of your website reserved for internal use (corporate extranet, CMS, etc.) be sure that Google Analytics' code is not present on those pages, unless you also want to track traffic to them.

Setup Intelligence Alerts

In the section "Intelligence Events" we covered the importance for Analytics Intelligence to automate the analysis of your reports. Set up custom alerts as well as signing up for default alerts. While you shouldn't rely on Analytics Intelligence as a replacement for regular review of your reports, it can assist you by identifying any issues or opportunities before you review your reports. This tool also uncovers issues you may have missed. The best way to monitor and measure your website's performance is by regular review of your KPI-based reports backed by automatic Intelligence alerts from Google Analytics.

How to Get the Most out of Google Analytics

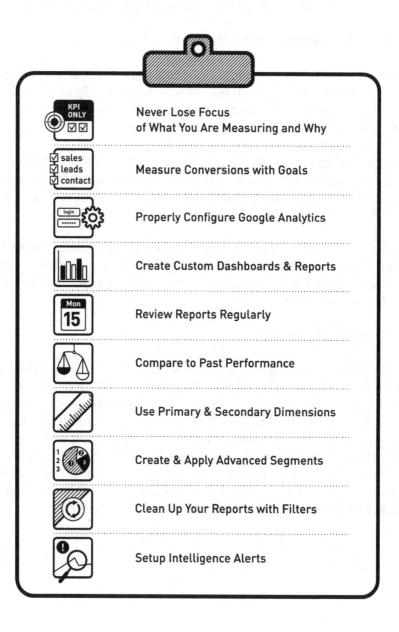

KPI ONLY ☑☑
Never Lose Focus
of What You Are Measuring and Why

☑ sales
☑ leads
☑ contact
Measure Conversions with Goals

login
Properly Configure Google Analytics

Create Custom Dashboards & Reports

Mon 15
Review Reports Regularly

Compare to Past Performance

Use Primary & Secondary Dimensions

1 2 3
Create & Apply Advanced Segments

Clean Up Your Reports with Filters

Setup Intelligence Alerts

Additional Tools

We have focused primarily on Google Analytics, which is a great product, but it does have limitations. First, the free account is limited to 10 million hits per month, and the premium version currently comes at a steep $150K in annual fees (yes, this is not a typo - $150,000). Google Analytics is also known for delayed reporting that can sometimes be as much as 24 hours.

Several alternatives and assorted tools offer capabilities similar to Google Analytics:

- **Clicky** (http://clicky.com/) is a popular alternative to Google Analytics that include a myriad of features including heat maps, split tests and even a Twitter monitoring feature.

- **Mixpanel** (https://mixpanel.com/) describes itself as the "most advanced analytics platform ever for mobile and the web." Interfaces are clean and easy to use with obvious emphasis on mobile analytics.

- **Mint** (http://haveamint.com/) is another choice that features simple interfaces and consolidated reports. Extra features include Bird Feeder – a subscription analyzer for your feeds, and Real Estate Agent that measures the above-the-fold-views on your website and more.

- **FoxMetrics** (http://foxmetrics.com/) is yet another alternative focusing on use interactions and actions of users, where data is centered on customers and not only page views.

- **GoSquared** (https://www.gosquared.com/) is primarily designed for an at-a-glance look at real-time analytics and boasts to be "the most accurate real-time tool." GoSquared has some nice features, like a daily digest that can be e-mailed to you by default. This is a nice feature for website owners who forget to check their reports regularly.

- **Chartbeat** (https://chartbeat.com/) Overwhelmed with the complexity of your analytics reports? ChartBeat is designed to make your data easy to understand as simple, beautiful insights. There are also nice features that measure user engagement.

These are just a few of the tools that you may want to consider. We will discuss a lot more in "Chapter 19 – How to Get the Most from Your Website" specifically section "Fine-Tune Your Website for Better Results"

Chapter 19 – How to Get the Most from Your Website

In the previous chapter, we covered the importance of measuring your website's KPIs in order to detect your website's performance. Well, simply measuring your website's KPIs is not enough.

Going back to your website objectives, the next letter "A" in S.M.A.R.T. stands for "Attainable". How can you attain these objectives within a reasonable amount of time? By continuously measuring your website's performance and making adjustments in response to your visitors' behavioral and conversion patterns, we not only achieve these objectives more quickly, but we can exceed them. Imagine outperforming your initial objectives by 5, 10, or even 20%? How would this affect your bottom line?

This chapter will teach you how to get the most from your website in the months and years following the new website's launch.

Schedule Ongoing Reviews with Your Web Developer

If you and your web developer treat your website as a one-time project, you will never realize its true potential. You and your web developer have put all your experience, technical knowledge and hard work into this project. This represents your best effort. Regardless of the high quality of your website, there is always room for improvement. The following recommendations will help you make educated decisions about ongoing improvements to your website:

Don't Wait until There is a Problem

Most companies don't contact their web developers until there is an urgent need or when they detect an issue with their current website. If you wait to analyze the effectiveness of your website until issues arise, it will result in missed business opportunities. Some issues aren't recognizable until it's too late, and in some cases, irreparable damage is done.

A better approach is to conduct regularly scheduled review sessions with your web developer. This proactive approach will provide opportunities to solve problems in a timely manner and prevent unnecessary costs when larger problems occur later.

Benefit from an Outside Perspective

Let's face it; you are not a web developer. You may not necessarily know what potential issues to look for but your web developer does. They are professionals at creating websites, and as they have progressed in their careers, they know exactly what works and what does not. An experienced web developer is likely to recognize problem areas before they happen or suggest opportunities to improve performance of your website. This may be anything from improving usability or conversion, to technical issues, search engine optimization or new features, and more.

Because you view your website continually, it is very common to develop a "tunnel vision" where you lose sight and perspective of important aspects of your website. This loss of peripheral vision will not be conducive to your long-term web site strategy. One of the key benefits in retaining an outside team to scrutinize your website on a regular basis is that it will be easier for them to detect problem areas missed by your tunnel vision.

Place Website Reviews on Your Calendar

As previously stated, the key to your website's long-term success is the ongoing effort directed toward continuous improvement. The concept is to be proactive and not wait for problems to arise. I recommend scheduling regular meetings and review sessions and have your web developer review the website regularly on all levels. I suggest that you create a calendar item for this action, and conduct quarterly reviews (or more often, if desired).

Pre-scheduling meetings and reviews will not only help maintain a structure to your long-term website planning, it will also allow you and your web developer prepare questions, ideas and topics to discuss prior to each session. Sure, this ongoing review service with your web developer will most likely incur charges, but it will be worth the investment.

Perform Routine Maintenance

Your website is like a car. If you fail to get routine oil changes, the vehicle's performance will continue to drop until the engine stalls. Don't let this happen to your site after all the hard work that was invested!

The following 10-item maintenance checklist should be followed by you, your web developer and your hosting company:

1. **Thoroughly review and test the entire website** (*annually or after any updates*)
    Set aside time to methodically and thoroughly review all pages of the website. You may find broken links, features that don't work or can use improvement. Pay special attention to:

    a. Overall user experience

    b. Load time

    c. Errors of any kind

    d. Broken links

    e. Missing or outdated content

    f. Missing page titles or meta tags

    g. Inconsistent styles or formatting

    h. Typos or grammatical errors

    i. Features and business logic

j. Compliance with accessibility standards (if applicable) such as ADA (Americans with Disabilities Act)

2. **Test your website forms/checkout process** (*quarterly or after any updates*)
Make sure to regularly test all calls to action and points of contact/sale, such as Contact Us forms and the checkout process on your website. There is nothing worse than discovering your contact form stopped working after a website update, and you lost business opportunities due to this flaw.

3. **Review your KPIs, SEO and analytics reports** (*monthly*)
In order to gauge your website's performance effectively, you must set and measure the KPIs (Key Performance Indicators), search engine ratings, and the general website analytics for at least a month. This process will indicate the effectiveness of the website and will help expose possible problems. We focused on KPIs and analytics in the previous chapter.

4. **Security updates & bug fixes** (*monthly or as patches are released*)
Be sure that both your web developer and hosting provider update the software and install any upgrades, security patches, bug fixes or any other software updates that may encompass the operating system, web server, database, CMS, etc. Ideally, patches should be installed as soon as they are released. Failure to install a security patch may compromise your website and make it vulnerable to attack.

5. **Renew your domain names** (*annually*)
Ensure that all your domain names are renewed in a timely manner. As discussed previously, your website's domain name is your most prized possession and allowing it to expire can mean a catastrophe.

6. **Check backups** (*annually*)
   Be sure that your entire website is backed up—the website itself and the data. Have your web developer or hosting company thoroughly check the backups to ensure they are working and that the data is retrievable.

7. **Design and compatibility with browsers** (*annually*)
   As time passes, the website layouts or technology may become incompatible with the new browsers. Regularly review and test your website in various versions of mainstream browsers: Microsoft Internet Explorer, Google Chrome, Mozilla Firefox and Apple Safari.

8. **Dates & copyright notices** (*annually*)
   Review and update any copyright dates or any date-specific text or references throughout your website. The homepage should contain no stale or outdated information (e.g., a year-old press release).

9. **Review contact information** (*annually or as needed*)
   Contact information on your website should always be up to date and accurate: team member names, addresses, phone numbers, etc. A change in staff responsibilities may require e-mails are routed to a different team member. Any real-time changes to your organization should automatically trigger you to think, "Should I update the website?"

10. **Review and update legal disclaimers** (*annually*)
    Review and update your privacy policy, site terms and conditions of use, terms of sale and any disclaimers to ensure they are compliant with policies and laws.

Be Ready for the Future

Will your website work on smart-watches or automobile dashboards as more and more Internet-connected devices propagate our lives every day? It is in the best interests of your business to stay current on industry offerings. Your primary focus should be on your business

Perform Routine Maintenance

☑		**Test the entire website** (Refer to the Website Quality Checklist)	annually or after any updates
☑		Review contact information	annually or as needed
☑	Ↄ.com	Renew your domain names	annually
☑		Check backups	annually
☑		Design and compatibility	annually
☑	©201...	Dates & copyright notices	annually
☑		Update Legal Disclaimers	annually
☑		Test your website forms	quarterly or after any updates
☑	KPI SEO	Review your KPIs/SEO	monthly
☑		Security Updates & Patches	monthly or as patches are released

Website Quality Checklist

Overall user experience	Load time	Errors	Broken links	Missing content	Missing titles/ meta tags	Incon- sistent styles	Typos grammatical errors	Features/ business logic	Compliance with standards
👍	☀	⚠	🔗		<...>	B I U	ABC...	⚙	☑ADA

rather than the latest Internet trends. This is the responsibility of your web developer. Not only should they anticipate the future of the Internet and its capabilities; they should take you there.

Discuss new features and applications with your web developer, and inquire how they may be incorporated into your website. Pay special attention to the following:

- New design trends and how your website compares

- New technologies and their applications

- Your website's appearance and functionality in new browsers and browser versions

- Your website's appearance and functionality on various mobile devices

Follow a Goal-Oriented Roadmap

Most website owners and web developers have no shortage of ideas for improvement to the website. How do you decide what to do next? A well-organized roadmap will help. A roadmap is a document that outlines proposed and planned website improvements. A roadmap should not end; it must be continually updated and evolve for the life of your website.

Maintain a Wish List

As part of website planning, I strongly recommend compiling a wish list. When you have an idea, or you like a recommendation from your customer feedback, make sure to record it immediately. Maintaining a wish list allows you to capture best ideas to review and implement at the appropriate time.

Best Roadmap Practices

Unlike a wish list, which is just a list of improvements you *want* to do at some point, a roadmap is a list of improvements you *will* do. The

Follow a Goal-Oriented Roadmap

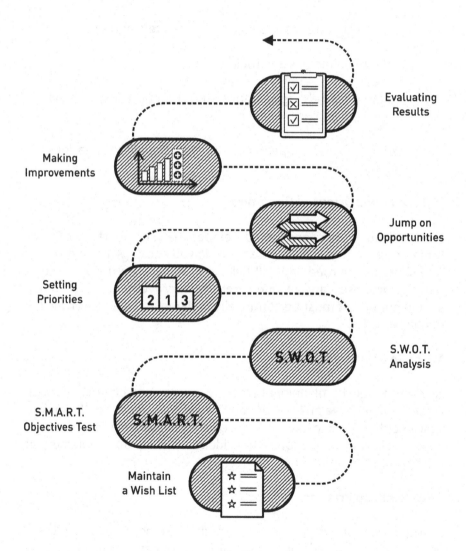

Evaluating Results

Making Improvements

Jump on Opportunities

Setting Priorities

S.W.O.T. Analysis

S.M.A.R.T. Objectives Test

Maintain a Wish List

roadmap is always prioritized allowing you to focus your resources on website improvements that will get you closer to reaching your business objectives.

S.M.A.R.T. Objectives Test

How do you decide what to include on the list? You need to be able to answer the question, "How does the proposed improvement help you get closer to your S.M.A.R.T. business objectives?" If you can't answer this question, it may be best to return the idea to your wish list.

Setting Priorities

The next decision is setting priorities for items on your list. Always focus on one improvement area at a time, as opposed to attempting to accomplish several tasks simultaneously. When deciding on priorities for items on your roadmap, you should consider the following five factors:

1. ROI – Will the improvement generate a quick Return on Investment? Focus on improvements that will create the biggest 'bang for the buck' from the business perspective.

2. *Time Constraints* – How long will the improvement take? If a major feature will take six months to complete, you may want to tackle the smallest features first, so you may reap the benefit of the improvement sooner.

3. *Resources* – Do you and your web developer have the necessary resources available to complete the improvement? These resources include a sufficient budget to complete the improvement in a smooth-running fashion.

4. *Complexity* – we already covered the fact that additional features can greatly complicate the entire project. Ideal feature candidates are those that are easiest to implement and have the biggest impact.

5. *Dependencies* –many features of your website have dependencies. For example, a specific improvement may require prior completion of another feature before it can be implemented, or there could be other outside constraining factors. You should also plan your priorities by factoring in the improvements' impact and/or support on each other.

Jump on Opportunities

On occasion, you may see an opportunity that scores off the charts with the S.M.A.R.T. Objectives. When this happens, you should capitalize on the opportunities as quickly as possible.

Some website improvements could have a compounding effect. For example, if you find that a specific improvement could significantly increase the conversion rate on your website, you should implement it as soon as possible. Over time, such improvements can result in thousands or even millions of dollars of added revenue; or in missed revenue, if you hesitate or procrastinate. If you uncover a truly unique opportunity, it could represent a significant competitive edge. In that case, you want to capitalize on it before your competition discovers it.

Always perform S.M.A.R.T. Objectives Test despite your enthusiasm about this seemingly lucrative concept. It may seem great "on paper," but if it requires millions of dollars and years to implement, it may not be feasible or realistic.

Making Improvements

Once your initial roadmap is established, you can start planning the execution. Agree on time and cost with your web developer prior to rolling out the project. Improvements are only beneficial when they can be achieved within time constraints and budget. If an improvement has a higher cost than anticipated, or takes longer to accomplish, it may not generate the return on investment you were expecting.

Implement new features and improvements one at a time. This single-faceted approach allows you to evaluate each improvement exclusively and make future adjustments as necessary. By focusing on one area at a time, you correctly analyze the level of impact these changes made.

Evaluating Results

After completion of each improvement or phase, it is imperative to evaluate the results. Be sure the improvements were strictly implemented as per plan, and more importantly, that the results have the positive impact you wanted to be achieved. Also, be certain that these results are aligned with your overall objectives. If they are not, other aspects of your planning may not stay on track, so it is recommended that you pause and re-evaluate before investing time and money into additional improvements. Further adjustments and re-evaluation of the overall roadmap may be necessary in order to continue working toward the business objectives in an efficient manner.

In "Chapter 18 – How Well is Your Website Really Doing?" I detail the principles of objectively evaluating and measuring performance of your website. You can use these principles to measure performance of individual components as well.

Collect Customer Feedback

The best way to learn how well your new website is received is through user feedback. This is true, especially in the beginning, before there is any data to analyze. Because your customers are the primary users of your website, their opinions not only matter, but these opinions are vital to your website's success. Your customers' collective feedback should be the guiding compass for your long-term website strategy. If you pay attention to this feedback and adjust the website appropriately, you will be more likely to create more customers like those who offered their feedback. If your website works for them, it will work for others too.

When requesting or collecting feedback, keep an open mind when reviewing comments. At this point, you are emotionally invested in your website, but it would be a waste of everyone's time (including yours), if you are going resist modifications or changes to your website. Seek feedback only if you are open to making changes so your website will continually improve.

Benefits of Getting Early Feedback

Following the announcement of your new website release, you will most likely immediately receive feedback from your customers right away. This early feedback is very valuable. People are new to your website, so this initial perspective is of paramount importance. When your customers frequent your website, the feedback content is typically not as rich.

Furthermore, since you and your web developer are currently working on the website, it will be much easier to implement changes at this stage. It will also be more cost-effective and efficient.

Finally and most importantly, incorporating feedback early in the game will make a big difference in the long run. Even a little issue that remains unattended regarding the website's ability to convert visitors into customers can result in significant losses over time. By the same token, a simple conversion improvement can result it impressive gains.

How Useful is your Feedback?

Feedback is just as valuable as the improvements you can make resulting from the feedback. If a person doesn't like the website without giving you any additional details, their feedback is not very useful to you. When someone says they don't like something on your website, you want to know specifically *what* they don't like and *why* they don't like it. This will allow you to make improvements.

When a bug or a usability issue is reported, get all the details from the source. Unless you or your web developer can recreate the issue, it cannot be detected and fixed. See "Quality Assurance & Repairs" in" Chapter 17 - Recommended Website Project Flow: How to Stay on Track and Achieve Results" for information the web developer will need to fix the issue.

When you receive feedback about your website, determine if this feedback is representative of your ideal customer demographic. If not, this feedback is of little or no value, and it could actually be misleading. You can obtain feedback from friends and family, but they could be biased and may not be representative of your customers. Scrutinize the objectivity contained in feedback offered.

How Accurate is your Feedback?

The statistical accuracy of your feedback is in the numbers. Polling several random individuals will not provide this accuracy. It will simply represent opinions of several individuals. Additionally, if you survey a broad range of individuals whose opinions are "polar opposites" of your customers, the feedback may be misleading or baseless.

How do you determine the number of people to survey to generate accurate and valuable feedback? To answer this question scientifically, it depends on several factors, including the size of the population, segmentation, degree of variance in responses and the tolerance for error. Dr. Van Bennekom of Northeastern University argues in his "Great Book - Organizational Effectiveness through Feedback Management", that as a rule of thumb, 200 responses are required for fairly good accuracy, 100 responses are needed for marginally acceptable accuracy, and 30 responses for acceptable accuracy, (only if you have little variance in responses and you are willing to accept low accuracy).[24]

The bottom line is to survey as many as possible to determine a genuine trend. For example, if a single individual doesn't like an element of your website, it shouldn't raise a significant concern; but if 5 out of 30 surveyed customers concur, there is a reason for concern and immediate attention.

Dealing with the Negative Feedback

It feels great to get praise for the hard work you have invested into the project, but you need to focus on negative comments that contain suggestions for improvement. You certainly don't want excessive criticism, but think of it this way: negative feedback is better than no feedback. Negative feedback is what perpetuates improvement. If you receive negative feedback, you should be grateful that your customers are direct and honest with you in addition to taking the time to offer

---

[24]   Fred Van Bennekom, Dr. B.A., Principal Great Book Consulting

constructive criticism. This feedback is what allows you to turn your website's weaknesses into strengths.

Do not be discouraged by negative feedback. While some feedback can be a learning opportunity, other feedback may be worthless. No matter how great your website you will always get feedback from individuals who "don't get it" or "don't like it." This doesn't mean you should necessarily act on this feedback. Some people are impossible to please, and given the opportunity, they will find something wrong with your website. You have to learn to filter out such feedback.

Before jumping to redoing or changing your website, determine if the feedback you've received is 1) useful and 2) statistically accurate (see previous sections).

Tools to Collect Customer Feedback

Many effective online tools provide in-depth testing and collection of feedback directly from your visitors. Here are some of my favorites:

- **UserVoice** (www.uservoice.com) is a widget that allows your website visitors to submit ideas and suggestions for the website; then responsively other visitors can vote these ideas up or down. This eliminates the guesswork, because it allows you to see what your customers really want to see on your website.

- **Get Satisfaction** (www.getsatisfaction.com) is an alternative to UserVoice that features a forum-like page for website visitors to field their questions, submit ideas and request support. You can delegate employees to provide assistance with specific issues and answer questions.

- **Usabilla** (www.usabilla.com) makes it easy for your website visitors to contact you and share their feedback. A floating widget allows users to leave website feedback, report bugs, and make suggestions in all areas of the website, specific pages or even sections of a page.

- **Feedbackify** (www.feedbackify.com) is a simple widget that lets you quickly collect feedback by asking specific questions (i.e., "Rate our new website from 1 to 10").

- **Kampyle** (www.kampyle.com) is an alternative to Feedbackify that not only provides a space for Q & A to specific questions, but also allows you to communicate with your websites users and even automatically provide them with relevant responses based on the feedback left.

- **Bugmuncher** (www.bugmuncher.com) is another feedback widget that is designed to submit annotated screenshots that are useful for bug tracking internally, as well as for getting feedback and bug reports from your website visitors.

Fine-Tune Your Website for Better Results

Earlier in the book, I compared a website to a high-performance car, using the analogy to explain the importance of regular maintenance in order to have continuous optimal performance. Let's take this analogy one step further.

When you compare your website to the competitors' websites, it can be observed as a drag race. In this race there is only one winner and one prize—the customer. You win the race, you get the customer. You come in second, you get nothing.

Now let's think about how these teams win their races. They meticulously fine-tune every possible component of the car. Each isolated, fine-tuned component doesn't win the race, but improvements to each component will shave off split seconds and get their car closer to the finish line. These collective improvements ultimately win the race.

It works the same way with websites. You may believe some improvements (or "tune-ups") are too small and insignificant. However, small improvements can be made and may produce results. Adding these to all other "tune-ups" amounts to a race victory.

The following recommendations, tools and resources will help you optimize and fine-tune your website for the best possible performance. The majority of these tools will require the assistance of your web developer to integrate them into your website:

Conversions Optimization

Are you missing conversion opportunities? Can something be done to improve the conversion rate so the website generates more leads or purchases? Conversion tracking and analysis allows you to identify and measure purchasing signs, optimize the checkout flow and remove all barriers that prevent prospects from converting to customers.

Conversion optimization can be a tricky business. Consider the following six steps that will make a positive difference:

1. Review "Chapter 12 - Is Your Website Built to Sell? Proven Ways to Convert Visitors into Customers" to be sure that you and your web developer haven't committed any cardinal sins that will diminish your business.

2. Experiment with various calls to action. For instance, make a call to action more prominent, experiment with various placements, or change the language for a more customer-centric experience, etc.

3. Simplify the checkout or Contact Us form. Make it as simple and user-friendly as possible with a minimum number of fields. Remove any possible distractions or barriers.

4. If you have access to the user's information (i.e., if the user is registered), consider targeted or personal calls to action based on their specific needs, wants and preferences.

5. If purchasing or indicating interest seems to be too large a leap, give your visitors a teaser (a whitepaper, a free sample or a consultation) in exchange for their information. They get a valued product or service, and you get a lead.

6. If your product or service offering is too extensive, consider guiding your visitors through the process by building a user-friendly, wizard-like interface.

You may also find the following online tools helpful to analyze and improve conversions:

- **Qualaroo** (https://qualaroo.com/) is a service designed to help you improve website conversions by gaining insights into the visitor's intent/preferences and by creating adaptive offers (targeted calls to action, lead generation forms) to drive conversions in real time.

- **Bounce Exchange** (http://bounceexchange.com) is a service that focuses on visitors who don't convert. It analyzes where a visitor is in the engagement funnel and applies the most effective conversion tactics in your strategy. The service promises to compel confused or disoriented visitors to stay on the site longer, collect unengaged, abandoned visitors, convert cart abandonments in real time, and more. All of the above has a hefty monthly price tag.

- **Picreel** (http://www.picreel.com/) is a more cost-effective alternative to Bounce Exchange. Their recovery technology constantly monitors the activity of your visitors, and in mere seconds before leaving the website (by hitting the back button or closing the window), they are presented with an offer designed to convert.

- **Exit Monitor** (http://exitmonitor.com/) is another alternative for a lead generation and conversion optimization tool. Like Bounce Exchange and Picreel, it detects the precise moment that a visitor is leaving your website and serves a perfectly timed, targeted offer so the visitor stays and converts to a lead.

- **WebEngage** (http://webengage.com/) is a service designed to help drive conversions and generate leads from visitors on your website by profiling website visitors, measuring customer satisfaction and push on-demand notifications.

- **OptinMonster** (http://optinmonster.com/) is a service that allows you to create attention-grabbing opt-in forms that convert website visitors to e-mail list subscribers and leads. It also supports A/B Testing and page level targeting.

User Experience & Behavior Insights

In order to improve the performance of your website, you want to know how people are using the website. This behavior analysis shows how people navigate the website, the paths they take, how many times they retrace their steps, how many pages deep they go into your website, etc. If you are measuring the success of your webpage against the expected user conversion routes defined early in the project, this tool is a clear indicator of your website's effectiveness. If you see that users are being sidetracked, and they are not using the website the way you intended, there may be usability issues that need to be addressed.

The following online tools and resources will be helpful in monitoring and evaluating behavior and user experience:

- **KissMetrics** (http://www.kissmetrics.com) provides a complete picture of user's focus and navigation on your website and where the revenue is generated. As their website states, "Google Analytics tells you what happened, and KISSmetrics tells you who did it." The service claims to fill this gap by illustrating every action of each user and every step they take.

- **Woopra** (http://www.woopra.com/) an alternative to Kissmetrics, this tool is easy to use and comes with several nice features to decipher and analyze the behavioral patterns and engagement of visitors on your website. Features include retention analytics, funnel analytics and segmented analysis.

- **Usability Tools** (http://usabilitytools.com/) is a suite of multiple tools that are typically offered separately. The UX Suite is designed to improve user experience. It includes web testing for improving usability and navigation, surveys to engage users, click testing, and more. The Conversion Suite is designed to optimize the website for higher conversion, and it includes a feedback form, click tracking (Heatmaps), form tester and visitor recording to capture mouse moves and keystrokes.

- **User Testing** (http://www.usertesting.com) is an online service that provides recording of real people and their commentary while using the website. You can select the demographic and the specific areas of the website you want analyzed. This tool employs a process that uncovers weak areas of your website.

- **UsabilityHub** (http://www.usabilityhub.com) is another tool to test your designs and mockups on real users. This tool shows visitors' interactions on your website, what they remember and where they make mistakes. This tool can also be used before your website goes live.

Speed Optimization

As described earlier, website speed plays an important part in your visitor's interaction with your website. Today's users expect the content to load quickly. If your website is slow to load, most visitors will move on quickly. Google Search also favors websites that are quick to load, so you should monitor your website's load times regularly.

The following tools will help you optimize your website for speed:

- **Pingdom** (http://tools.pingdom.com/fpt/) is a free tool that allows testing the load time of your website, analyzing it and detecting potential bottlenecks.

- **GTmetric** (http://www.gtmetrix.com/) is an online service that analyzes your website for speed and assists in optimizing your website for speed, efficiency and an all-encompassing improved website experience for your visitors.

- **Webpagetest** (http://www.webpagetest.org) is another tool that conducts website load speed testing from multiple locations around the world using real browsers and at actual consumer connection speeds.

Heatmaps & Scrollmaps

Sometimes it is helpful to know where people click and what they select on a page: Are your users not clicking on the calls to action? Are you wasting prime real estate on "stuff" that no one cares about? What percentage of users clicked the primary button versus a smaller link below it?

You will learn a lot by viewing the visual representation of clicks overlaid on your website. This can show you quickly whether calls to action are working the way you expected, or if users are wandering off elsewhere. A Heatmap is a visual representation of clicks. A Heatmap resembles thermal imaging. The hot (red) zones are the areas that get the most clicks, yellow represent fewer clicks, green hardly sees any activity and blue see no action at all.

It's not just about what is clicked, but also who clicks it. Heatmap analysis is particularly helpful when combined with user experience analysis and behavior insights.

Scrollmaps (like Heatmaps) show you how far down the page the user scrolls and where attention fades or disappears. If you have important information below the fold of the page (the point on the page that requires scrolling), most users may not even get to it. The scroll map will show you exactly how far most people go.

The following online tools can help you set up and analyze Heatmaps for your website:

- **Crazy Egg** (http://www.crazyegg.com) is one of the most popular solutions to generate Heatmaps and Scrollmaps with overlays (seeing numbers or percentages of clicks) and confetti (distribution of traffic—based on source or destination) for your website.

- **ClickTale** (http://www.clicktale.com) is another tool designed to visualize and measure website behaviors. The tool allows visitor mouse-movement recordings and mouse-move Heatmaps (strongly correlated to eye movements) as well as traditional click Heatmaps.

- **Clickdensity** (http://www.clickdensity.com) is the original Heatmap analytics tool that includes Heatmaps, click maps and hover stats.

A/B & MV Testing

When you and your web developer detect weak spots on your website and plan improvements, how do you know what works and what doesn't? You won't really know until you try it.

A/B testing takes guesswork out of the game and makes improving by experimentation more effective. For example, A/B testing allows you to compare two different versions of a form, a call to action, design or a piece of content. It then reveals which version performs more effectively. The concept is improving your website by running two variations, measuring results and keeping the variation that works better.

MV Testing stands for Multivariate Testing. The concept is similar to A/B testing; but where A/B tests are usually performed to determine the better of two variations, multivariate testing can test multiple (more than two) combinations.

Many tools listed in this chapter have some built-in A/B capabilities, but the tools below take it one step further.

- **Unbounce** (http://unbounce.com/) is a tool designed for building high-converting landing pages without the need for assistance from your web developer with an A/B testing component as the centerpiece.

- **Optimizely** (https://www.optimizely.com/) is the leader in A/B testing that allows you to visually try different variations and easily set up tests on promotions, pricing, buttons, sale text, banners, colors and more. You can then track the performance of each variation: clicks, conversions, engagement, revenue or virtually any other custom goal, and then select those that made a positive impact.

- **Visual Website Optimizer** (http://visualwebsiteoptimizer.com/) is an alternative to Optimizely that also includes Heatmaps, geo-targeting and usability tracking for improved A/B testing.

Surveys & Market Research

Sometimes the best way to find out what your customers think about your company and its products or services is to ask them directly. Your customers and other participants can provide you with valuable feedback that can in turn be used not only to improve your website but your offering as well. Online surveys on or off your website are a low-cost way to conduct basic market research to learn if an idea or a product is appealing to website visitors.

- **Google Consumer Surveys** (http://www.google.com/insights/consumersurveys/) a great tool that harnesses the scope of Google to reach everyday people, not only those who choose to participate in research panels. You can run a number of questions in various forms, specify the demographic and get thorough analytical results.

- **SurveyMonkey** (https://www.surveymonkey.com/) one of the most popular and easy to use tools to create, design and analyze surveys online. You also can obtain feedback from your target audience via SurveyMonkey's pool at a nominal fee.

- **AYTM** (http://aytm.com) a powerhouse in online market research reaching 20M+ people; offers video questions and responses, demographic filters, psychographic filters, allows you to prequalify responders, includes real-time results, and more.

Professional Testing

If you feel you are still not getting the most from your website, it may be time to ask for professional help. Although your web developer has a high level of expertise, they may not possess superior skills in a specific area (outside of their core competency). Additionally, they may not have sufficient resources available to trouble-shoot and solve all problems. Remember, at this point, after working on the website for this length of time, both you and your web developer have developed tunnel vision. This means that elements go unnoticed where it would likely be obvious to a fresh eye.

Bring in a fresh, new perspective. Luckily, there are services and resources designed for just that--to get constructive review and critique from other professionals in the industry:

- **Notable** (http://www.notableapp.com) is designed for web developers to get feedback from their peers on wireframes, designs and finished websites. This may be a great tool to audit your website for potential issues and missed opportunities.

- **Concept Feedback** (http://www.conceptfeedback. com) is another website feedback community for web designers and web developers. This is great way to collect expert analyses and recommendations from other web professionals.

Stay Ahead of Your Competition

By the time, you finish reading this chapter, thousands of new websites will have appeared on the Internet. Many will become your direct competitors. Your existing competition will notice your new website quickly. Some will blatantly copy ideas from your website; others will develop their own ideas and strategies that may be better than yours.

The only way to beat your competition, *every* time, is to make your website better in *every* way. This can be achieved by monitoring your competition, comparing their results to yours, improving your website while protecting your content and information. Following are some of the resources and recommendations that will help you with this vital process:

How Does Your Website Stand Up to Competition?

One of the best ways to beat your competition online is to follow proven successful strategies. Once you see what works and what doesn't, you can adopt these winning strategies and improve on them. You can develop your own unique strategies, but it will take more time and money. Instead of reinventing the wheel, direct resources to improve what is already proven to deliver results in your industry.

You need to continually review and monitor at least five websites of your closest competitors. The following scorecard will help you objectively evaluate the effectiveness of competitors' websites as compared to yours. Simply assign a score from one to 10 (1 for least effective and 10 for most effective) for each of the following criteria on your competitors' websites. Later in the chapter, I will list some tools that will help you in this step.

By totaling these scores, you will be able to discern the winner. You can then compare these scores to your own website, and decide on the next items for your roadmap:

1. Rate your overall perception and your first impression of the website.

2. How effective are their messages and value propositions?

3. How effective is the design in delivering and supporting messages?

4. How effective are their calls to actions?

5. How fast does the website load?

6. How easy is it to use and navigate?

7. How easy is it to use on mobile devices?

8. How are their positions in search engines?

9. How effective is their content marketing strategy?

10. How effective is their social media presence?

✳ **Download:** *You may download this worksheet at* <u>www.Results OnInternet.com</u>

Competitive Intelligence & Research Tools

Wouldn't it be nice to keep tabs on what exactly your competition is doing online and how well their website is performing? There are several online tools designed specifically for this purpose. With the help of the following resources and tools, you can monitor your competition and compare your website to theirs:

- **Alexa** (<u>http://www.alexa.com</u>) is like having access to your competitor's Google Analytics. You can view the analytics of your website as well as the competitor's website. It estimates website's ranking in the United States and worldwide, demographics breakdown, top search engine queries, other sites that link to the site, bounce rate and more.

- **Quancast** (https://www.quantcast.com/) is an alternative to Alexa, Quancast provides detailed demographics, geographic and lifestyle information for a website's audience.

- **Compete** (https://www.compete.com) is a suite of products designed to help research competitor's traffic, engagement and demographic, as well as benchmark your performance and market share in the industry. Additional tools include keyword research, websites that competitors use to drive traffic, and more.

- **Google Alerts** (http://www.google.com/alerts) is a great tool for keeping current on a competitor or the industry in general. You can set up a keyword search, and it will automatically send you an e-mail containing the latest matching Google results (web, news, etc.) based on your query. For example, you can monitor any mentions of your competitor online.

- **SEMRush** (http://www.semrush.com/) is another tool that allows you to see search engine and ads traffic of your competitors' websites, broken down by geographical regions. You can see whom you are competing against in search engines, the complete breakdown of their positions, and much more.

- **Marketing Grader by HubSpot** (http://marketing.grader. com) is an online tool that lets you check how your website stacks up against your key competitors. Each website is assigned a score from 0 to 100. This score is based on a number of factors like the content on your website, readability level, social media presence, domain name authority, etc.

- **SpyFu** (http://www.spyfu.com/) allows you to expose the successful search marketing formulas of your competitors. You can see their rankings on Google, keywords they have purchased on Adwords, and ads they have purchased in the last six years.

- **Change Detection** (http://www.changedetection.com/) allows you to monitor competitor websites and be notified with any changes on their websites. This could be an incredibly useful tool to monitor how your competition is fine-tuning their websites.

- **Social Crawlytics** (https://www.socialcrawlytics.com/) is an online service designed to identify your competitors' most shared content. This offers great insight into your competitors' content marketing strategy.

- **Cromonitor** (http://www.cromonitor.com/) is another useful tool from the makers of Social Crawlytics that allows you to monitor your competitor's A/B and MVT tests, showing you exactly how they are tweaking their websites to improve conversions and overall performance.

- **Wildfire Social** (http://monitor.wildfireapp.com) is a simple social media monitoring tool that allows you to compare the performance of your website and your competition on social media (Facebook, Twitter and Google+).

- **SocialMention** (http://socialmention.com/) is a tool that can be used to look up mentions in social media. It allows you to track and determine what the public is buzzing about, and if you and your competitors are included in this buzz.

Resources for Content Protection

Content theft is become an increasingly serious problem on the Web. If your website has valuable, unique content, such as articles, posts, reviews, images or even well-written information about your products or services, it is just a matter of time before your competition will "borrow it" without attributing it to your organization.

United States Copyright Office (www.copyright.gov) is the logical place to start. Please note that in accordance with the U.S. Laws (as well as the European Union) the original work is automatically copyrighted from the moment of creation. Since 1989, you no longer need to display a public copyright notice ("© All rights reserved") on your website[25], even though it may be a good idea to include it, since laws differ in other countries.

You may want to consider filing a copyright registration. Registering a copyright creates a public record of ownership (stored with the Library of Congress) and will serve in your favor before filing an infringement lawsuit in court, should it escalate to that level. The U.S. Copyright Office eCO online system (http://www.copyright.gov/eco/) allows you to file for a copyright registration for your website's content (original text or images). Refer to the online guide (http://www.copyright.gov/circs/circ66.pdf) for more information.

The following additional resources will also help you protect your content and intellectual property:

- **Creative Commons** (www.creativecommons.org) provides licenses to give the public permission to share and use your work on the specific conditions of your choice. For example, sharing content but not allowing companies to sell it; encourage readers to re-publish your articles if they give credit, etc.

- **Copyscape** (www.copyscape.com) is a tool you can use to protect your website from online plagiarism. The premium service automatically monitors the Web for copies of your content, notifying you if any plagiarized content appears.

- **TinEye** (www.tineye.com) is a reverse image search engine that allows checking if anyone else is using your images, even modified versions. Similar to Copyscape, there is also a premium service to check the locations automatically where your images appear online.

---

[25]   http://www.copyright.gov/circs/circ01.pdf

- **Distil** (www.distilnetworks.com) protects your website against web scraping (automatically mining your website for content), price scraping (copying and matching or beating your prices) competitive data mining, form spam and click fraud.

- **DMCA** (www.dmca.com) is an online service that assists you in forcing your stolen content to be taken down in accordance with DMCA (Digital Millennium Copyright Act). DMCA requires hosting providers to remove content that infringes on intellectual property rights. This service assists you with filing DMCA takedown requests if you find content that violates your rights.

Chapter 20 – How to Grow Traffic and Market Your Website

So, your website is up and running and you want to know: How do I quickly drive more traffic to the website? After all, the more traffic the website gets, the quicker the website generates revenue and meets business objectives, right?

Not quite! Marketing your website is important, but you have to proceed strategically. First, ask yourself: Is your website ready for additional traffic? How effective is your website in converting visitors into customers? Do you know your website's present conversion rate?

Unless you are absolutely convinced that your website is a lean, mean conversion machine, even the best marketing will not prevail in realizing its true potential. Remember, your website is a like a funnel: visitors go in, customers come out. If your funnel has a bottleneck, pouring more traffic into it won't be an optimal use of your marketing dollars. You will be investing extra time and money to produce results that can be achieved with a lot less if your website is optimized for conversions.

Without fully understanding your visitors, their behaviors, and your website's effectiveness in converting them, simply scaling up traffic will equate to pouring your marketing dollars down the drain. Please make sure you've read the previous two chapters before proceeding: "Chapter 18 – How Well is Your Website Really Doing?" and "Chapter 19 – How to Get the Most from Your Website" If you feel that your website is set up to get the biggest bang for your marketing buck and you have the proper tools to measure the effectiveness of your marketing campaigns, let's gets started.

10 Common Online Marketing Mistakes to Avoid

It is impossible to teach everything about marketing in one chapter. One can easily write a book exclusively devoted to marketing (actually more like ten books). In this chapter, we will focus on the basics. The recommendations in this chapter are universal and can be applied to any kind of marketing: inbound or outbound, SEO, social, e-mail or paid advertising. The following tips will help you get started and will steer you away from making potentially costly mistakes:

Not Marketing Your Website

I can't tell you how many times I've seen very smart business people come to us with the naïve idea that when the new website is live, it will somehow magically market itself, and visitors will flock to the website by millions in number.

There are over 1 billion (yes billion) websites on the Internet today. What are the chances of someone stumbling upon your website? What makes you think anyone would have the cognitive reasoning to seek your website?

Just as your company's sales would dry up without marketing, your website would also have little or no traffic without marketing. Without traffic, you website is a dead weight in the digital universe. There will be no visitors, no leads and no sales. Regardless of your website's purpose or objective, proper marketing is always the key to its success.

Having Unrealistic Expectations

Another common problem that I see with many website marketing plans is unrealistic expectations exist. Many stakeholders set unrealistic goals on the returns from marketing and the timing of such returns. On occasion, it is caused by the assumption that online initiatives produce immediate results. Overestimating user engagement can also skew expectations.

For example, a client recently approached us with a goal for a new website: 500,000 users in the first year. Here is the kick. They didn't want 500,000 visitors. No, they wanted half a million *paid* customers during the first year of the website.

Most reasonable people, even those without a degree of online marketing experience, will know that it is unrealistic. Sure, there are real cases of exceptional successes, but these are rare at best. A business person should not expect an overnight success for a start-up website.

Marketing requires a substantial investment of money, time and lots of hard work. There are no shortcuts or tricks. Unfortunately, when a plan fails to meet expectations, many will resort to a quick fix, which brings us to the next marketing mistake.

Engaging in Shady Practices

You have undoubtedly seen these e-mails: "Top 10 in Google. Guaranteed." Sounds tempting, doesn't it? A quick fix, and your website gets plenty of traffic, and you don't have to worry about anything.

Be careful. While there are many reputable SEO firms, there are just as many (if not more) that will promise instant results. These companies employ, what's called "black hat" methods that may involve "tricking" the search engine into giving your website a better position for certain keywords.

While you might experience a short-term gain, you will also be playing with fire. Search engines specialize in providing users with quality search results. They want you to achieve the positions your website has rightfully earned. In fact, all search engines, Google in particular, have been taking aggressive steps to impose penalties and even ban websites that try to cheat the system.

Don't try to outsmart Google. They spend millions to combat cheating. You will eventually lose. Getting penalized or being banned from Google is extremely difficult to fix and causes irreversible damage to your marketing efforts and your website's reputation.

Instead, hire a reputable company that will walk you through what are called "white hat" techniques. These techniques provide methods that are guaranteed to produce results now and in the future. That's what search engines want you to do and what they recommend you do. Following these guidelines requires more time and expense, but it produces long-term results.

Marketing to Anyone and Everyone

Most companies make the mistake of focusing exclusively on the number of visitors when analyzing traffic to their website. If the traffic is growing, they are happy, and they will do anything to bring more visitors to the website, regardless of whether these people will become customers.

In reality, your website needs the "right" traffic. You need visitors that can be converted into customers. When I refer to the "right" visitors, I am not referring to only demographic parameters. You should be marketing to a niche, not a demographic. A well-defined subset directly correlates to successful marketing. Your marketing efforts should be focused on the personas you defined (your High Value Customers).

Not Having a Right Partner or Tools

Today's online marketing is very complex. There are so many different factors, components and intricacies, that you can spend an entire lifetime becoming knowledgeable on just one small subset. In fact, after eighteen years in the industry, I still rely on an army of professionals to lead the way and hold my hand every day. My company subscribes to and licenses dozens of various tools that help us with day-to-day marketing activities. It just doesn't work any other way.

My point is that you and your team can't do it alone. If you think you can, you are wrong. As I argued earlier in the book, it takes a team to build a world-class website. It also takes a team to deliver world-class marketing results. I've never met a person who is an expert in all aspects of online marketing and excels in everything from search engine marketing and social media to e-mail marketing and PPC. There are certainly experts in multiple fields, but they don't solely manage these areas. They count on other people with various skill sets to collaborate on the work.

Same applies to tools. Just the sheer amount of data to process and update on daily basis will easily overwhelm you. Don't waste your time on tedious tasks and mundane reports. There are tools that will automate monitoring your website's positions in search engines and update all your social media accounts simultaneously.

This book starts with my recommendation that you spend time and effort to retain the right web developer for your website project. The book concludes with my recommendation that you retain the right marketing partner for your website. It may be your web developer, or your developer may recommend a partner. Regardless, be certain they know what they are doing. This marketing professional has a marketing history and can demonstrate results with previous clientele.

Underestimating Marketing Costs

"But we spent all our money on the website," I have heard in the past. We then warned our clients in the beginning of a relationship that they budget funds for marketing. It's a common misconception that online marketing is free. Even if you plan to focus your efforts on types of marketing that don't incur direct expenses for advertising (such as search engine optimization), the expertise that produces results never comes cheap.

Spending money on a website and having no budget for marketing is like buying a car and having no money for gas. It precludes the need for a website. While this scenario may be extreme, you should understand that website marketing always incurs cost. Whether you hire an in-house expert or an outside agency, this service presents a significant expense that requires proper allocation of funds.

I recommend setting a budget that will cover a year's cost of marketing expenses. The exact amount may vary depending on objectives and the aggressiveness of the marketing strategies selected, but ideally, the budget amount should start at between 20% and 50% of your website's cost.

Relying Solely on Paid Advertising

What's good about paid advertising (such as PPC in search results, paid ads on other websites or on social media) is that it is reliable and will always produce results. It is also the quickest way to get the right traffic to your website, and it is easy to calculate ROI (Return on Investment). As appealing as paid advertising sounds, it also has some major drawbacks. First, it is expensive, and when compared to other forms of marketing, you may find that there often cheaper alternatives that produce better ROI in the long run.

Secondly, paid advertising has no long-term residual benefits. This means that if your marketing budget changes or dries up, you could be in trouble. A marketer's nightmare is that you stop paid advertising, and all traffic to your website stops as well. This is not good. In fact, I have seen companies run out of money and literally go out of business because they did not invest in long-term marketing strategies in addition to paid advertising.

You should never rely on paid advertising as your only source of traffic. In fact, you shouldn't rely on any single method of marketing. You should always invest in long-term strategies, such as SEO, social media, e-mail or better yet, a combination of multiple methods. It is true that some of these marketing methods require time to start achieving noticeable results. However, these results are there to stay, and you will be reaping the benefits for the long run, as opposed to fleeting and sporadic injections of traffic offered by paid advertising.

Paid advertising does have its place, however. I recommend it in two situations. First, it will take time for your other marketing efforts to start generating traffic, especially for new websites. Paid advertising can be a quick temporary fix and may be your only option. Secondly, when you have exhausted all other options, and you have unused dollars in your marketing budget. This is especially true for larger, well-established companies who can afford to budget extra marketing dollars to drive traffic to their website with paid advertising. As long as it shows ROI, this can be a nice addition to your marketing efforts.

Not Measuring Returns on Marketing

Neglecting to measure your marketing results is one of the worst sins in marketing. How can you know if something is working if you are not measuring results? You can't. Yet, many businesses make this mistake. They sporadically pour time and money into different forms of marketing, and as long as their traffic stays the same or grows, they are happy.

Implementing marketing strategies blindly without measuring return on investment is a terrible way to spend your company's money. This means you are not in control. You are relying on luck and gambling the money away.

Another common problem is that most companies who measure results do so incorrectly. They look at "vanity metrics" like traffic or overall leads or sales without an in-depth understanding of how individual marketing campaigns contribute to these numbers. We will focus more on how to measure marketing results later in this chapter.

Not Having a Marketing Plan

Now we get to the cardinal sin – not having a marketing plan. Just as I argued in" Chapter 2 – Defining Business Requirements" that you can't expect to build a successful website without a plan, the same applies to your marketing efforts. Before you commit a single dollar to marketing your website, you must establish a basic marketing plan.

Having a marketing plan is essential to your website and your company's success. Without a plan, you will be spinning your wheels burning through resources and getting little traction. There is nothing worse than sporadic marketing without the proper strategy in place. You will be spending money and effort "here and there" without realizing the effect it has. Worse, you will have very little or no understanding of whether your actions are producing any results. This approach will suck your budget dry and will waste your time.

In contrast, a comprehensive marketing plan will help direct your day-to-day activities, will guide your approach, help measure your successes and failures and will ensure that you are getting the most from available resources. A marketing plan facilitates making clear and concise decisions and combines long-term planning with short-term execution (i.e., what's next?).

Making Excuses

Still not convinced that you need a marketing plan for your website? If not, you no doubt have reasons. I have news for you: these reasons are excuses. Don't believe it? Let's take a closer look:

- *Marketing plans are for big business, not for us.* A business of any size needs a marketing plan. Your marketing plan is a roadmap for increasing your sales and growing your company. Your website is a tool that allows you to compete with all companies: big or small. The size of your company is irrelevant, because a good marketing plan can be a game changer that will fuel the growth of your company.

- *Marketing plans are for businesses, not for websites.* Isn't your website a business tool? If the success of your business depends on your website, why wouldn't you extend the same care and consideration to your website?

- *I don't have the time to put together a plan.* If you have time for marketing, you should find time to put together a plan. In fact, a good marketing plan will save time several times over. You will become so much more efficient in your marketing efforts. The time you initially invested will pay dividends later and will provide time later on to devote to additional projects.

- *I want to be flexible; I don't need a plan.* Having flexibility is great, and you definitely want to be responsive to emerging opportunities. But, how do you know if pursuing these opportunities is worth the expense and the effort? A marketing plan will help you make informed decisions about what's best for your company. You won't lose flexibility; instead, you will actually gain a tool to discover, analyze and compare opportunities.

- *I don't know how to put one together.* Next section will help you with that.

How to Put Together a Marketing Plan for Your Website

You may still be intimidated by the idea of developing a marketing plan for your website, but it is actually easier than you think. The good news is that an effective marketing plan doesn't have to be complicated and time consuming. Just answer the following ten simple questions that will help you form a marketing plan:

1. What are the goals you want to accomplish?

2. Who is your High Value Customer (HVC)?

3. How are you going to reach them?

4. What are your marketing tactics?

5. What is your competition doing?

6. What motivates and engages your customers?

7. How can you get potential or existing customers to the site?

8. How much money are you going to spend?

9. How is the marketing plan going to be implemented?

10. How are you going to measure marketing performance?

Simply writing down answers to these questions will actually produce your basic website marketing plan. Let's look at each of these separately:

✳ *Download: You may download a sample marketing plan at* www.ResultsOnInternet.com. *You can use it as a template to create your own.*

Set S.M.A.R.T. Marketing Goals

The goals for your marketing should be the same as those you defined for your website. Start with your website's S.M.A.R.T. (Specific, Measurable, Attainable, Relevant and Timely) business objectives and think about how you can use marketing to achieve these goals. Then set S.M.A.R.T. goals for each of your marketing campaigns.

- *Specific* – Ask yourself: what do I want marketing to accomplish? Be specific. Do you just want to drive more traffic to the website, or do you want to generate more leads or sales? Are you interested in increasing brand recognition or improving the brand perception?

- *Measurable* – Figure out how you will measure results of your marketing campaigns (We will focus more on that in the next section of this chapter).

- *Attainable* – Be realistic about whether the goal is attainable with your budget, and time and resources. With any kind of marketing activity, it is easy to lose track of time and money. Setting specific budgets and time limits will prevent overextending your resources on a phase that may or may not produce desirable results.

- *Relevant* – Next, ask yourself how reaching your marketing goals will help reach your business objectives. It is very easy to get excited by the increase in traffic to your website, followers on Twitter or positions in Google, but how does all this benefit your business' bottom line? There has to be a direct correlation.

- *Timely* – set time limits for all your marketing campaigns so your expenses are capped, and measure performance in time increments that allows you to compare results side by side.

Target High-Value Customers (HVC)

In "10 Common Online Marketing Mistakes to Avoid" we talked about the importance of knowing your target audience and focusing on a specific niche. In fact, you should take it one step further. Your website should be designed for your ideal High-Value Customers (HVC). Naturally, the visitors you want to come to the website must fit the same profile.

You want visitors be converted into high-value customers who generate most profits for your company. Think about loyal customers, who will remain loyal for the long run and generate recurring revenue to your business. That is whom you want.

Research done by Monetate.com shows that as many as 66% of marketing professionals don't know how much their customers are actually worth[26]. If you have trouble defining your ideal customer, you should go back to the drawing board. Otherwise, your marketing strategy will be flawed.

As I discussed in Section "Audience Analysis" of "Chapter 18 – How Well is Your Website Really Doing?", if your website's visitors don't represent the target audience for which the website was built, this traffic has very little value. You will see high bounce rates with very little traction. Even if some of these visitors do convert, they probably won't be your best customers.

On the other hand, by knowing and understanding your market and your target audience, you can create marketing campaigns specifically designed to appeal to them. You can also prequalify potential customers by focusing on ideal customers who are most valuable to your business, and weeding out the rest.

Understand How to Reach Your Targets

Now that you know your target audience, you will need to identify the best ways to reach it. From there you can design tactical programs that can be turned into effective marketing campaigns.

To do that, ask yourself the following questions about your existing customers, or better yet, ask them. Remember, you should always focus on your highest-value customers. Think of your best customers that you'd love to clone if it were possible. You want to talk to these customers. You want to find a way to bring in more customers like them. Understanding how they think and understanding the path they would take to reach your website allows you to focus your efforts on a marketing strategy tailored specifically for them.

I find that most customers are happy to share this information. Just call some of your best customers, and talk to them about their experience. Here are some of the topics to cover in the process:

---

[26]   http://monetate.com/infographic/what-does-it-mean-to-be-customer-centric/

1. How did your customers find you? Ask about not only the medium and channel but also the specifics; for example, if they found you through a search engine, which one did they use?

2. What keywords do your customers use in search engines when they are looking for your products or services? Understanding this will allow you to focus on search engine marketing as well as PPC.

3. Are there specific professional learning materials (articles, whitepapers, infographics, reports, videos, etc.) that your customers would find useful and valuable? Equipped with this knowledge you can attract them with content marketing.

4. Are your customers active on social media? Which social networks do they use? Do they use any of them for professional purposes? Having these answers will allow you to market effectively on social media.

5. Do many of your customers subscribe to e-mail newsletters? Are any of them professional newsletters that they read on a regular basis? If yes, you should consider e-mail marketing.

6. What online media do your customers read? Are there certain professional websites that they visit regularly? This will help you with content marketing as well as paid advertising strategies.

7. Do your customers have memberships in associations and professional organizations? Do these organizations have popular websites? If the answer is yes, you may want to consider doing paid advertising with these organizations.

8. What type of online marketing is your competition using? Are there specific marketing tools that are clearly producing results for them? Following and improving on

strategies that have been proven to work is often the best way to go.

9. What type of marketing messages and calls to action have your customers responded to successfully in the past? Why should they care about what you have to offer? What are some of the pains they experience that you can eliminate? Equipped with this information you can develop effective messages across multiple channels and campaigns.

10. How can you motivate your customers to act? Is there an effective solution to their problems that you can demonstrate? How can you create a sense of urgency? How can you make it safe and risk-free for them? Having these answers in your arsenal will empower you to produce effective calls to actions.

For best results, interview as many customers as possible. Write down their answers and look for trends and similarities. You should be able to detect emerging patterns in ways your customers reach out to companies like yours.

This information is invaluable, because you just got a head start. Marketing is often performed through trial and error. By learning the hard way, you eventually determine what works best. Conducting this homework before your marketing plan is implemented allows you to cut to the chase and direct your energy and resources on these proven methods.

Plan Your Tactics

At this point, you should already have a great deal of information about your customers. You know who they are and you have a strategy to reach them. Now let's go into the tactics of this strategy.

Think of your marketing dollars as soldiers, and you are a general who sends them to war. You want your soldiers to win or capture the prisoners. You don't want to be losing your soldiers in the battlefield. If all your soldiers are dead, you just lost the war.

Good tactics are essential to your ultimate success. In marketing, tactics are often called campaigns. Webster's Dictionary defines campaign as "a series of military battles or attacks designed to produce a particular result in a war".[27] Remember your soldiers? Let's look at Webster's second definition for campaign "a series of activities designed to produce a particular result".[28]

Organize all your marketing activities into campaigns (i.e., "battles"). Your ultimate goal is to win the war. Winning each campaign will help you get closer to your goal.

As you may know, there are many ways to market your website: search engine optimization, social media marketing, content marketing, pay-per-click, e-mail, etc. There is no magic formula for marketing success that will work for everyone. While a certain tactic may work for another company, it could be a complete waste of time and money for you. After all, ask yourself, if there were indeed such a tactic, wouldn't everyone be using it?

What works and what doesn't depend on a number of elements, such as your business model, your industry, the target audience, your products and services, the pricing model, you sales cycle, your competition and sometimes even luck. Never rely on a single tactic. Instead, use an integrated approach to deliver a consistent message across multiple platforms. Experiment with several tactics to determine what works best for your company.

You already know your best customers, you understand how they think and you have a plan in place for reaching them. Put this information to good use. Use it to assemble your initial campaigns.

In the next chapter, we will review specific strategies and tactics that have been proven successful in marketing websites. I invite you to try all of them.

---

[27] Webster Dictionary: http://www.merriam-webster.com/dictionary/campaign
[28] Webster Dictionary: http://www.merriam-webster.com/dictionary/campaign

Research Your Competitor's Marketing

One of the best things you can do for your marketing strategy is to research and study your competitor's marketing techniques. You can then adopt a proven marketing strategy and even improve on it. This is not an invitation to copy someone else's work. This is your chance to create a *better* marketing plan, based on your knowledge of what works.

The best marketing results come from experimentation and trial and error. This is how you ultimately learn about what works and what doesn't. However, you have to be clever about it. Don't learn from your own mistakes. It's too costly. Instead, learn by research.

In the "Stay Ahead of Your Competition" section of "Chapter 19 – How to Get the Most from Your Website" we talked about competitive research and intelligence. There are tools that show your competitors' use of SEO and social media. You can even estimate their traffic and the associated demographic. Factor your research results into your marketing plan as much as possible.

Finally, don't forget to talk to your existing and prospective customers. If they have working experience or history with your competitors, they may be able to offer valuable insight regarding the competitor's marketing strengths and weaknesses.

Engage with Customer-Centric Marketing

In "Chapter 12 - Is Your Website Built to Sell? Proven Ways to Convert Visitors into Customers" we covered the importance of designing a customer-centric website. Your approach to marketing should be the same. Online marketing is about generating quality traffic to your website by creating compelling reasons for visitors to come to your website.

Don't make the mistake of becoming product-oriented, which is the opposite of being customer-centric. People just don't care about your company or your products or services. You have to explain what's in it for them. You have to paint the picture.

All of your marketing campaigns should be laser-focused on addressing the needs and solving the problems of your customers. In order to achieve this, you need to understand their beliefs and desires. Talk to your customers, tell them a story and show empathy.

At this point, you know the profile of your ideal customer. The same research you have conducted to create the website needs to be applied to your marketing.

As stated previously, most effective marketing campaigns are those that focus on the needs and wants of your customers, not just *any* customers, but your *best* customers. Remember, customer centricity is not focusing on your average customer; you want to attract the best.

Motivate to Act

As with customer centricity, guiding visitors to take action is equally important. No matter how great your marketing is, it will fail if you fail to get people to act. To succeed, you have to make people cross the bridge; you want them to come to your website, craving for more.

Effective calls to action will draw visitors to your website through their interest and curiosity. We talked about best practices for calls to action on your website in section "Create Effective Calls to Action" of "Chapter 12 - Is Your Website Built to Sell? Proven Ways to Convert Visitors into Customers" You should use the same principles in your marketing: make visitors feel safe and comfortable, influence their behavior by creating a sense of urgency, but make the steps easy and risk-free.

The best way to get people to act is by reinforcing their perceptions and experiences. You have to make the process clearly visible, show that with every step they advance toward the ultimate prize. In fact, the most successful websites are not only successful in driving traffic. They start converting visitors into customers well before people even arrive on the websites. They do this by creating an experience and telling a story—beginning with the first encounter and ending with the sale.

Your marketing should be effective in bringing people *to the site* and continue converting them *on the site*. These are not separate processes. They are part of the same process. Your *internal* marketing (i.e., marketing on your website) should be consistent with your external marketing (i.e., outbound or inbound marketing). People don't differentiate. A message from your company is a message from your company, no matter where they see it. After all, if people believe they are moving in the right direction, that progress makes them feel great, and they will be more likely to convert.

Set Fixed Budgets and Caps

When planning your budget, start with a figure that is affordable for the initial marketing campaigns. Then distribute budget dollars between campaigns. Alternatively, you can determine your tactics and price them out separately to see where the numbers fall in your total marketing budget.

In either case, it is important that you have a separate budget for each campaign, as well as a total budget for all marketing costs. You should track them independently.

Budgeting individual campaigns will allow you to calculate ROI for each campaign, as well as control costs on each level of the campaign. Tracking your total marketing budget will allow you to focus on your total spend and prioritize when necessary. You can always adjust the distribution between campaigns when you determine if a set of tactics is effective or not. You want to retain this flexibility.

Today it is very easy to spend your marketing dollars, and it is even easier to overspend. If you turn on an ad and neglect monitoring it, or worse, abandon it completely, you can see how the cost mounts. Unmonitored ads can rapidly rack up thousands of dollars in unplanned expenses. To prevent this, always set caps on time (how long for the ad runs) and on expense (the maximum budget you are willing to spend).

Most of your marketing activities will require an investment in some form. In addition to cash, your time is also money, so you need to spend your marketing dollars sparingly.

Decide on the Implementation Specifics

A marketing plan is no good if it remains on paper. An important and necessary component of your plan is a concrete, realistic, step-by-step implementation strategy. This plan includes the detailed methods implemented in your marketing strategy, assigned resources to each phase, the procedure to be used in executing all phases and associated lengths of time projected for each phase.

A common marketing problem is that companies frequently overextend their resources. This is the case, especially with human capital. It doesn't matter if you have an entire marketing team or if you perform all marketing tasks. There are only 24 hours in a day, and you can't devote all your hours exclusively to marketing. Your plan should be realistic. Ask the following questions:

- How many of you will implement the plan?

- What are the specific roles, based on their strengths and levels of experience?

- Do you have the bandwidth to manage all these channels and campaigns?

- How many team members can you or your PM manage simultaneously?

- How much time will you need to allocate for learning new tools and channels?

- How much time will you need to allocate to measure results?

- Do you have the bandwidth to generate the necessary creative spaces (ads, landing pages, etc.)?

Set a realistic implementation plan based on the number of people involved, their availability and their strengths. I would also suggest padding your plan by approximately 20% to accommodate unforeseen marketing-related tasks and activities that will undoubtedly arise.

Frequently Analyze & Look for Ways to Improve

How do you know what works and what doesn't if you don't measure? We talked about it in "Chapter 18 – How Well is Your Website Really Doing?" These principles apply to marketing as well.

You should plan on running several tests in your marketing plan. These tests will reveal what works best; this also helps you realize the greatest returns by focusing your marketing dollars on effective tactics. Later in the book we will be itemize common marketing campaigns; however, there is no guarantee all of them will work for your business. You must test the waters and select the marketing tactics that work for you. You have to learn to walk before you can run.

You will be making mistakes along the way. There is no way around it, and you should anticipate and prepare for them. When you make a mistake, you have to learn from it. You must take quick action to fix a problem or improve a process, or you will pay a hefty price in time and money. Rather, channel your resources toward effective revenue-building marketing strategies and avoid ones that don't deliver a return on your investment.

To determine what works and what doesn't, to learn from your mistakes and to seek methods toward improvement, monitor and analyze results of your marketing campaigns as often as possible. You have to teach yourself this discipline. Check your KPIs daily. Put it on the calendar, or set a reminder. Whatever works.

As previously outlined, the first step is to separate all marketing activities into campaigns. Then track them separately (see "Campaigns" under "Acquisition Analysis" in "Chapter 18 – How Well is Your Website Really Doing?"). Google Analytics (and many other tools) allows you to set up and track your marketing campaigns in real time. We will focus on the KPIs you need to track for all your marketing campaigns later in the book.

How to Put Together
a Marketing Plan for Your Website?

Remember the "soldiers" analogy? Your marketing dollars are soldiers. When you send them to war, you want them to come back with prisoners. Count your wins and losses daily. Look for ways to send out fewer soldiers who bring back more prisoners. That's what effective marketing is all about.

How to Measure Your Marketing Results

Just as you track Key Performance Indicators (KPIs) for the overall website's performance, you also need to establish and measure KPIs for each of your marketing campaigns. This will clearly show what works and what doesn't. You can then direct your marketing dollars toward the most effective campaigns.

Following are some of the common KPIs you should measure for each of your campaigns, regardless of the type, channel or medium:

- *Return on Investment (ROI)* – Measures the sales revenue a campaign brings on every dollar spent. For example, if John spent $1,000 on a campaign that generated $5,000 in sales, John's ROI is $4,000 or 400%. This is the best KPI to measure the effectiveness of all marketing campaigns because it also measures the quality of leads these campaigns generate.

- *Cost per Win (Sale)* – The Cost per Win measures the expense of each sale. Let's say that John's campaign resulted in five sales. With a $1,000 budget, that is $200 per sale. This important metric compares the campaigns to each other.

- *Cost per Lead* – measures the cost-effectiveness of marketing campaigns. This metric focuses entirely on the leads generated by the campaign. Since it factors out the sales process it doesn't measure the quality of leads. Using the example from above, let's say the five sales resulted from 10 leads. With the same $1,000 budget, that is a cost of $100 per lead.

- *Conversion Rate (or Goal Completion Rate)* – Just as you measure your website's conversion rate (percentage of visitors converted into leads or customers), you should also measure the same for individual campaigns. For example, if a campaign brought 1000 visitors, from which John got 10 leads, that is a 1% conversion rate. The conversion rate combined with bounce rate and other behavior information reveals a great deal about the quality of traffic to the website.

- *Incremental Sales* – this measures the contribution of marketing efforts toward the sales numbers. Incremental sales show the effectiveness of your marketing campaigns in generating sales, and are a great way to compare your marketing efforts. For example, if John's sales for the month were $500,000, the campaign from above resulted in 1% of his total sales.

- *Purchase Funnel* – with the help of Google Analytics (or similar tools) you should also measure and analyze the sales process for the leads generated by each marketing campaign (for example, conversions and percentages for visits, interactions, leads and sale), as there could be drop off points that will tell you more about your traffic or your sales cycle. See Section "Goals" in "Conversion Analysis" in "Chapter 18 – How Well is Your Website Really Doing?" for more information.

- *Customer Lifetime Value (CLV)* – this metric should measure all your customers. It measures the lifetime value of your customers by utilizing the following formula: "average sale per customer" multiplied by "average number of times a customer buys per year" multiplied by "average retention time in years for a typical customer." This data will certainly take time to compile but by calculating the CLV, you can see which of the marketing efforts generate your best customers.

- *Multi-Channel Funnels and Attribution* – While you want to measure each of your campaigns and marketing channels separately, in reality there will always be overlaps. For example, a customer learns about your website on social media and then returns to it via a search engine. If you want to see a more precise picture of your marketing, you should use multi-channel funnels and apply attribution modeling. See Section "Multi-Channel Funnels" and "Attribution Modeling" and "Conversion Analysis" in "Chapter 18 – How Well is Your Website Really Doing?" for more information.

- *Other Metrics* – depending on your marketing channel and medium, you may want to measure other KPIs. We will cover these KPIs for each of the following marketing channels: Search Engine Optimization, Social Media, Content Marketing and Paid Advertising.

*Download: You may download this competitive analysis worksheet at www.ResultsOnInternet.com

Chapter 21 – Inbound Marketing as a Proven Strategy for Promoting Your Website

Consumers are becoming increasingly savvy at controlling the information overload. Consider these facts: 86% of TV viewers use DVRs to fast-forward through commercials, 200 million Americans are registered with the "Do Not Call List" and about half of direct mail never gets opened. The Web is no different: over 90% of e-mail users have unsubscribed from mailing lists for which they have previously opted, and about 84% of Internet users have abandoned a favorite website because of intrusive advertising. [29]

With traditional marketing becoming less effective, industry professionals understand that there has to be a strategy to diversify their traditional marketing efforts. And there is. It is called inbound marketing.

Inbound marketing has been proven as one of the best ways to market your website. Recent marketing research demonstrates that adopting inbound marketing more than doubles average website conversion rates and produces higher quality and quantity of leads compared to traditional marketing. [30]

So, what exactly is inbound marketing, and how can you put it to work?

Inbound Marketing 101

Inbound marketing is a term that was coined in 2006 by Brian Halligan and Dharmesh Shah, founders of HubSpot, one of the leading providers of marketing solutions. They explain the benefits of inbound marketing the following way: "*Inbound marketing pulls customers to your company and creates lasting relationships. More than just a tactic, inbound is a philosophy. It's fundamentally rooted in the principles that people*

---

[29] http://blog.hubspot.com/blog/tabid/6307/bid/28330/23-Reasons-Inbound-Marketing-Trumps-Outbound-Marketing-Infographic.aspx

[30] http://www.stateofinboundmarketing.com

value—personalized, relevant content and connections, not interruptive messages, and that marketing can and should be more lovable."[31]

This sounds great but how does inbound marketing compare to traditional forms of marketing?

Inbound vs. Outbound Marketing

Inbound marketing is promoting your website and your business with various forms of quality content through blogs, search engine optimization, social media, videos, infographics, newsletters, podcasts, whitepapers, eBooks, and more. The idea behind inbound marketing is to create and distribute relevant and valuable content that the customers want. The useful content pulls visitors toward your website, brings them closer to your brand, engages them and converts them into customers as well as loyal followers.

In contrast, outbound marketing includes traditional approaches, such as direct mail, cold calling, radio ads, television ads, trade shows and telemarketing. Outbound marketing is also often called interruption marketing. This term is easily understood by anyone who has had his or her dinner interrupted by an unwanted telemarketing call.

In his book "The New Rules of Marketing and PR" David Scott argues that using inbound marketing businesses can "earn their way in" (for example, by publishing useful articles on their website) in contrast to outbound marketing where they "buy, beg, or bug their way in"[32] (through traditional forms of advertising or through cold calling).

Let's compare both forms of marketing in more detail to see why inbound marketing is becoming a favorite with marketing professionals:

Benefits of Inbound Marketing

Inbound marketing benefits everyone. Customers appreciate it because they get the information they want, when they want it and in the format that is most useful for them. Companies love it because inbound

---

[31] http://www.stateofinboundmarketing.com
[32] David Meerman Scott. (2010). The New Rules of Marketing and PR

Inbound Marketing	Outbound Marketing
Customers coming to you	Seeking out customers
Two way communication	One way communication
Encouraging feedback and interaction	Not interactive
Work across multiple channels	Focusing on one channel at a time
Builds up confidence and credibility	Relies on impulse decisions

marketing makes them heard, generates quality leads and generates long-lasting relationships with their customers.

With inbound marketing, companies can nurture leads throughout the entire lifecycle: from the initial visit to closing the sale. As companies learn more about their leads over time, they can create better messages that are personalized to customers' needs, making each interaction focus on the needs and desires of the individual.

Finally, inbound marketing is multi-channel by nature. It allows for a more natural and integrated approach to reach people through channels they prefer and at their convenience. With a good strategy, your marketing efforts will have a compounding effect across all channels.

How Does Inbound Marketing Work?

The inbound methodology described by HubSpot[33] is designed to obtain visitors and generate customers through the following four steps: *Attract, Convert, Close* and *Delight*. Let's review each of these steps and see how you can use them as part of your inbound marketing strategy:

- *Attract* – By creating and publishing useful and targeted content, you can attract the right type of visitors to your website. Today, most people begin their buying process using a search engine to gather necessary information

---

[33] http://www.hubspot.com/inbound-marketing

in order to make a purchasing decision. You can attract such prospects to your website by providing easy access to this information through search engines. By sharing the same content on social media, you can also make it more personable, and you can engage strangers to turn them into visitors to your website. You also optimize your website to appeal to buyer personas or visitors who represent your ideal customers.

- *Convert* – Once you have visitors on your website, you need to convert them into leads. One effective method is to ask for their contact information in exchange for something of value. You can think of contact information as a currency. To have a lead offer this detail willingly, you have to give them something in return: a useful article, an eBook, a whitepaper, etc. With the help of landing pages, calls-to-actions and forms, you can collect contact information and build a centralized marketing database that can be used further for lead nurturing.

- *Close* – The next step is transforming leads into customers through lead nurturing. At this point, you built a database of leads who appreciate the useful information you provided but are not quite ready to become customers. Using a series of e-mails focused on useful, relevant content, you can continue building trust while extending a helpful hand every time. With the help of marketing automation software, you can personalize messages and information to every lead's specific needs. By integrating your marketing activities with your Customer Relationship Management (CRM) solution, your marketing and sales teams will work together like never before.

- *Delight* – Current customers should not be taken for granted. In fact, inbound marketing is as much about nurturing your existing customer base as acquiring new customers. Existing customers are the lowest hanging fruit that is often overlooked. They can and should be a source of recurring sales, but unfortunately, companies frequently take them for granted and ignore their needs. Engaging (or delighting) your existing customers through e-mail and social media will allow you to up-sell additional products and services as new needs emerge. You can also turn your happy customers into promoters and brand ambassadors for your company.

Successful Inbound Marketing Tactics

Before we review each of the inbound marketing tactics, let's first look at some of the popular tactics of inbound marketing that make it so effective:

- *Content Marketing* – Inbound marketing starts with good content. Content marketing is based on creating useful and relevant content that customers want and are seeking online. The content helps customers, answers their questions, addresses their needs, and makes their jobs easier or their lives more enjoyable. It also establishes credibility and presents your company as the expert in the field. You will see that most of the inbound marketing tactics revolve around useful, relevant content, so creating and producing such content will be our starting point.

- *Search Engine Optimization* – As most people begin their purchasing process in search engines, they conduct research and seek information that helps with this process. This is why SEO should be one of your main tactics, so your helpful content is found under the right keywords in Google, Yahoo, Bing, etc. We will be looking at ways to choose the right keywords, optimize your content and build links in order to improve your website's position in search engines.

- *Social Media Marketing* – When interesting and useful content is combined with a presence in social media, it puts a human face on your brand and makes your site more personable. Engaged prospects and happy customers will be more than glad to share your useful content with their connections. The prospects will not be willing to do for run of the mill, boring information about your company or its products or services. We will focus on making your marketing "social and fun" while capitalizing on the reach of social media.

- *E-mail Marketing* – Sending unsolicited e-mail simply doesn't work. People resent unwanted e-mails, and it is illegal to send unsolicited e-mail. However, delivering useful and relevant content that people want (and are willingly to subscribe) is a sure way to keep your prospects and customers engaged and interested.

- *Viral Marketing* – Some content may be so good and have informative or entertaining value that people will take the time to share it. This type of content can be easily shared outside of your network and can literally become an overnight sensation. It certainly requires some luck, but with hard work and the right approach, you can create content that has potential to go viral beyond your wildest dreams.

- *Paid Delivery* – As you may have noticed, I am not a proponent of paid online advertising, and I rarely recommend it to customers. There are exceptions though. Targeted paid campaigns (press releases or paid content distribution) can often be the quickest and the most cost-effective way to jump-start your campaign.

Content Recipe for Successful Marketing

Content marketing is an important foundation of inbound marketing. The whole idea of inbound marketing is to attract potential customers to your website by offering them something of value, something they are seeking and something they want. Original and useful content that helps potential customers solve their problems and makes their job easier or life more enjoyable is a sure way to attract them, engage them and bring them back to seal the deal.

Bluntly, if you want to make the most out of your website, you will have to start producing quality, original and relevant content. There is no better strategy for inbound marketing. Here is why:

How to Use Content to Generate Revenue

Earlier in the book, I compared visitor's contact information to a currency. People value and protect their contact information. No one would give you his or her phone number or an e-mail address unless he or she wanted something of value from you in return. Saying "we are so good at what we do" is not enough. You have to prove it.

Content marketing is what enables you to build trust and complete this exchange. Think of your content as a valuable product that a website visitor purchases using their currency: their time, their contact information and eventually, their business. Here is how it works using the *Attract, Convert, Close* and *Delight* methodology:

1. You are giving away some of your useful content to *attract* visitors (perhaps in the form of a relevant blog post or video). Visitors arrive on your website through search engines and social media.

2. Once visitors get a taste and want more, you exchange some of the more valuable content (whitepapers, marketing research, etc.) for visitor's contact information to *convert* them.

3. Now that you know who they are and what their needs are, you can provide them (through e-mail and social media) with personalized content designed to address their needs to build trust and *close* the sale.

4. Having acquired a new customer, you continue to *delight* them with your useful content (through blog, e-mail and social media) that they have grown to enjoy and appreciate. Happy customers will turn to you every time a need emerges while becoming your most loyal brand ambassadors.

Hidden Benefits of Content Marketing

As you can see, content is essential to successful inbound marketing. However, content has many other benefits you should consider as well:

1. *Improves Search Engine Exposure* –Your website may consist of 10 pages or 100 pages. You can only write a finite amount of content about your company and your products or services. To make matters worse, this content is usually static and, let's be honest, quite boring. However, if you produce one blog post per week, in one year you would add about 50 new pages to your website. Think about it: 50 new pages filled with the content that your customers *want*. Google loves fresh, relevant content that people want, and the search engine will continually give your blog posts good positions in search results. As the result, every new post becomes an additional page of your website that will generate traffic that you wouldn't get otherwise.

2. *Makes Your Company More Sociable* – Unless you have a cool and trendy consumer brand, people are not going to be particularly interested in interacting with your company on social media. The harsh truth is that no one cares about your company or your products/services. Many companies go out of their way to generate hype about themselves, and they fail. There is a better way. By creating customer-centric content that people find useful, educational or entertaining, they will engage and distribute or promote the content for you while representing your brand.

3. *Opens Lines of Communication* – By allowing people to interact with your content (i.e., comments on your blog, shares or likes or social media) you can create stimulating conversations and generate buzz around important issues, as well as grow a long-term audience. As a result, you can learn a great deal about your customers' needs, their perceptions of your company, as well as your competition. You will get valuable feedback that can be incorporated into both your marketing and product or service offerings.

4. *Encourages Employee Participation* – Engaging with and sharing excellent content should not be limited to your prospects or customers. You may find that your employees (even those not involved in sales or marketing) will be more than happy to participate. After all, good content validates everyone's efforts and gives your employees a voice and an outlet to connect with your customers. It can do miracles for employee participation in your marketing efforts and the overall morale.

5. *Attracts the Right Employees* – In addition to attracting customers, your content can attract top talent who understand your company's culture, the value that you bring to your customers and who wants to be part of it. Hiring the right talent is like marketing, and good content gives you a recruiting edge.

6. *Works for Any Industry* – The commons misconception is that content marketing works for only certain industries—like consumer brands. I often hear, "Our customers wouldn't read our blog." Nothing is further from the truth. If done well, content marketing can do miracles for *any* industry. You may manufacture cardboard boxes and still generate excitement about your products. There is always an angle, including providing tips for packing and environmental issues relating to recycling packaging materials.

7. *Works Across all Marketing Channels* – Great content is versatile, and you will always find applications for it across all other marketing channels and throughout the company. If you wrote a phenomenal piece for your blog that your customers loved, why leave it at that? You can convert it into a whitepaper, make it a centerpiece of an e-mail newsletter, share on social media, create a printed brochure or even incorporate it into your sales pitch. Good content will always find its way into the hearts and minds of people, so don't limit content to one channel or application.

8. *Numerous Other Benefits* – Content marketing creates informed buyers, educates your employees, reduces your dependence on third parties and helps you manage your reputation. The list goes on. I could provide more reasons that would fill this book. It really works.

Content Marketing Tactics

At this point I have illustrated that producing great content is one of the best ways to market your website. Let's now look at some of the best content marketing tactics.

- *Blogging* – Most people think of blogging where it applies to content marketing. They are partly correct. Running a blog on your website is a great way to feature your content in an informal and familiar format. Even traditional corporate websites are slowly replacing old-school "company news" and "press releases" with friendlier blogs.

  Effective blogs are designed to attract, interact with and engage visitors by providing the content people want in a casual and welcoming format. In fact, with proper inbound marketing, your website's blog could be the most visited section of your website. Good content will eventually bring visitors to your website, and new content appearing on a regular basis will keep them coming back for more.

  Regardless of the purpose of your website, you should consider running a blog as a part of your website. It will act as a starting platform for your content and will be tightly integrated with your inbound marketing campaigns. Maintaining a blog is not limited to writing articles. Some of the most engaging blogs feature a lot of visual content such as images, infographics or videos.

- *Guest Blogging* – Guest blogging is contributing your content to third-party blogs and websites that are willing to publish it in exchange for a credit or a link to your website. It's a great way to build an audience, especially in the beginning when very few people are aware of your blog's existence. When your content is well liked and appreciated, readers will naturally follow it to you blog. Guest blogging also allows you to build partnerships and affiliations with other blogs and websites to exchange good content on a regular basis.

- *eBooks* – an eBook is an electronic version of a book that is designed for view on a computer or an electronic reader. eBooks may be the length of a book (this book also comes as an eBook), or just few pages in length with focus on a particular topic for readers strapped for time. Unlike whitepapers, eBook are generally more casual and more visual, often containing images, interactive presentations and even videos.

  Content marketing often utilizes eBooks as a product that can be downloaded in exchange for a website visitor's information. That information (like an e-mail address) can then be used for lead nurturing to convert and close. For example, Hubspot.com makes great use of eBooks in a wide range of marketing topics that can be downloaded your information is submitted. Every company, including yours, has similar material that can be converted into an eBook that your visitors would love to download and read. In this scenario, they won't mind providing their e-mail address.

  The key is to determine what information really interests your prospects. It could be a "how-to" guide, market research or a guide into the state of your industry. A blog is a wonderful platform to test the content and give your visitors a "teaser." It could then lead to a downloadable eBook that will request their information, join a mailing list, or similar action.

- *Whitepapers* – Whitepapers are slowly being replaced with more casual and visual eBooks in content marketing. However, whitepapers do have many applications. Whitepapers are generally technical documents or reports focusing on a particulartopic.TheyaremoreacademicandformalthaneBooks and typically consist of mostly text with minimal graphics. Consider using whitepapers to share any information that is data-centric, technical or based on quantifiable research. Whitepapers are often created in PDF format and can be downloaded, just as eBooks, in exchange for a visitor's contact information. A common strategy is to offer whitepapers via e-mail, which requires their email address for delivery.

- *Infographics* – Infographics are fun. People love them because they make even the most technical and complex information visually attractive and easy to digest. Infographics are great for incorporating into blog posts or when used on their own. They are often favorites on social media as their visual nature makes them great for sharing.

- *Videos* – We talked about using videos as an effective communication tool for your website. The same concept applies to marketing. Videos can be effectively used on your blog. People love sharing videos on social media. Google includes videos in its search results that create yet another avenue. Finally, there are entire communities such as YouTube or Vimeo through which you can get even more exposure by uploading your videos there.

  Some of the most effective videos in marketing have compelling content. Videos are great for educating and entertaining. Think about how you can use videos to help your customers: video tutorials, screencasts, product demonstrations, interviews, and more.

- *Webinars* – Of all content marketing tactics, the webinar is probably the most immersive, with attendees focusing all their attention for as long as an hour. Unlike a static video, the webinar format allows for interaction with others, including asking questions. This makes the webinar an incredibly effective tool.

362

- *Podcasts* – A podcast is an amazing way to deliver your content on the go. Thanks to mobile devices, people now have quick access to their favorite content in their car or on the train while commuting to work, going for a walk or travelling.

  It may seem like a lot of work. However, podcasts can actually be the same recycled content that you and your team record and release on a regular basis. Some of the best podcasts are informal and conversational.

How to Blog Like a Star

The number one challenge in content marketing is producing quality content. And all good content (whether an article, an eBook, a whitepaper or a script for a video) starts with writing. Writing is an essential part of content marketing. As previously outlined, you need good content in order to apply any of the successful inbound marketing strategies.

Most people don't like to write and avoid it at all costs. You may say, "But I don't have time to blog," and "I am not a writer." Well, let me tell you something. I work between fifty and sixty hours a week as a CEO of a fast-growing web design agency. English is not my first language, and I never had any formal training in writing. If I can write, you can.

You may not enjoy writing because you haven't experienced the reward that writing can bring to your business, your job and to you personally. It's not that you don't like to write, you choose not to write. The main reason people do not like to write is because they think it's mundane, tedious and unnecessary. Remember when you had to write papers in school, and you absolutely hated it? Well, you are not in school anymore. Many people carry this dislike toward writing into adulthood.

Writing doesn't have to be tedious and difficult. You don't have to be Ernest Hemingway or Mark Twain to write. In fact, one style of writing has become incredibly popular because it's fun, quick and simple. It's called blogging. Blogging is the type of writing that anyone can enjoy and master with very little time and effort.

363

Blogging as a Rewarding Experience

Blogging is a great starting point for your inbound marketing. You will find it to be a rewarding experience. In addition to clear business benefits, you will benefit from it personally. Yes, blogging could be a personally rewarding experience. Still not convinced? Here is how blogging will benefit *you*:

1. *Build a Reputation* – Writing on relevant topics automatically boosts your credibility and establishes trust. It helps position you as the expert in the field. For example, when consulting on website projects, my customers have questions and I often provide them with links to the articles I've written. When a prospect is talking to me and I happen to be the same person who wrote an article on a subject that they found extremely helpful, you can see what that does to my credibility.

2. *Make a Difference* – Nobody else knows more about your business and the industry than you do. You are the expert. Wouldn't be great to share your knowledge and expertise with the rest of the world? Wouldn't that feel good? Your customers are craving it, your prospects want it, and even your colleagues will enjoy what you have to share. As the result, you will help and inspire others, you will meet new people and you will have a rewarding sense of importance and standing in the industry.

   You will also get a feeling of accomplishment every time someone will find your article useful, will quote it on social media or will leave you a positive comment on your blog. You will become known by others and your contribution will be appreciated. It's quite a rush and a great feeling to know that you are making a difference.

3. *Grow Professionally* – When you write, you think, you read what others write and you do research. All of this not only makes you a better writer, it helps you learn new things about your business and the industry and grow

professionally. With every article that you write you will learn something new, you will get new ideas, you will come up with ways to tie everything together cohesively and you will find better ways to express your thoughts. All of these newly acquired experiences will help advance your career and your skills in communications, marketing, sales, creative, technical and many other fields. You will grow as a professional. As a personal example, I can tell you that I have learned more about web development during the year I spent working on this book than in the previous three or four. I also acquired new skills, became a better presenter and generated a number of opportunities for my business.

4. *Discover & Express Yourself* – Writing is a great outlet to learn a thing or two about yourself and to express your inner thoughts, ideas and feelings. Human brain is full of mysteries and writing allows you to unleash your imagination, nurture your ideas and tap into the farthest corners of your brain. By writing, you will become well rounded in your way of thinking. Spending some alone time with your thoughts is also very therapeutic. It's like meditating while staying productive.

   Writing is always challenging for me to start, but at the end, I find it strangely satisfying. And then it becomes hard to stop. The ideas and creative juices just start flowing. By the time I finish what I set out to write, I often formulate new ideas for my business that I wouldn't have otherwise realized.

5. *Have it Lead to Bigger Things* – Writing something as simple as a blog could easily lead to bigger things. Take my example: with English as a second language, writing has always been a challenge for me. I started blogging as an experiment for inbound marketing for my company and my first blog posts were so bad I am still ashamed to show them to anyone. Five years later and I am a published book author. I am now pursuing other things such as public speaking engagements and interviews.

I found that blogging helps you discover more confidence, opens new horizons and is a great starting platform that could lead to bigger things. My writing has supplied our entire company with invaluable content that we now use everywhere from our marketing literature to sales presentations.

Why You Shouldn't Hire Others to Write for You

If you have been reading this chapter from the very beginning you might have already uncovered my cunning strategy. First, I made a case for inbound marketing as a methodology to promote your website. Then I argued that producing quality content is crucial to this marketing strategy. Finally, I convinced you that you should write and produce this content.

At this point, you might be asking yourself: Why can't I hire someone to write for me? The answer is you can. Many freelance authors and companies would be happy to provide you with content and even manage your blog for you. I have many wonderful experiences with authors that we hired for various projects and we still purchase content from them on a regular basis.

The difference is that you want to be in control. Keep in mind that outside authors don't know much about your business, don't understand your products and services and don't know your customers the way that you do. No one knows this detail better than you do. That's why you must be in control.

You do have the option of retaining others to do the writing, conduct research, proofread, and edit. However, at the end of the day, every word that is posted on your blog should have your stamp of approval. After all, by posting it on your company's blog you are putting your name on it. Any material that is poorly written, inaccurate or is not in alignment with your marketing strategy and company values will backfire, reflect directly on you and potentially have an irreversible, negative impact on your reputation.

This is why it is important to set standards and guidelines for your blog by producing your own content internally. When you know what works, and you have the infrastructure and system in place, you can delegate an individual internally or externally to assist. Here are some of the options:

- *Purchase Content from Outside Authors* – There are many online resources (such as http://www.textbroker.com/, http://www.bloggingpro.com/jobs/, http://jobs.problogger.net/) where you can find experienced writers that will provide you with quality content. Typically, the rate ranges from $10 to $100 per post, depending on the length, quality of writing and the research involved. If you consider hiring an outside writer, make sure to look at their previous work and pay special attention to their quality and style of writing, their experience with subjects in your industry, as well as the recognition and following (comments, social media, etc.). This will give you a good indicator of the effectiveness of their previously produced content.

- *Invite Guest Bloggers* – We spoke about the importance of guest blogging on additional blogs in "Content Marketing Tactics." The same logic applies to inviting guest bloggers to write for your blog. You get free content in exchange for giving them credit (i.e., link to their website).

- *Encourage Employee Participation* – Sometimes the best help comes from within your organization. Ask around who would be willing to contribute to the blog. You may be surprised to find out that many of your colleagues would be happy to contribute to the blog for the reasons we discussed in the previous section. Some may need guidance or editorial assistance with their writing, but retaining several authors from within your organization makes your blog more interesting and versatile. For example, you can have technically oriented people write about their expertise, and business team members will focus on business-related topics.

- *Hire a Content Manager* – If your organization is serious about content marketing, and your budget allows, you should consider hiring a content manager. The responsibilities for this position would include daily review of new content, editorial management of authors, editorial calendar, tracking effectiveness of the content, etc. A great content manager should be highly organized and detail-oriented, have solid writing and editorial skills and be social-media savvy.

How to Create Amazing Content

You are now ready to invest some time and effort into producing your own original content, with or without outside help. Let's look at recommendations that will, not only make this process easier, but will also help produce content that will deliver marketing results. Here are ten proven ways to produce amazing content that will do miracles for your marketing:

1. *Listen to Your Customers* – A sure way to come up with great ideas for your content is by listening to your customers. Your customers are asking questions and by producing content that answers these specific questions, you are essentially answering your customers directly. Pay attention to what your customers want to know and focus on addressing this subject matter. Customer-centric content will help attract new customers and delight existing ones.

2. *Do Your Homework* – The best content is always preceded by research. You should closely examine what others have written before embarking on your own content. Thorough research provides new ideas, and the opportunity to include subject matter you would have otherwise missed. A proven course of action is to read others' content and improve on it in your content. It is commonly referred do as content curation.

3. *Make it Easy to Read* – One of the key characteristics of successful blog posts is that they are easy to read and digest. Ensure that your content flows nicely, and interject descriptive

subtitles, insert quotes and use bullet points or numbered lists. In fact, I chose this format for my book because busy professionals find it easy to scan so they can quickly focus on the information they need. Subheadings and lists can help the reader quickly navigate to the desired information.

Finally, keep your posts short. If a post runs too long, break it up into two separate articles or parts. Limit the length of your posts to 1,000 words.

4. *Use Visuals* – Renowned psychologist Albert Mehrabian demonstrated that a whopping 93% [34] of communications are non-verbal. It is important to use visuals like diagrams, schematics, infographics, and screenshots throughout your posts to support and expand on your information. Videos may also be embedded into posts. Posts with videos get 267% more links[35] than those without videos. Visuals are important because they help break up and support the information, and they provide "resting points" for eyes when reading and absorbing an article. This is the reason it typically requires a lot less effort to read most magazines than the Wall Street Journal. Visuals make a huge difference in information presentation.

    Additionally, you should have a visual representation associated with each of your posts to attract attention and to help distinguish them visually. You can purchase quality stock photography at websites like (http://www.istockphoto.com/ or http://www.shutterstock.com/) for a couple of dollars per image. Ask your web developer for guidance with the types and style of images that will be original and will integrate well with the design of your website.

5. *Maintain a List* – You may not have the resources and bandwidth to produce a lot of content in one writing session. You will get new ideas and suggestions along the way. You may see an article you enjoyed, or a conversation

---

34 http://en.wikipedia.org/wiki/Albert_Mehrabian
35 http://moz.com/blog/what-makes-a-link-worthy-post-part-1

with a client or a colleague may give you an idea for the next post. Write all of them down. A continuously updated list of ideas and topics will ensure that you don't run out of ideas for your blog.

6. *Maintain a Schedule* – You need to maintain a schedule for posting content: daily, weekly or monthly. Determine the frequency you want of blog posting, and adhere to that schedule. Plan new content accordingly so you ready for each new posting date. Keep track of "red letter dates" for seasonal content (to be covered later).

7. *Create Effective Titles* – In order to get the most from your post, you have to treat titles as calls to action. No matter how great your post is, an ineffective title will prevent people from engaging. Effective titles are short, descriptive, witty, intriguing and use the right keywords. Anyone's first encounter with your post would be his or her attention to its title. The title needs to tell users what your post is about and compel them to click. Think about what people want to see when searching for information in your post. For example, "How to Create Amazing Content for your Blog?" is a good title. People will search for this information, and this title has all the right keywords and ingredients for an effective call to action.

8. *Identify Keywords* – Once great content is created, it will not fulfill its mission unless people can find it on the Web. This is why it's essential to focus on the right keywords. Ask yourself, "How will people search for this content? Which keywords or phrases will they use?" Be sure that your content can be found organically by search engines. Keywords are especially important in your posts' titles.

9. *Don't Plagiarize* – Not only can plagiarism get you into legal trouble, it is unethical and can permanently tarnish your reputation. Always reference your sources, and never

(I mean *never*) copy anything from someone else's blog, either text or images.

10. *Measure Results* – Recommendations in this chapter give you a good starting point, but every business and target audience is different. Something that works for one company may not work for you and vice versa. That's why it is very important to measure the performance of each of your posts individually. Apply the same principles discussed in "Chapter 18 How Well is Your Website Really Doing?" to measure the performance of all your posts. You can then focus your efforts on producing the type of content that delivers the best ROI.

12 Best Tips for Effective Blog Posts

As we just reviewed, the type of content that will work for your marketing depends on your business and your audience. This is why it is important to experiment to determine what works and what doesn't.

Subjects described below have been demonstrated to be effective in general. They are used by some of the most successful blogs across many industries. These principles are universal, and with a little thought, you should be able to apply them to your business:

1. *How-To Guides* – "How to..?" tutorials do extremely well. You can focus on any subject matter and help your readers solve a problem, explain a complex process or guide them to complete a task. Give your readers simple step-by-step instructions they can follow, and they will love you for it (i.e., "How to Blog Like a Star?").

   With these types of posts, you demonstrate your subject expertise and immediately establish a connection with a happy and educated visitor.

How to Create Amazing Content

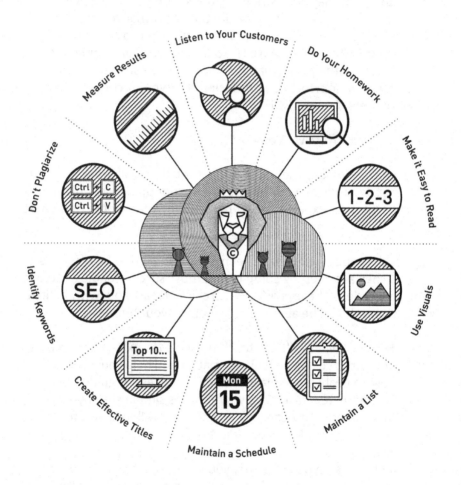

Listen to Your Customers

Measure Results

Do Your Homework

Don't Plagiarize

Make it Easy to Read

Ctrl + C
Ctrl + V

1-2-3

Identify Keywords

SEO

Use Visuals

Top 10...

Mon
15

Maintain a List

Create Effective Titles

Maintain a Schedule

2. *Lists* – Readers love lists. Give them numbered lists, bulleted lists, checklists. Lists draw twice as much traffic as other types of posts[36]. Numbered lists work great: "12 Best Tips for Effective Blog Posts." The list tells the reader exactly what to expect, and the information is broken down for them so they can focus on one item at a time or skip to those of interest. The longer list doesn't necessarily mean its better, but numbers over 5 are generally perceived as "more complete." Don't go overboard though. I recommend focusing on quality and subject matter that your readers find useful: "Top 20 Ways to...", "10 Websites for...", "15 Tips for..."

3. *The Best / Top* – Another commonly searched post is "The Best" or "The Top" lists: "Best Ideas for...", "Best Blogs for...", "Top Tools for...", "Best Anything". The keyword "Best" subconsciously makes your list *better* than the others and implies that you've done the research and legwork to find and select "the best of the best" and save the reader substantial time.

   Compare these two titles and decide which one you would choose: "10 Ideas" or "10 Best Ideas". People also love ratings or charts. When a "Best / Top" list is numbered, it implies that the items are in order of greatness. You can use the keyword "Best" or "Top" to jazz up any post "12 Best Tips for Effective Blog Posts". Another spin on this concept would be "The Worst" list.

4. Tips – People love quick tips and actively search for them. Think of ways you can help your customers by giving them quick tips. "Tips for ..." are very popular and can be easily converted into "The Best" lists, making them even more effective. This is what I've done with this section entitled "12 Best Tips for Effective Blog Posts." I could have named it "Ideas for Effective Blog Posts," but that would be far less effective.

---

[36] http://moz.com/blog/what-makes-a-link-worthy-post-part-1

In addition to tips on what to do, people often search for tips on what *not* to do. This leads us to the next popular post subject:

5. *Mistakes & Myths* – No one likes learning from their own mistakes, and many will make a concerted effort to avoid mistakes. This is why "Mistakes to Avoid" is another popular post subject. What are some of the common mistakes that your customers make? Write a post to help avoid them.

   Another effective approach is myth busting. What are some common misconceptions in your industry? Write a post to bust those myths, and position you as an expert.

6. *Series and Follow-ups* – Once you have enough content, you can start grouping your posts in series based on subject matter or sequence. The idea is to create a list post that references your other posts. For example, I could have posts titled "How to Create Amazing Content" or "12 Best Tips for Effective Blog Posts," and then tie them together in a series "How to Blog Like a Star"

   A "Follow-up" is a similar idea where follow up is done, expanding on a post that has been successful. Remember, you can always do a "Part II" post and link them. The new post will piggyback on to the first popular post, and eventually both posts will mutually benefit in traffic.

7. *Trends & Predictions* – Trends and predictions are always sought-after because people want to keep up with trends now and in the future. By making these predictions and declaring trends, you literally position yourself and your company as an expert in the field. Consider writing a post on "Top 10 Trends for [next year]".

   Many writers are reticent to make predictions, because they don't want to be wrong. You should look at this as an opportunity. First, if you are wrong, it will stir discussions, and direct attention to you. Controversial posts actually work very well, and a lively discussion around your prediction (even though erroneous) is great PR. Second, even if you *are* wrong, it will be years before anyone can point it out, and by then, it is old news.

8. *Reviews and Opinions* – Write unbiased reviews to provide your commentary and opinions about any solutions, tools, vendors, books, products or services that your customers may find useful. Consider doing competitive comparisons and cite differences, benefits, shortcomings and the overall experience. When writing reviews, be sure they are unbiased. Stay away from directly comparing your own products or services to those of your competition.

   Another similar subject is voicing your opinions, objections and rebuttals to anything in the industry. Controversy sells and will help attract traffic to your website. However, you should be ready for heated discussion and potential criticism.

9. *Interviews* – Interview an expert, and include the transcript of their interview (or a video interview) with their short profile (bio and credentials). You can interview experts from within your organization as well as clients, professional associations, independent consultants, vendors and even your competitors.

   Interviews add massive credibility to your blog, because the content doesn't come from within your organization. By hosting someone else's interview, you get a type of indirect endorsement. Celebrity power works great. Securing an interview with someone known or influential is always a challenge, but it's worth a try. Don't underestimate a person's ego. With the right approach, you would be surprised how many people would enjoy an interview for your blog. They will most likely share the interview on their social networks as well.

10. *Recaps* – Consider recapping events, conferences, seminars, tradeshows, presentations or training exercises in which you or a team member may have participated. Don't simply tell readers you were present. Turn it into an informative, educational and entertaining experience for the reader so that they can enjoy it vicariously.

   For example, several years ago, I was invited to the White House with a delegation of business leaders from Chicago. I blogged about the overall experience, and even though it had little to do with web development, our customers enjoyed reading the article.

11. *Newsjacking* – Newsjacking is riding the wave of breaking news in your industry, which generates a ton of traffic to your website when done properly. In order to catch that wave you have to produce a post early in the game, (and promote the heck out of it), as public excitement grows and well before it peaks. The key to this approach is to monitor news, recognize specific pieces of news that will be big, and jump on it first. Then, as people search for news of the event on the Internet, your post will appear in the results, other websites will link to it, and people will share it on social media. All of this will produce the effect you desire.

12. *Seasonal* – Regardless of your company's product or line of service, you can always find an angle to write relevant content on annual events or holidays like Christmas, Thanksgiving, New Years, Valentine's, etc. It is certainly easier for consumer brands, but even B2B services can benefit from seasonal content. Your customers are people who enjoy holidays. Posting lighter material around holidays is entertaining and ultimately rewarding.

Chapter 22 –Search Engine Optimization Strategies Guaranteed to Work

SEO (Search Engine Optimization) is the practice of promoting your website through search engines. As Internet users typically begin their quest by searching (in Google, Bing or Yahoo), ranking high for strategic keywords in search results is of paramount importance. Search engines remain one of the most common methods (with social media coming in second) for Internet users to learn of your existence. People "Google" something they need and land on your website. It is that simple.

Getting continuous traffic to your website through people naturally finding your website in search engines is called "organic search." This happens when your website gets ranked high in search results, because the search engine thinks it is relevant for the keyword and contains useful information. This is the opposite of Pay-Per-Click (PPC) or paid advertising where you pay to be listed or to get traffic to your website.

Because of obvious business benefits, SEO is arguably one of the best, long-term marketing strategies for your website. Because it is not easy to master, it can take a long time and a tie up lots of resources before you get significant results. The dividends will most often be worth the investment. Imagine a constant stream of traffic to your website that it relevant and doesn't depend on paid advertising (it's free). That's what SEO can help you achieve. Interested? Let's get started.

Getting Started with SEO

The first order of business is to understand what you want from your SEO. Set objectives for your SEO campaigns just as you did with your website project and other activities. SEO goals usually involve getting your website listed on the first page of search results. People very rarely go past the first page in search results so your goal should be appearance in the top ten, or better yet, top five results. Also, keep in mind that search results are keyword-specific, so identifying and selecting the strategic keywords will be the major part of your SEO strategy.

Recommendations in this section are not intended to be a "Do It Yourself" guide. We can't possibly cover everything in one chapter, and even a book devoted exclusively to the topic is not enough to make you an SEO expert. The purpose of this section is to familiarize you with safe and effective SEO strategies, so you can be an educated website manager when working with an SEO partner.

Your first action item should be to team with a reliable and experienced SEO partner. Your web developer may be a partner candidate, or they can recommend a qualified SEO partner. Either way, unless you have a team of dedicated in-house SEO experts, you shouldn't be doing SEO internally (detailed later in this chapter).

Search Engines Basics You Should Know

Before we dive into SEO strategies, we should briefly review the basics of search engines and their operation. Without this basic knowledge, it would be hard for you to understand the SEO strategy presented in the book.

Introducing the King of Search

When people talk about search engines, they typically refer to Google, Bing and Yahoo (Yahoo search is powered by Microsoft). These "Big Three" represent over 95% of all online searches in the U.S[37]. There are many other major search engines in other countries, like Baidu in China, but the collective amount of searches they produce in the U.S. is insignificant.

The king of search is obviously Google. What made Google so popular is that it revolutionized the search engine industry by using link popularity to measure relevance of content. The method proved to be so effective that Google became a household word. Because roughly two-thirds[38] of all searches are conducted on Google, we will focus on it primarily to define your SEO strategy.

---

[37] http://searchenginewatch.com/article/2345837/Google-Search-Engine-Market-Share-Nears-68

[38] https://www.comscore.com/Insights/Market-Rankings/comScore-Releases-June-2014-US-Search-Engine-Rankings

How Does Google Work?

The web today is made up of billions of websites consisting of over 60 trillion individual web pages[39], and that number is growing every day. Google (and other search engines) work by crawling the Web, following links from page to page. Site owners can tell Google what to crawl, but Google also does a fine job on its own.

Google then sorts the pages based on their content (and hundreds of other factors), and maintains this data in what's called "the index." The index is Google's massive database of all meta-data on the Web.

As you search for something, Google uses a number of programs and formulas (algorithms) to determine what you are trying to find (spelling, auto complete, synonyms, and much more). Based on these clues, Google pulls the relevant web pages from the index. Then Google ranks the results using more than 200 factors[40] (such as content quality and freshness) to provide you the best possible matching results.

Why is Ranking Important?

When people talk about search engine optimization, they are usually referring to improving SERP ranking of your website. The SERP stands for Search Engine Results Page, that's the results listings page returned by a search engine in response to a keyword query. Ranking high on that page is the ultimate prize, and SEO is the process of getting there.

People rarely go past the first page of search results. More often, they just look at the first three to five results. Consider the following distribution of traffic in Google based on positions in search results:[41]

1. 18% of all traffic

2. 10% of all traffic

---

39   http://www.google.com/insidesearch/howsearchworks/thestory/
40   http://www.google.com/insidesearch/howsearchworks/algorithms.html
41   http://moz.com/beginners-guide-to-seo/how-people-interact-with-search
       -engines

3. 7% of all traffic

4. 5% of all traffic

5. Under 2%

That's why ranking high in search results is critical. If your website is ranked #57 for a keyword, no one will ever get to it. Ranking that low is like not ranking at all. That's why SEO is all about improving your positions for important keywords.

How Does Google Rank Websites?

Google uses over 200 criteria to determine a ranking of a webpage for every keyword. Search engine algorithms are closely guarded secrets and there are armies of marketing and SEO professionals trying to reverse-engineer what affects ranking. We know many things starting with the quality and freshness of your content to load speed of your website and your activity on social media.

One factor stands above all: link popularity. This is what made Google what it is today. Link popularity measures the number of other relevant websites linking to yours. In other words, the more other websites link to yours, the more highly it is likely to rank.

When another website links to yours, Google looks at it as a signal that there is something of value on your website. When you have multiple websites linking to you, Google sums up these links so the more links you get, the better. However, not every link is counted with equal value. The most valuable links are from websites that have high link popularity themselves. If a popular website links to yours, they transfer some of this link popularity to you. If the same website also links to websites other than yours, the value of the link to you is diluted and divided between all other websites.

How Does Google Determine Keywords?

It all begins with a keyword. Someone types in a keyword into a search box and gets a myriad of results. We already talked about the

380

importance of ranking high, but since search results are keyword-specific, how does Google know which keywords are associated with your website's pages?

Google analyzes the content of your website to determine the keywords. It looks at the text on your website, page titles and subheadings, navigation and even filenames of your images and documents. In addition, Google looks at the keywords of the websites linking to you. If these websites are related or have similar content, Google considers these links as votes of confidence for a particular keyword. This is why related links from websites are typically better than unrelated links.

What Is Google Doing to Improve Quality?

Google is determined to improve the quality and relevance of search results in a continuous manner. After all, that's what Google is all about. They see anyone trying to cheat the system as a threat. Deceiving, low quality or irrelevant content doesn't align with Google's vision of good user experience. That's why continuously fight spam by devaluing and removing websites that produce bad content or try to manipulate the system.

Google openly fights the following to be types of spam: unnatural links, hacked websites, cloaking (displaying different content to search engines), content with little or no added value, parked domains, hidden text or keyword stuffing and a lot more.

As you can see, Google does a lot to maintain the quality and relevance of search results, and you should adopt the same priorities for your website. The most effective and safest SEO strategy is to play by the rules.

Important SEO Definitions

SEO can get technical, and a separate lingo includes terms that may be unfamiliar. You will be seeing some of these terms later in this chapter and when working with your SEO partner. Below is a quick reference sheet for your convenience:

- *Link Popularity (Link Juice)* – Credibility of a one-page web page passed to another page through a link.

- *PageRank* – Google's metric for measuring link popularity of a web page that is named after Larry Page, Google's co-founder. PageRank is measured with a number on a scale of 1 to 10.

- *MozRank* - An alternative metric measuring a web page's popularity. Managed by MOZ (leader in SEO tools) on a scale of 1 to 100.

- *Domain Authority* – Another metric managed by MOZ that manages credibility of the entire domain (website) on a scale of 1 to 100.

- *SERP* – Search Engine Results Page is the results listings page returned by a search engine in response to a keyword query.

- *Inbound Links* – Links from other (third party) websites to your website.

- *Internal Links* –Links from within your website (i.e., one page of your website linking to another page on your website).

- *Anchor Text* – Refers to the visible text inside the link that describes the linked content. For example if the link says: SEO Practices, it is likely the linked content is about SEO Practices.

- *Link Bait (Link Magnet)* – Content that is designed to encourage others to link to it from another website adding to link credibility and the overall SEO benefits.

- *Trackback (Pingback)* – A type of comment that is created when your blog post is linked from another website.

- *Authors Rank* – Authorship system to rank the quality of content associated with a Google Plus profile (the Author of the content). Google now tracks authors of content and the rating is primarily compiled based on the number +1 and shares of the content you've written.

- *Publisher Rank* – Similar to Authors Rank, only for businesses on Google+.

SEO Mistakes to Avoid

Unfortunately, the following SEO mistakes are too common and many can lead to disastrous results. Because SEO is not an exact science, it is surrounded by many myths and misleading or straight-out wrong information. Working with the wrong company or following bad advice is not only a colossal waste of time and money, but it can result in an imposed penalty or a ban from search engines.

This is why the first order of business is to study these common mistakes and avoid them at all costs:

Doing Your Own SEO Instead of Hiring an Expert

SEO is a full time job and requires advanced knowledge of the latest trends, strategies and algorithm changes. Many marketing professionals know the basics and believe they can do their own SEO. The truth is they can't, and they learn it the hard way. Trying to manage your own SEO without extensive experience and day-to-day, hands-on approach will simply waste your valuable time and produce little results.

SEO is highly competitive. After all, your competition will be trying to outsmart you and beat you in this game. For the same reasons you choose to hire an expert to do your website, you should consider hiring a true expert to manage your SEO. True SEO professionals stay on top of all the latest trends and know from experience what works and what doesn't. You don't want to experiment with your website and create problems that will take more time and money to fix.

Falling for Unrealistic SEO Promises

When hiring an SEO partner, it is very important to select a reputable company that uses safe methods. Partnering with the wrong company is ineffective and can lead to disaster. Engaging in shady SEO techniques could get your website penalized, or worse banned from search engines.

Unfortunately, many SEO firms promising instantaneous results utilize what's called "black hat" methods. You probably get e-mails with these offers every day promising to get you on the front page of Google search results quickly and inexpensively. If it sounds too good to be true, it probably is. The techniques employed by these companies involve tricking search engines to gain better positions in search results with certain keywords. This is often done by using spam-like techniques to get more inbound links, participating in link exchanges or purchasing links, stuffing your website with keywords and engaging in tactics that search engines specifically guard against.

Relying on these methods is a ticking time bomb. Search engines (Google in particular) have been taking very serious steps to detect, penalize and even ban websites that are trying to cheat the system. The problem lies with the fact that some companies don't really care about the long-term success of your SEO. Their business model is designed to generate quick cash from you while "black hat" techniques are working, and when these techniques stop working, they won't assist in restoring good search results placement. They will move on to the next unsuspecting paying customer.

Using "Black Hat" Methods for Quick Gains

Before you can make a decision about whether the SEO vendor is right for you, you need to study their methods. If the vendor is not willing to disclose their methods, this should be a red flag. There is nothing secretive about SEO. Effective SEO is more about due diligence, research and analysis, as opposed to having a "secret proprietary method" that many "black hat" companies claim.

Let's get the number one SEO myth out of the way. There is no SEO "magic" trick. No one can provide inexpensive, instantaneous SEO results. Don't try to outsmart Google, and don't work with a company that tries to game the system. You will lose every time.

Let's look at the fundamental differences between the "black hat" and "white hat" SEO approaches:

- *Black Hat* – are methods to influence search engine rankings in ways that are disapproved by search engines. This often involves using unethical manners and techniques trying to cheat or manipulate the system for quick gain. Some examples include keyword stuffing, purchased links, link exchanges (or farming), hidden text and links, blog comment spam, etc. These techniques go against search engines' guidelines and will eventually be penalized through lower rankings or a permanent ban.

- *White Hat* – are respectable practices that are accepted and encouraged by search engines. They include a great deal of research and analysis, as well as continuous content improvement and technical enhancements to your website. They last for a long time, improve the overall user experience and make your website and accuracy of search results better for everyone. This chapter focuses *only* on white hat techniques that are endorsed by search engines and are assured to work. You and your SEO vendor should only be using white hat techniques.

Not Adapting to Search Engine Changes

Search engines continually change their algorithms to improve the quality of searches and to combat cheaters who try to manipulate the system. Google said in the past they do approximately two adjustments to their algorithms per day[42]. It averages to about 500 changes a year. Ask yourself: do you have the bandwidth to keep up with these frequent, changing trends? If the answer is no, that's another reason to team up with SEO experts who will stay on top of latest trends and changes and will tweak your strategy as necessary.

---

[42] http://www.forbes.com/sites/cherylsnappconner/2013/12/21/5-top-seo-and-online-marketing-trends-for-2014/

As search engines update their algorithms, it is very important that you and your SEO jump on these changes to reduce risks associated with updates as well as to take advantage of the new opportunities that will emerge following each major update.

There have been at least three several major changes to the Google algorithms at the time this book was written. You may have heard the code names: Panda, Penguin and Hummingbird.

- *Panda* was first introduced in 2011 and was specifically designed to stop websites with poor content to make their way into Google top search results. This filter runs periodically to sift out content that Google deems to lack substance. The main target was content farms – websites with large quantities of content aggregated from other websites, specifically aimed to match popular searches.

- *Penguin* update was introduced in 2012 to filter out websites that tried to improve their search rankings by buying links or obtaining them through networks designed to boost rankings in search results. The update was specifically designed to target "spammy" and "unnatural" links.

- *Hummingbird* was rolled out in 2013. This complete algorithm replacement was designed to better predict what the person wants and make the search more conversational. For example, if you search for "Where can I get lunch?" Google will understand that you are looking for restaurants and will suggest the ones that are in the area with accompanying customer reviews. This was a big shift from the keyword-centric search to predicting the needs and wants of the end user.

Choosing Keywords without Research

One common mistake made with SEO strategies is focusing on keywords that are far from ideal strategic choices. Many companies target wrong keywords based on assumptions and lacking due diligence. They select keywords because they *think* people search for them. This may not be the case. The wrong keywords can also generate competitive search results that are not worth pursuing.

There are strategies and tools for selecting the right keywords. We will discuss them later in the chapter. In a nutshell, you want to select keywords that are the lowest hanging fruit (i.e., generate the most searches with the least amount of competition). You should also look at keyword synonyms, competitor brands and related topics your customers may be researching.

To summarize, don't embark on your SEO campaigns without careful research and analysis of your hand-picked keywords. Without this list, you will be creating a lot of smoke but getting very little traction. In addition, it will be impossible for you to measure the results of your SEO campaign.

Producing Low Quality Content

The most important advice from Google for your website's SEO success is to have original, high-quality content. That's it. SEO is synonymous with quality content. You simply cannot effectively market your website without it. This applies not only to SEO, but also to social media marketing and e-mail marketing.

In my experience, I have seen website owner's expectations that their website will be ranked for keywords not even included in their content. It is ridiculous to expect search engines to find your website without relevant content, especially when considering that your competitors' websites may have superior quality content.

The single goal of search engines is to help people find quality and relevant information quickly, and they are very good at it. If you want people to find your website under keywords describing your products or services, a page or two about these products or services is no longer enough. You must invest time and money in producing quality content that will inform, educate and even entertain your prospects (see "Content Recipe for Successful Marketing" under "Chapter 21 – Inbound Marketing as a Proven Strategy for Promoting Your Website")

Google and the like are continuously improving their understanding of your quality content. Search engines are also increasingly more effective in filtering poor content. Specifically, Google's' Penguin update was designed to filter content that is spammy, irrelevant or repetitive. Beware of purchasing low-quality content just for the sake of having content. Content marketing and SEO is becoming increasingly more about quality, not quantity.

Having Duplicate Content

Duplicate content is that which appears in more than one place on the Internet. It could be the same text used on several pages on your website, or that you republished from another website. In both cases, this is considered duplicate content.

Duplicate content is bad and will most likely have an adverse impact on your SEO; even worse, your content may be entirely excluded. Search engines rarely show duplicate content, and when it appears, they are forced to ascertain which version is the original content. By hosting duplicate content on your website, you are taking the large risk of traffic and ranking losses, due to being excluded in search results. Google's Panda update specifically targeted duplicate content.

As a rule of thumb, be sure that all your content is unique and original. Don't reuse or recycle the same content on different areas of your website.

There are some situations where search engines may deduct that the same page is actually two different pages. This happens with capitalization of URLs, print versions of pages, session IDs, etc. Work with your web developer to ensure that you don't have duplicate content, and have the developer set "canonical" tags to resolve any duplicate content issues.

Stuffing Your Website with Keywords

One of the biggest myths of search engine optimization is that stuffing your website with keywords will help improve your positions in search engines. The idea comes from the belief that search engines determine content relevance based on keywords that appear on the website. This mentality is that the greater the number of keywords, the higher the website will rank.

While this thinking may have been the case fifteen years ago, distancing from this method is what allowed Google to crush its rivals like AltaVista and Lycos. Search engines were easy to manipulate then, and people would place multiple keywords at the bottom of each page in the same color as the background so they weren't visible to regular users, while search engines would devour these keywords.

Stuffing your website with keywords is now considered a "black hat" technique. Not only is it ineffective, but you will actually hurt your rankings, and you may be penalized or banned. Search engines have become incredibly good at identifying the overuse of keywords, so don't make this mistake. Instead, invest in good content with an emphasis on a particular topic.

Building Spammy Links

Another popular "black hat" SEO technique is obtaining additional links to your website through shady practices (termed "unnatural" by Google). This usually involves the following practices that today produce little effect and can lead to website penalties:

- Buying links from spammy websites with questionable reputation.

- Participating in link farms or link exchanges where websites link to each other.

- Participating in blog networks where members pay bloggers to place links in their websites.

- Posting and "spinning" articles (article marketing) on websites designed for users to submit their articles solely for SEO purposes.

- Joining disreputable directories with low quality and spammy websites.

- Spamming links on forums and online communities.

- Posting excessive links in blog comments.

Ignoring User Experience

Google repeatedly stated that its number one priority is to provide the best possible user experience to the masses. That's why your website will never rank high if it does not meet Google's criteria of the acceptable user experience.

User experience is very important to any website. Poor user experience can result in a ruined reputation, a high bounce rate and few conversions, so SEO would be the least of your problems. There are, however, certain aspects that are changing, and some are often overlooked. The following factors could affect your positions if not properly addressed:

- *Speed* – Users today want websites to load quickly. Google does measure the speed with which websites load, and if yours is slow to load, it may adversely affect your rankings.

- *Mobile Support* – Mobile use is on the rise, so Google is naturally giving attention to mobile-friendly content on your website. If your website is not mobile-friendly, your positions will most definitely get a hit.

- *Safety* – If you website is considered unsafe by Google (contains malware, viruses or any potentially dangerous materials), Google may block it or display a warning.

- *Flash* – Adobe Flash is generally bad news for SEO. Search engines cannot effectively see all the text inside the Flash, cannot navigate the links, etc. There are better and newer technologies (HTML5/CSS3) that can often replace Flash, so try to stay away from it.

Best Ongoing SEO Practices for Your Website

Whether working on the content of your website or preparing a new blog post, you should always employ the following best SEO practices. Practices recommended here may have little impact individually (Remember, Google uses over 200 factors to rank your website.), but they do accumulate quickly. The difference between several positions in search results could be a matter of whether you followed these guidelines:

Create Great Dedicated Pages

Every page you are trying to optimize should have target keywords, and every keyword you select should have a dedicated page optimized for it. You shouldn't expect that your selected keywords would generate traffic unless you have great dedicated pages focusing on the same topics. Remember, search engines don't rank websites, they rank individual web pages.

Avoid creating multiple pages on the same topic. This will simply dilute the effectiveness and impact of the topic. You should have one page per topic that is laser-focused on a particular keyword group.

Don't focus too much on SEO. Focus on the reader. Do your best to create a dedicated page that provides great information on the topic at hand. Invest due diligence on research, and create content that makes your page the most useful on the Web.

Then view your page as though you were Google, and scrutinize the details of your page for all the content you want the search engine to see. You can always beef up the content by using examples, industry trends, research studies, quotes from experts, reviews or any other materials that will help support your message.

Use Header Tags

Header tags (<h1>, <h2>, <h3>, etc.) should be used to mark up and separate the content of your page. The most important one is obviously

<h1>. That should be used for all page titles and needs to include your target keyword for the page. Use the keyword only once.

For subheadings use <h2> and <h3>. It is also a good idea to include some keywords, but don't overdo it. Your Content Management System needs to be equipped with header tags and apply them correctly.

Create Effective TITLE Tags

The title tag of your page (<title>) is equally important for search engines and website visitors. It is displayed in your browser's tab, gets saved when bookmarking the page and shows in the search results. Search engines also look at titles to determine the subject of the page, so use the following best practices when creating titles:

1. Place important keywords in front of the title. The search engine will pick them up for rankings and will emphasize (bold) them in search results.

2. Use your brand name in the title to increase recognition of your brand. Some of the common techniques are to follow.

3. Use the same advice for creating accurate, descriptive and compelling titles as recommended in "Content Recipe for Successful Marketing" of "Chapter 21 – Inbound Marketing as a Proven Strategy for Promoting Your Website". Treat titles as calls to action, and create them in a descriptive and compelling manner.

4. Titles should be no longer than 65-75 characters (approx. 10-15 words). Most search engines will truncate titles any longer than that.

Most Content Management Systems create default title tags but will allow you to modify them. Customize titles for all your pages.

Set META Description

Meta tags were originally created to help provide search engines with all kinds of information about the page's content. However, search engines no longer rely on most of them. For example, Meta keywords are no longer valuable or important for SEO. In fact, the presence of Meta keywords on your website tells your competitors the specific keywords you are pursuing.

While most content management systems give control for customizing Meta tags, only Meta description still matters today. While they are not as important in search engine rankings, they are instrumental in encouraging users to click on your link from SERP (search engine results page). Your page's description is displayed below the title of your page and just as with title tags, search engines highlight keywords the users keyed in to their searches.

For best results write compelling Meta descriptions using the same principles as titles, keep them between 150 and 160 characters in length and use keywords. Also, avoid using duplicate Meta tags.

Use Image ALT Attributes

You may be shopping for a new iPhone, and find a great picture of a stylish iPhone and a complementary carbon fiber case. That's what you see on a picture but search engines don't perceive images the same way a shopper sees it. They rely on ALT attributes that describe images. By using an ALT attribute "iPhone with a complementary carbon fiber case", you are essentially describing the image to search engines.

Image ALT attributes is a good place for your keywords. Make them descriptive, thorough and accurate. This not only helps with the consumer's web search, but it enables your images to be searchable in image search, and this can produce a great deal of traffic. For this reason, you should always use ALT attributes for important images on your website.

Create Human-Friendly URLs

URLs (or web addresses) of your pages are important and show up in several places: on search results pages between the title and the description, in the browser URL bar and when someone is referencing a page on your website (in an e-mail for example).

It is a good practice to maintain clean and descriptive URLs that give the user a good understanding of the page without actually visiting the page. A clean URL also implies the structure of your website. The best URLs are those that allow users to predict the content (for example, http://www.intechnic.com/web-development/).

Keep URLs short. Shorter is more convenient in that it's easier to share URLs (text messages, e-mail, Twitter, etc.). It is also a good idea to include keywords in URLs, but don't overdo it. This could trigger spam filters. Finally, if you have multiple words that need to be separated, use hyphens (-) and stay away from underscore "_" and other characters.

Most CMS create URLs for new pages automatically but do allow modification to custom URLs. This is sometimes an advanced feature, so talk to you web developer to learn the latitude you will have.

Set Internal Links

This tactic is designed to boost rankings of certain pages by passing credibility to them from other pages (note, this tactic doesn't add credibility, it just transfers it). This works by linking related pages using contextual links (i.e., referencing a "target" page from a "donor" page within the body of an article). You can do this in three easy steps:

Determine Donor Pages – The key to this tactic is to find pages from which you want to link and to which you want to link. Pages from which you want to link (donor pages) are the pages that are linked most often from other websites. You can reference these pages in Google's Webmaster Tools (Search Traffic > Links to Your Site) or see which pages are most visited using Google Analytics (Behavior > Site Content > Landing Pages).

Determine Target Pages – The next step is to find pages to which you want to link (target pages). The pages that need most link credibility are the ones which are "almost ranking" on the first page in search results and need an extra "boost" to get to the first page. To find these pages go to Google Analytics (Acquisition > Search Engine Optimization > Queries) and filter results by the average position greater than 10. Then filter results by the average position, starting with the lowest position. These pages should receive your focus.

Create Links – Now you are ready to link the pages, you must create links within the text of the page using keywords that best describe the subject of the page to which you are linking. Remember, you are linking in order to pass link credibility. In this example, the link for "link credibility" was used contextually. It is focusing on the target keyword and should be set to another page on your website containing this subject. If you are linking from more than one donor page, use different keywords and mix it up.

Use internal linking sparingly, and don't overdo it. You shouldn't have more than 5-6 internal links per page (navigation doesn't count).

Note that broken links (internal and external) are bad for SEO so you should regularly examine your website meticulously for broken links and fix them.

Vary Anchor Text in Links

As you already know, links to your website as well as internal links are great for SEO because they transfer link popularity. What also makes a difference is the anchor text of the link. Anchor text is the visible text inside the link that describes the linked content. For example: SEO Practices, where it is clearly implied that the text describes the content of the linked page.

That's exactly how search engines look at it, so use descriptive anchor text and include your target keywords instead of using "click here" or "read more." It is good to have links that include keywords, but, again, don't overdo it. Having too many links with the same keywords will look spammy and may be considered "unnatural." Instead, use variations and sometimes omit keywords entirely.

Turn Old Content into Link Magnets

Most marketers focus their SEO efforts on the latest blog post. They promote content on social media for a couple days and then move on to the content topic.

The problem with this strategy is that it may take longer than a couple days or a couple social shares to get the traction you need. SEO is the process that takes time, work, experimentation and measurement, so by abandoning SEO efforts on old posts, you are preventing them from realizing their true potential. So how do you make the most from your older posts? Create link magnets. Link magnets involve creating content that is designed to encourage others to link to it from other websites. This sounds good in theory, but how do you get others to do it? You can achieve this in five steps:

1. First, identify the posts with the most SEO potential. These posts are close to the first page of SERP for good keywords. You can use the same approach recommended for creating internal links: go to Google Analytics (Acquisition > Search Engine Optimization > Queries), and filter results by the average position greater than 10. This will provide old posts that have the most potential.

2. Check all principles described here and conduct additional optimization as needed. Remember, the difference between ranking on the first and second page may be a detail as small as missing an <h1> (header) tag or insufficient keywords in the body of the text. Check everything, and make improvements, but be careful not to overdo it.

3. Link to the post from other old posts (see: "Set Internal Links") to pass some link juice to the post with potential.

4. Look for ways to improve the content of your post. In order for this strategy to work, you must have good content, and I

mean *very* good content. If you think you have a great topic, selected perfect keywords and followed all the practices described here, but somehow you are still not getting enough traction, perhaps the content is good, but not great. Look for ways to improve it: add illustrations, graphs, evidence, screenshots, examples, statistics, quotes, etc. Follow the advice in "How to Blog Like a Star" in "Chapter 21 – Inbound Marketing as a Proven Strategy for Promoting Your Website". Create the best post possible on the subject. Make it such a useful piece of content that you would have used it in your own research. When you do this, others will too.

5. After you have followed all these steps, it is time to give your post a new life. Run another promotion campaign with higher intensity: re-share it across social media, include it in your mailing, add the link to it in your e-mail signature block, run a paid ad campaign on Facebook, LinkedIn and Twitter, reach out to other bloggers to see if they would like to reference your content.

Review Technical SEO

When search engines can't index your website, they cannot show it in search results. A number of technical aspects can assist or prevent indexing of your website by search engines. You should review them with your web developer to ensure your website is optimized from a technical standpoint:

1. *Webmaster Tools* – Between you, your web developer and your SEO partner, you should set up an account for your website in Google Webmaster Tools (https://www.google.com/webmasters/tools/). It is a free service that will help you understand how Google sees the website and if there are any problems or recommendations. Bing also has a similar tool (http://www.bing.com/webmaster).

2. *Sitemap* – Your website should have a sitemap in the XMP format that includes the entire structure of your website (including your blog posts) that should then be submitted

to Google using Webmaster Tools. This will help Google index your website and inform it of updates.

3. *Permanent Redirects* – If the URL structure of your website is changing (for example, when redoing the website), it is vital to set up permanent redirects (code 301) from your old pages to new pages. That's how search engines (as well as users) will be redirected to new versions of the old pages.

4. *Nofollow / Noindex* – Make sure that your website's pages are "open" to indexing by search engines. There is one tag in particular that will stop search engines in their tracks: <meta name="robots" content="noindex, nofollow">. Be sure you don't have it set if you want your website indexed.

5. *Robots.txt* – a file on your web server that can restrict access to your website for search engines. It works the same way as "noindex, nofollow" tags, so be sure that it does not prevent search engines from indexing your website.

6. *Forms/Passwords* – Search engines cannot complete forms, so if any content behind a form has to be completed in order to access it, search engines won't be able to reach it. The same applies to password-protected content.

SEO Strategy that Will Always Work

Effective search engine optimization strategy has five pillars: Keyword Research, Producing Quality Content, Use of Social Media, Building Links and Analyzing Results. The strategy is all about understanding what content your readers want, producing quality content, measuring response and delivering more good content.

If you stick to these five main principles, you will be on the road to SEO results. Why will this strategy always work? Because this is precisely what Google wants you to do. They say, "Our advice for publishers continues to be to focus on delivering the best possible user experience on your websites and not to focus too much on what they think are Google's current ranking algorithms or signals."[43]

Let's look at one of the steps closer:

Research Perfect Keywords

Successful SEO begins with a strategy and a SEO strategy begins with researching keywords. The search always begins with words typed into a search box. If you don't know what people are searching for you won't be able to deliver the content that they want. You will also not attract the visitors that you want.

Remember, it's not just about getting traffic to your website. It is about getting the right traffic. Researching keywords is like reading the minds of your customers. By doing this you can learn about your customers, their behaviors, and you can predict shifts in demand and changes in market conditions. You will find keyword research a hugely rewarding experience.

Before embarking on keyword research let's first define a perfect keyword. A keyword delivers the most volume for the least amount of competition. Think of it as the lowest hanging juicy fruit. Targeting a keyword that no one searches is like picking a fruit that isn't ripe. At the same time going after the fruit at the very top of the tree requires a lot more energy, so why not focus efforts on the lowest hanging fruit in the first place.

With this approach in mind, let's select and target optimal keywords using the following five steps:

Step 1

Begin by establishing what people term your product or service and how they will search for it online? What terminology do people use? What are some of the related services and products people are looking for? What are some of the queries already generating traffic to your website (Google Analytics: Acquisition > Search Engine Optimization > Queries)? Can you expand or improve those?

---

[43] http://googlewebmastercentral.blogspot.com/2011/05/more-guidance-on-building-high-quality.html

The Low Hanging Fruit

Step 2

Next, let's look at the popularity of the keyword and the search volume that it produces. We will be using two tools for this:

1. *Google AdWords Keyword Planner* (https://adwords.google.com/ko/KeywordPlanner/Home) gives you estimated numbers of monthly searches and suggestions.

2. *Google Trends* (http://www.google.com/trends/) shows trending for a search phrase over time, and allows you to compare them as well as suggests alternatives.

   First, use Google's Keyword Planner to narrow down your list to the "lowest hanging fruit". The idea is to focus on keywords that have the most monthly searches but the least competition. Note that because Keyword Planner is designed for AdWords it shows competition within AdWords and not the organic search; therefore, real competition data may be different. After you compiled this list, compare your findings to Google Trends.

Step 3

Expand your keyword search by using the 'suggest' feature in both tools. Also, try Ubersuggest (http://ubersuggest.org/) which is a great tool that includes all Google's suggestions from various sources. Look for synonyms and variations or derivatives of the same keyword. Then group these keywords in keyword groups.

Talk to your team members and your customers to learn keywords they use to search. For all new suggestions go back to Step 2, and retest the keywords for volume and competition.

Step 4

Assign each keyword group to various pages of the website based on the keywords' correlation to them. To help with that you can split your website into zones. I suggest at least three:

401

1. First zone would be your homepage. You should select more competitive keywords that closely describe what your company does and with the number of searches in thousands.

2. Second zone would be your inside pages, such as pages for your products and services. These keywords may be more specific and less competitive with monthly searches in hundreds.

3. Third zone would be your blog or other section of your website where you conduct ongoing content marketing (whitepapers, articles, videos, etc.). These keywords may be very specific and naturally have lower monthly search numbers (less than a hundred). These keywords are often referred to as "long tail" keywords. They may be long and very specific, which is good, because they will have little if any competition. A lot of content targeting long tail keywords could be cumulatively producing massive amounts of traffic to your website.

Step 5

When you have narrowed down the keywords, you need to analyze the size and activity of the competition for these keywords. First, search for it in Google. I recommend using Google's Ad Preview tool (http:// adwords.google.com/d/AdPreview/), which shows search results without factoring your personal preferences, geographic location, etc. Think of it as a stripped SERP. Look at the following:

1. The number of search results – with how many pages are you competing? The number of pay-per-click ads on the page – how many companies know the keyword is so valuable that they are willing to pay for it?

2. Who is ranking in top positions – does it appear they are employing SEO strategies described in this book? Will you be able to compete with these websites?

3. A great tool that allows you to compare how your website stacks up to your completion is Moz's Site Explorer Tool (http://www.opensiteexplorer.org/). Look at domain authority, PageRank and other factors.

Create Quality and Optimized Content

Now that you have determined some good keywords for your website, and you know there is an opportunity to rank for them, you should focus your efforts on creating and optimizing your content for these keywords.

The important rule of thumb is to be sure that the keywords you are choosing are relevant to your website's content. When arriving at your website through a search engine, people should always get the content they expect and be happy with its quality. This is the main rule of SEO.

There is nothing, however, preventing you from producing original quality content to target specific keywords that represent opportunities. As long as the new content is in line with your website and your company's vision, you can actually create content to attract additional traffic. After all, this is what content marketing is all about.

Once you have the content that nicely aligns with the keywords you have chosen, you should spend some time optimizing it. Go through one keyword at a time, and focus on the page of your website that corresponds to that particular keyword. You want to be certain that the keyword appears in several places on your page, but don't over-populate the keyword. Spamming or overloading a page with a keyword will actually hurt the ranking.

Specifically, you should place your keyword in the following areas:

1. In the beginning of the page title tag (<title>) at least once. Try to keep the keyword as close to the beginning of the title as possible.

2. In the top header tag (<h1>) of the page or prominently near the top of the page.

3. Three to five times in the body of the page. Spread keywords out and use variations such as singular and plural, abbreviations, synonyms, etc.

4. At least once as an alt attribute for the image used on the page.

5. Once in the URL of the page.

6. At least once in the Meta description of the page. It doesn't affect rankings, but it is displayed on search results.

7. In internal links from other pages (see "Set Internal Links" in the next section).

Utilize Social Media for Social SEO

Google uses hundreds of criteria to determine web pages' rankings. There is recent data[44] that shows Google is starting to rely more on signals from social media, specially its own Google Plus network.

Likes, Tweets and Plusses on social media are like votes of confidence for your content. They tell Google the content is good, because real people find it valuable and are willing to share or express their appreciation for it. It is called Social SEO.

Social SEO is hard to fake, so Google and other search engines are starting to put more trust in social media all the time. If you don't have a social media strategy and your competition does, you will be at a disadvantage regarding SEO.

Here are five simple tips you can use to start implementing your social SEO strategy today:

1. Optimize your social media profiles. Complete the information meticulously, including your address, categories and description (often skipped under "About"

---

[44] http://searchenginewatch.com/article/2281153/2013-Search-Ranking-Factors-Survey-Results-From-Moz

or "Information" sections). Use your strategic keywords. Always include links to your website.

2. You should give special attention to Google Plus. Google owns G+ and uses that leverage to grow it. Google Plus is already tightly integrated with Google Search, so you should be active on this social network in particular. Ask your web developer or SEO vendor to link Google Plus profiles of all your blog authors to show them next to search results in Google Search as well as to build on Authors Rank (the system Google uses to track the quality of content by each author). Also, set up a publisher's association to show your company's G+ account in Google Search when someone searches for your company.

3. In order to make full use of social SEO, try to incorporate relevant keywords in your social network updates. Another technique is using your company's name in social posts. For example, when you do status updates on Facebook or tweet something on Twitter "sign it" with the company name: "Another busy day at Company" or "Daily tip from Company."

4. Your content may be great, but if no one sees it, it will not fulfill its purpose. Social media can be a great starting point to promote your new original content, and it may give it a slight boost. As soon as you post new content (especially blog posts), immediately share it across your social networks (Facebook, Twitter, Google Plus, LinkedIn and others). Focus especially on Twitter (because it helps Google index your content faster), and Google Plus (for the reasons explained above).

5. Add social media badges (buttons to share or like your content) so that others can share, like and comment on it easily. Every time this happens, social media sends a signal that there is good content on your website. Once again, content quality is the key. The better the content, the more likes and shares you will get.

As you can see, social media marketing and search engine optimization are becoming more intertwined. In "Chapter 23 – Effective Social Media Marketing Strategy", we will review social media strategies in more depth.

Build Links to Your Website

As we know the more links you get, the more it helps the page's ranking. As previously stated, purchasing spam my and low quality links is ill advised. So how do you get people to voluntarily link to you from quality sites?

Content quality is the key. You should think of your link building as *earning* links not purchasing them. You earn them with the quality of your content. Without that quality factor, the entire effort of obtaining links will be an uphill battle.

Let's look at some ways to earn links to your website:

- *Natural Editorial Links* – This is others choosing to link to your content at will. In order for someone to want to link to your content, it has to be very good. It has to be so good that you would want to share it. By producing great content and raising awareness you will inevitably perpetuate others linking to you as well.

- *Manual Outreach* – Share your content with others. If you think a person could benefit from referencing your content (for example, another blog referencing the market research that you've done), contact them to see if they are open to referencing your content.

- *Guest Blogging* – This remains one of the most popular methods that is also white hat and reliable. If you are producing good content, offer to write for others' websites. It is generally acceptable to ask for a link to your website to be added to your bio.

- *Press Releases* – If your company has announcements, new projects, product, innovations, or other newsworthy information, issue a press release to draw attention that can result in legitimate links from bloggers and news websites or at least, the mention of the brand.

- *Ask Customers / Partners* – Why not ask your loyal customers or partners link to you from a prominent place on their websites? If they love your product or brand, they would likely be open to this idea.

- *Through Sponsorships* – Consider sponsoring a local charity, an event or a scholarship that is worthy of earning you a link.

- *Through Participation* – If you or your colleagues are members of associations or professional organizations or frequently participate in tradeshows, seminars or conferences, why not ask for a link from their website?

Analyze Your SEO Performance

Just as you measure your website's effectiveness, measurement of your SEO campaigns is of utmost importance. Because SEO isn't an exact science, it involves constant experimenting, so if you can measure the results, you can improve them.

What SEO KPIs to Measure

You should measure and analyze the following SEO metrics at least once a month:

- *Visits through Organic Search* – How many visits do you get via search engines? Are you getting searches from all three: Google, Bing and Yahoo? How do the numbers compare to the previous month? Are they growing, the same or declining? Watch out for gains or drops in specific search engines (Google Analytics: Acquisition > Overview).

- *Keywords* – What keywords have generated most traffic to your website? Compare the number of impressions to clicks and the resulting CRT (click-through-ratio). What are your positions for these keywords? Are there any unexpected keywords or trends that you can detect? Can you optimize and improve the current positions or capitalize on new good keywords that you just discovered (Google Analytics: Acquisition > Search Engine Optimization > Queries, Google Analytics: Acquisition > Keywords > Organic, Google Webmaster Tools: Search Traffic > Search Queries)?

- *Conversions Per Keyword* – which of the keywords resulted in conversions (Google Analytics: Acquisition > Keywords > Organic)? Unfortunately, in 2011 Google announced that it started encrypting search queries of logged-in users. This means that you no longer had easy access to data showing which keywords were used for every session (to see which keywords corresponded to conversions, for example). Expect to see the infamous "(not provided)" for many of your keywords.

- *Landing Pages* – What are the most frequently accessed pages on your website (Google Webmaster Tools: Search Traffic > Landing Pages)?

- *Link to Your Site* – Who is linking to your website? What content is most-often linked? How is your content linked (what is the anchor text used)? (Google Webmaster Tools: Search Traffic > Links to Your Site)

- *Internal Links* – What are the most cross-linked pages on your website internally (Google Webmaster Tools: Search Traffic > Internal Links)?

Applying the Data

The reports above will provide a great deal of insight, but it is just as important to apply this data correctly in order to draw conclusions and make adjustments to improve your SEO strategy. To help you with this step, let's review possible trends and what they really tell you about your SEO performance:

- *Fluctuations* – All of your SEO metrics will fluctuate from time to time. You will see natural fluctuations in the number of indexed pages, inbound links and positions of your keywords. It's normal as search engines re-crawl websites, update their indexes, add and remove web pages, change their algorithms, etc. Minor fluctuations shouldn't be grounds for concern unless a clear, negative trend prevails, and fluctuations are accompanied by drops in referral traffic to the website.

6. *Negative Trends* – If you notice a significant drop in traffic referrals from a certain search engine and the results are consistent over time (don't bounce back within a month), it could mean one of the following:

   1. Your website has suffered a penalty for violating the search engine's guidelines. Check the Webmaster tools for any warnings or notices.

   2. The search engine has updated their ranking algorithm, and the update is not in your website's favor. This most often occurs when search engines devalue links pointing to your website. Research what SEO experts have determined about the most recent update to learn how you may have been affected by it and what action to take.

   3. You might have accidentally blocked access to a search engine's crawler. See "Review Technical SEO" in the next section for more details.

   4. Your competition may have seriously overtaken your positions. Check to see how you rank compares to them.

- *Positive Trends* –SEO is considered successful when positive trends outweigh negative trends (in other words, when your website's positions and SEO traffic increases over time). This process is slow. As previously covered, it is unrealistic to expect instant and great SEO results. In fact, I've only experienced it once when Panda penalized a large share of our competition. We gained positions literally overnight. However, this was the result of our competitor's use of black-hat techniques and not due to our strategy.

SEO is always a long-term strategy. Be patient, create quality content and apply practices described in this chapter and you will be successful.

Tools to Help Your SEO

In addition to Google Analytics and Webmaster tools, you may want to consider the following tools:

- **MOZ** (http://moz.com/) is one of the favorites in SEO Tools that offers everything in one place: keyword research and optimization, technical analysis, link reports, competitive comparison and intelligence. Also includes a number of tools for inbound marketing: social analysis and optimization, social mentions, etc.

- **Raven** (http://raventools.com/) originally designed for SEO by an SEO agency and includes a number of features and integrations with Wordtracker, Facebook, Twitter, Social Mention, etc.

- **WebCEO** (http://www.webceo.com/) is another industry veteran and an alternative to MOZ and Raven, and includes a great number of features.

- **Wordtracker** (http://www.wordtracker.com/) a popular tool for keyword research that saves time and automates your keyword research by recommending popular keywords.

- **Buzzstream** (http://raventools.com/) is designed primarily for link building and management. It's a great tool that saves your team a lot of time when researching influencers and tracking relationships.

Chapter 23 – Effective Social Media Marketing Strategy

Social Media Marketing (SMM) is big and is getting only bigger. Did you know that every second two new members join LinkedIn[45], 80% of Internet users prefer to connect with brands on Facebook, and the number of worldwide social media users will surpass the 2 billion mark by 2016[46]?

Social media is already an important part of our lives. It is also integral to business. If you are serious about marketing, you should make social media a major component of your marketing strategy. Regardless of the nature your industry or the function of your website, social media integration is no longer optional. When done properly and combined with content marketing and SEO, social media can do wonders for your website and your business. When dismissed or handled poorly, social media could be the reason for losing business to your competition.

This chapter is not going to make you an overnight social media marketing guru, but it will give you a head start and will steer you away from costly mistakes. Let's begin.

Common SMM Mistakes to Avoid

"Social media marketing doesn't work," I often hear. "It doesn't work for *you* because you are not doing it right," is typically my response. Most companies do not incorporate SMM successfully. In fact, they are following the trend of others and quickly become discouraged by the lack of positive results.

The explosion in social media popularity caught most businesses off guard. SMM is so different from the traditional forms of marketing that many companies simply don't know what they are doing. They

---

[45] http://www.fastcompany.com/3021749/work-smart/10-surprising-social-media-statistics-that-will-make-you-rethink-your-social-stra

[46] http://www.mediabistro.com/alltwitter/social-media-growth-worldwide_b51877

are learning on the job. This confusion often contributes to numerous myths, misconceptions and rookie mistakes. Let's look at some of the common ones:

Dismissing Social Marketing as Ineffective

If you believe social media is not right for your demographic or your industry, you are wrong. It is a common misconception that social media is only for teenagers and the tech savvy. That is no longer the case. For example, did you know that the fastest growing demographic on Twitter is the 55-64 year age bracket and that the fastest growing demographic on Facebook and Google+ is 45-54 year olds. [47] You will find that other demographics are represented as well. Social media has penetrated all layers of our society. Social media is for everyone.

You must not avoid social media, regardless of the nature of your business or it's targeted demographic. You may have had a poor experience with SMM already. In most cases it is because you didn't have a good plan, you made poor choices or have fallen victim to mistakes outlined in this chapter. Regardless, there is no reason to dismiss social media marketing as ineffective. In fact, you should look at it as an opportunity. This is where you can turn your weakness into strength by discovering a method to make SMM work for your business.

Consider this simple fact: you are not alone in this struggle with social media. Your competition may also be struggling. If you manage to put together an effective social media strategy ahead of the competition, you will have an upper hand. At the same time, if you are falling behind, this could be a wake-up call to do something about it—quickly.

Not Having a Social Media Marketing Plan

Your social media efforts need to be planned the same way as any other type of marketing. In fact, SMM should be a part of your marketing plan (see "How to Put Together a Marketing Plan for Your Website" in "Chapter 20 – How to Grow Traffic and Market Your Website")

---

[47]   http://www.fastcompany.com/3021749/work-smart/10-surprising-social-media-statistics-that-will-make-you-rethink-your-social-stra

Social Media Marketing can be a colossal waste of time without a proper plan of action. Many companies fall into this trap. They sporadically post things to their social media accounts, share some of their content here and there and try to attract followers or fans. That's not social media marketing; that's having no plan.

Social media marketing must be approached the same way you approach your planning for PPC, a direct mail campaign or a tradeshow. You should have specific goals, budgets and a concrete plan of action:

- What are you trying to accomplish?

- How are you going to achieve it?

- How are you going to measure results?

- What resources are you willing and able to allocate?

Measuring the Wrong KPIs

Measuring results is instrumental to any form of business activity. You improve by measuring and making adjustment. Social media marketing is no different.

Unfortunately, when measuring Key Performance Indicators (KPIs) of your social media marketing, many marketers fall into the trap of vanity metrics. They measure the number of fans on Facebook or followers on Twitter, and if these numbers are growing, they are happy.

In reality, social media marketing is no different from any other marketing channel. You should measure the success, not by the numbers of fans or followers, but by the impact your SMM has on your business. Ask yourself: How many leads did I get from Facebook last month? How many leads from Twitter resulted in sales? If you can't answer these questions, you are not measuring the right KPIs.

You need to measure conversions from every social network as well as the ROI (see "How to Measure Your Marketing Results" in "Chapter 20 – How to Grow Traffic and Market Your Website"). Remember, there is no such thing as "free marketing." Time is money, and the time you spend on social media is the same expense as PPC or paid advertising. In addition to return on investment, you need to monitor the Acquisition-Behavior-Conversion (ABC) breakdown as well as Multi-Channel Funnels and Attribution Modeling (see "Chapter 18 – How Well is Your Website Really Doing?") since visits from social media are often preceded or followed by visits through other channels like search or e-mail.

Treating All Social Media the Same

You probably wouldn't speak Spanish in Germany, yet many businesses make the mistake of speaking the wrong language on social media. Every social network has its own customs, language, audience and type of content. Addressing the audience in a way that's inconsistent with the traditions of the social network is ineffective and counter-productive.

What makes social media marketing great is that in addition to demographic criteria, you can reach out to specific audiences as well as target specific professionals, personal tastes and interests. However, in order for your efforts to be effective, you need to account for differences between social networks. It is important to learn how people communicate on every social network. We will focus on common social networks' strategies and differences later in this chapter, but as you explore and experiment, keep this in mind.

Failing to Engage in Conversations

Social media is all about communicating, not just posting. If you have time to do only one type of activity on social media, you should engage in conversations on your network. Your one-way posts are useless if no one cares to share them and respond to them. Communication is always a two-way street. This is why your posts and your content should be designed to elicit conversations with your audience. You want comments, shares, tweets, likes and discussions. If you don't get these reactions, your overall strategy and the content should be revisited.

When a person responds or comments, be sure to reply. Failing to respond to customers on social media is one of the cardinal sins in social media marketing. Either positive or negative, every comment a customer posts presents an opportunity to communicate with the customer directly. Ask them about their experiences, offer assistance and thank them for their patronage. Be friendly and personable; after all, this is what social media is about.

Don't limit your company's social interactions only through the marketing department. Your business consists of many other departments that interact with customers, such as sales, customer service, billing, production, etc. Involve them in your social media strategy to communicate with your customers on all levels.

Connecting as Opposed to Networking

In addition to communicating, social media is just as much about networking. By building and expanding your network, you will gain better access to prospects and other professionals and will increase the exposure for your messages and your content. The size of your network matters, but so does the quality. Interacting with a group of ten followers will simply not produce desirable results. Having thousands of random followers who don't represent your ideal customers and have little to contribute would be just as ineffective. You want to attract and engage prospects, peers or professionals who share same views and interests and who will be instrumental in the success of your marketing efforts.

Many companies believe networking on social media is simply following someone or sharing their content with them. This is another common mistake. Following someone on Twitter or even connecting with them on LinkedIn is not proper networking. Networking is just as much about giving as receiving. It's about adding value to the relationship. You should set aside the time to reach out and write personalized messages, engage in discussions, share and comment on someone else's content as opposed to just pushing yours down everyone's throat. Treat these relationships the same way you want to be treated. By adding value to these relationships, others will be more likely to pay attention to what you have to say.

Making It All about You

How would you like hanging out with a person who only talks about himself? That gets old quickly, right? Well, that's the very mistake many companies make on social media. It's all about them—their news, their events, their products, their projects, etc. Here is the truth: nobody cares.

In order to succeed in social media you not only have to speak the language of the audience, but you have to tell them what they want to hear. The content that you post should be of high quality, of significant interest and be in line with the deeply rooted traditions of the social network and your followers. Make it about them. Make it for them. To learn how to create quality customer-centric content, refer to "Content Recipe for Successful Marketing" in "Chapter 21 – Inbound Marketing as a Proven Strategy for Promoting Your Website".

Relying too Much on Automation

One of the most common mistakes companies make is relying too much on automatic (canned) posting to their social media accounts. Some go as far as to resort only to automatic posting of their new blog posts. That's not what social media is all about. People use social media because they want to interact with others. If all they want is to read your blog, they will go to your blog.

Your social media presence must have a personal touch. If people can tell that your posts are automated, or if they feel the exchange is impersonal, they will distance themselves to your brand. In extreme cases, if you spam them with too much irrelevant automatic content, you will start losing them. Be careful not to alienate your audience by posting content automatically and instead think of ways to delight, entertain and inspire by posting content that is personalized and authentic.

Having Too Many Accounts to Manage

There are thousands of social networking websites out there. Many businesses make the mistake of jumping on every social network possible, setting up accounts and trying to manage them all only to realize that they are stretching their marketing resources thin and producing very little results in the process. In my experience, one dedicated marketing professional can effectively manage no more than 2-4 social media accounts. If your organization's social media strategy is in the hands of a single team member, you should focus your resources and energy on the "Big Four": Facebook, Twitter, LinkedIn and Google Plus. You then should further prioritize your efforts on the social network that produces the most results for your business.

Not Having a Social Media Policy

Not having a company-wide social media policy is clearly dangerous and can often result in unexpected public embarrassments. Regardless of who manages your social media accounts, you should adopt a policy outlining what is and is not acceptable. For most companies content that is sexist, racist, religious, offensive, obscene, sexually suggestive, derogatory or discriminatory in any way is off limits. Make sure that all your employees know the policy and adhere to it.

Be sure that the same policy covers the creation and management of "official" company accounts. As new social networks and features within those networks emerge, you want to be in full control of any content that officially represents your company. There should be rules regarding opening such accounts.

Finally, keep access to these accounts restricted and maintain a list of all accounts, usernames and passwords. Make sure that credentials are different for each account, and change passwords regularly, especially with employees who leave or change their roles. A single post by a disgruntled employee could be a PR nightmare for your organization.

Proven Social Media Marketing Tactics

Social Media Marketing remains an uncharted territory for many businesses as far as a proving it as a successful marketing strategy. Many are confused and overwhelmed by the abundance of social networks and the saturation of content. They don't know where to start or how to focus their efforts. The 10-Step SMM strategy below will help you get started towards producing tangible results.

417

Hire a Knowledgeable SMM Partner

Just as with search engine optimization, social media marketing requires a great deal of time and expertise. You simply might not have the bandwidth to manage your social media accounts effectively. You might also not have the experience required to know what works and what doesn't. Instead of sporadically posting content here and there, poking around and learning from your own mistakes, why not hire a professional? An experienced SMM partner can help create and implement an effective social media strategy: from choosing the right social networks for your business to helping produce the content. With systems in place, you can them run on their own or have them continue managing it for you. Either way, chances are it will take less time and cost less money, and it will produce better results.

When selecting an SMM partner, make sure they can demonstrate previous results, particularly in your industry. Another option is to reach out to other professionals in the industry for recommendations. Remember to always perform due diligence before hiring a vendor that will represent your company across social media. You want to make sure that they are experienced, reputable and that they know what they are doing. Ask for a specific plan of action before committing to anything. Your web developer may be a good starting point to finding a reliable an SMM partner.

Go Where Your Customers Are

The first order of business for you and your SMM partner will be to determine where your customers are. Marketing 101 is going where your customers are. With the abundance of social networks out there, you should primarily focus your efforts on social platforms where your customers and prospects are most active. This largely depends on your demographic.

I recommend starting with the "Big Four": Facebook, Twitter, LinkedIn and Google Plus and analyzing each to see if it is a good fit for your business. One way to determine which platforms are the best is by researching what your competition is doing and where they are most active. Pay attention to not only their activity, but more importantly the responses and the engagement that they get from their customers and followers. If it works for them, it will probably work for you. One of the safest and quickest marketing strategies is adopting successful strategies adopted by your competition and improving upon them.

Produce and Curate Valuable Content

Just like all other forms of Inbound Marketing, effective Social Media Marketing requires quality, useful, relevant and engaging content to unlock the potential of what SMM can do for your business. Revisit principles discussed in "Chapter 21 – Inbound Marketing as a Proven Strategy for Promoting Your Website" for tips on how to produce amazing content that you can use throughout your social media channels.

One of the obstacles in producing quality content is the level of content saturation, so it is rarely possible to produce original content. The workaround for this obstacle is content curation. Content curation is the process of collecting, organizing and presenting content in a way that it is useful and informative. It is an art of improving on someone else's content, usually from multiple sources, by researching, arranging and presenting it in a way that is efficient and easy to digest.

An experienced SMM partner will be able to assist you with producing and curating quality content that is not only optimized for social media but also for the very social networks that you decided to target. Together, you can experiment with content to see what works and what doesn't on various social networks. Keep an eye on what kind of content entices the best responses from your customers.

Integrate Your Social Presence

For best results, your social media should be tightly integrated into your other marketing channels. SMM often provides a support role and acts as a stepping-stone toward converting or closing a visitor as well as to delight and support existing customers. That's why it is important for SMM to be consistent with other forms of marketing and be part of the overall experience. Consider integrating your social media marketing the following ways:

- Promote and link to your social accounts from your website, your e-mail signatures, mailing lists and offline materials.

- Add social media badges to your blog or any other pages on the website where you feature engaging quality content to help promote and share it across social media.

- Many social media accounts allow you to connect and integrate them with other social networks. Make use of this to entice people to follow you across social networks.

- Integrate your social presence with live or virtual events. For example, ask people to RSVP for events on Facebook, Twitter or LinkedIn.

- Check out the list of the tools at the end of this chapter to help automate many social media management tasks and deploy your efforts across multiple social networks at once.

Make the Most out of Social Media Accounts

Each social network has numerous features and capabilities of which many companies fail to take full advantage. Some of the more common ones have to do with customizing and branding profiles. Almost all social networks give you the ability to customize your avatar, header images to support and solidify your marketing messages. At the very least, that should be changed from default and made consistent with your branding and marketing guidelines. Ideally, you should treat your social media profiles the same way as your website. They should have the same value propositions, customer-centric messaging, calls to actions, etc. For every social account, you should be creative and make your presence stand out. An experienced SMM partner will help here.

Another part that is often overlooked is the company bio. Many companies put in the basic information or skip this step completely. Include your website's URL, your mission statement, your locations and contact information. Take the time to provide as much information as possible; it will come in handy for your fans or followers, as well as benefit you for SEO purposes. Finally, take time to learn capabilities and features of every social network to see how you can make the best use of your account. The best way is to read up on network-specific tips and suggestions as well as to research what the competition is doing.

Build a Social Media Audience

Social media marketing is all about building and expanding your social audience. We will focus on network-specific strategies for Facebook, Twitter, LinkedIn and Google Plus further in the chapter. For now, let's focus on universal tactics you can apply to grow your network.

As we previously discussed, the quality of your network is more important than its size. That's why it is very important to know from the beginning the type of the audience you want to attract and how you are planning on growing your network. Here are some ideas you might find useful:

- Make an effort to seek out social media presence of your clients, prospects, vendors and business associates continually. Connect with them and follow them. Many will follow you back.

- Consider allocating small budgets to pay to promote your accounts within social networks at least initially to grow it to a critical mass. For example, you can pay to promote your Facebook page to potential prospects or to promote your LinkedIn page.

- Run contests, sweepstakes and giveaways to create brand affinity, show appreciation for existing customers and engage potential prospects.

- Offer exclusive content that is highly desired and valuable but is only available to those who follow you on social media.

Network with Influencers

Some of the more valuable connections in social media are influencers. Influencers are users with large followings and voices in the industry such as renowned writers, celebrities or business leaders. They are power users who influence others. Having a single influencer endorsing your company or sharing your content could produce an Oprah Winfrey effect.

Connecting with and engaging influencers should be an important part of your networking strategy. Of course, connecting with Oprah Winfrey may be a long shot, but many others may be within your reach. Here is one tactic that may be useful:

1. First, find your industry influencers on each social network where you have a presence and start following them. Focus on influencers whose views are aligned with those of your company. Interact with their content by commenting, sharing and liking, but be authentic and don't overdo it.

2. Then, utilize an "ego bait" strategy to engage them. Quote them on social media and in your blog and mention their name in a positive context. You would be surprised the results this may produce. Influencers might share your mention with their audience, and they may link to your content or follow you.

3. If that fails, try another tactic. Reach out to them directly. Compliment them on their content and ask if you could commission an article for your blog. Yes, this may cost you some serious money, but it will be more likely to get their attention. Having even one article from an influencer will be a huge credibility boost and will help attract others.

When all fails, don't be discouraged and focus your efforts on other influencers who may not be as hard to attract.

Become an Influencer

The ultimate goal of your SMM strategy should be to become an influencer yourself. An influencer status will do miracles for your social media marketing as well as your own career.

Working toward earning an influencer status is a long journey that starts with producing amazing content, continuously improving it, networking tirelessly and working your way up to earn the respect and trust of the industry.

By networking and interacting with other influencers (see the previous tactic) you can learn a great deal about becoming one yourself. Here are some suggestions:

- As an aspiring influencer, you have to be ready to contribute by producing and curating a lot of quality content.

- Discover where other influencers contribute their content and pitch some of your best material.

- Be prepared to be rejected at first. Use the criticism to improve on your content, and don't give up. Practice makes perfect.

- Participate in discussions and conversations. Respond to all comments; engage others by discussing their content across multiple platforms.

- Join Tribes (lists of influencers). In particular, join Triberr (http://triberr.com/) home of influencers.

- Associate all of your posts with your Google Plus account by requesting an authorship status (http://plus.google.com/authorship).

- Be ubiquitous by applying your name and face to every piece of content that you produce. It's all about building recognition.

- Post frequently across multiple social networks. Use automation tools to help schedule your posts.

- Utilize your personal social media accounts and channels to distribute your content as well as to receive feedback.

- Be helpful to others by offering advice and assistance. Helping others grow will grow your network as well.

- Be active offline. Attend networking events, seminars, conferences; try to land some speaking engagements or interviews. Anything that will help to get your name out there.

Allocate Realistic Budgets

Let's address the elephant in the room: social media marketing is not free. Successful SMM costs money. You should expect fixed costs such as staff salaries, training, cost of producing and curating content, subscriptions and licenses for various software and tools. Variable costs and unplanned extra expenses will also occur.

Set aside an adequate budget for social media marketing. The difference between successful SMM and lack of traction is often measured by the size of your marketing budget and its application. Sometimes a small paid campaign to promote content that you spend a ton of money producing is worth the investment. Without it, you may not get the traction you need.

Measure Performance

You should continuously measure the performance of your SMM campaigns. Measuring is what will allow you make educated adjustments and improvements. Let's look at some of the KPIs you should look at monthly:

- *Visits through Social Media* – How many visits are you getting from social networks? Which social networks are sending the most visitors? How do the numbers compare to the previous month? Are they growing, the same or declining? (Google Analytics: Acquisition > Social > Network Referrals)

- *Content Visits* – What content or pages on your website have attracted the most traffic? Compare the number of visits. Are there any content that is unexpected or developing trends that you noticed? Can you produce follow up content to ride on this wave? (Google Analytics: Acquisition > Social > Landing Pages)

- *Engagement* – How engaging was your content? How many likes, shares, tweets or pluses did you get? Which content was most engaging and on what social networks? Can you repeat this success? (Review insights and analytics from within each of the social networks)

- *Conversions*– which of the social networks have resulted in most conversions? What's the conversion value? (Google Analytics: Acquisition > Social > Conversions)

- *ROI* – What's the return on investment when it comes to your time and the SMM expenses you incurred?

- *Audience Growth* – How many new fans have you acquired on Facebook? How many followers on Twitter, Google+ and LinkedIn? How does it compare to the previous period? Is your audience growing? Review new followers' profiles. Are you attracting the audience you want? (Review insights and analytics from within each of the social networks)

Facebook Marketing Tactics

Facebook is the world's largest social network. In fact, at the time this book was written, Facebook had more monthly visitors than Twitter and LinkedIn combined. With exposure like this, almost every business wants to set up a presence on Facebook but very few manage to do it in a way that truly benefits their business. Recommendations below will help you make the most of your Facebook presence:

How Can Facebook Help Your Business?

Facebook is a great tool for businesses to build and engage with their fan base. The world's most successful brands use Facebook to enhance their brand recognition and to support and interact with their customers. It is also a great tool for market research.

Facebook is more social than other social networks. This means that most people use feedback for recreational and entertainment purposes, not for business.

If you are a consumer brand then Facebook may be a great choice for you. It is a little more challenging for B2B companies. Your company may not be the perfect fit. You can, however, still use Facebook by making your content more social in nature as opposed to business oriented. The recommended rule of thumb for Facebook is the 80/20 content rule (80% of original content and 20% promotional).

Facebook Lingo You Should Know

The following is some basic Facebook lingo you might encounter:

- *Profile* – Your Facebook account. Profiles are for personal use and represent real people.

- *Page* – Pages are profiles for businesses, brands or organizations. The right way to set up a presence for business on Facebook is by creating a page.

- *Group* – Groups are for people that share common interests.

- *Timeline* – a chronological list of your posts, photos, videos or anything else that you might have posted.

- *Status* – Updates that you post (may include text, links, photos or videos) that your fans and followers will see in their newsfeed.

- *Cover Photo* – The large image that is displayed across the top of your page.

- *Profile Picture* – Your company's avatar that is used to identify you throughout Facebook.

- *Fans* – Facebook users who have "liked" your page and are following your updates.

- *Apps* – Software (usually third party) to extend the functionality and experience that Facebook offers.

- *Tagging* – Identifying a person or a brand in a post, photo or video.

Getting Started with Facebook

Facebook is very useful to a business, but for the purpose of this chapter, we will focus on the most common practices that will get you started:

1. *Set up a Business Page* – The first order of business setting up a business page. A business page is like a separate profile for your business. It is linked to your personal user profile so you don't need to create a separate login. Notice, that you can designate other team members as additional administrators.

2. *Customize the Page* – At the very least change the profile picture and the cover image. Choose images (or better yet, have them created professionally) that reflect your brand and support your marketing messages. For the profile picture choose something that will make your posts stand out. For the cover image, include your company name, website URL and some descriptive taglines. You can have your web developer or SMM partner help you with that. There is also a lot of information you should contain on your business page profile.

3. *Set Permissions* – You should set permissions for who can post on your business' page, otherwise you can expect to get a great deal of spam. I recommend allowing comments but disabling direct posts to the page's timeline.

4. *Upload Photos and Videos* – If you have media content such as photos and videos that you have created for the website, upload them into photos and videos sections of your page.

5. *Invite People to "Like"* – Getting the initial critical mass of fans is important so you want to start building your audience right away. To do that you can invite e-mail contacts by uploading an e-mail list of your customers (up to 5,000 contacts).

6. *Run Ads* – Consider running a small ad campaign to promote your Facebook Page and build the audience. What's great about Facebook ads is that you can laser-target by interests, keywords and location.

7. *Suggest the Page* – Another way to get the page going is to suggest it to friends in your personal network. You can also ask your colleagues to do the same.

8. *Get a Vanity URL* – Once you get a certain number of fans (currently 25), you can request a custom user-friendly URL like http://www.fb.com/yourbusiness.

Best Facebook Practices

Because of the recreational nature of Facebook, most of the content that you will find is entertaining in nature. There are, however, many good examples where companies run successful campaigns educating and informing their followers. The following are some of the practices that have been proven to work:

- Keep your posts short and use images and videos as much as possible.

- Always respond to all comments.

- Post visually stunning content such as images or videos. Anything visual works great on Facebook.

- Share some of your best articles or blog posts and encourage others to comment on them.

- Create a page to raise awareness for important issues or common pains that your customers experience.

- Build a community and encourage discussions around controversial issues that affect your customers personally.

- Share your experiences, provide guidance and answer questions your customers have regarding their daily lives.

- Run polls and gather customer opinions or feedback on industry trends, products or services.

- Share industry news and repost (through sharing) the content that is posted by leading influencers.

- Run contents sponsored by your company and establish prizes.

- Post exclusive information (information that you share only through Facebook).

- Reward your fans by offering promotions, discounts, announce special deals and sales.

- Post content that is humorous in nature. This works really well on Facebook but it might be challenging to do it as a business, especially B2B.

- Pin and highlight most effective posts or posts that you want to emphasize.

- Promote company events, webinars, seminars, tradeshows, etc.

- Consider paying to boost (get additional exposure) some of your best posts. You can select and customize the target audience.

- Try targeting your posts to specific audience (you can choose who can see your posts) to increase their effectiveness.

- Use custom tabs that allow you to create custom pages or integrate third-party applications.

- Use post scheduler to schedule posts in the future.

- Study your page insights (analytics that show impressions, page views, unique page views, etc.)

- Do a substantial amount of A/B testing to determine which types of posts/content works best for your audience.

Twitter Marketing Tactics

Twitter is a micro-blogging social network that became popular thanks to its 140-character limit. It is the second most popular social networking website in the U.S. after Facebook. Twitter is finally getting traction in B2B making it a great social network for businesses.

How can Twitter be Used for Business?

Twitter is becoming as important for businesses as Facebook. In fact, some argue that Twitter is more business-friendly than Facebook, and the community is more welcoming to business content. It is great for establishing industry authority and to create a loyal following of either consumers or other businesses. Twitter also has proven SEO benefits.

Twitter is all about conversations, and it is a great tool to engage existing customers, prospects and partners. Twitter is also an effective way to find and connect with other professionals in the industry.

Twitter etiquette is similar to other social networks: spend less time talking about yourself and more time talking about others. Social Media Expert, Chris Brogan recommends a 12-1 rule: Tweet about other people 12 times as often as you tweet about your own company[48].

Twitter Lingo That You Will Find Useful

The following basic Twitter lingo will help you get started:

- *Tweet* – A post of 140 characters or less.

- *Retweet / RT* – An equivalent of a share when someone reposts someone else's tweet.

- *Direct Message / DM* – A private tweet between two users. The recipient must be following the sender to receive a DM.

- *Timeline* – A chronological list of tweets, your own, someone else's or in a list.

- *Following* – Subscribing to someone's tweets to see them on your own timeline.

- *Follower* – Users that are *following* you (i.e., choosing to see your tweets). Following is one way, and it is not required to follow someone in return.

- *Hashtag* – Keywords preceded by a "#" symbol that are used to identify the subject matter of tweet. Twitter links them to quickly search for or see related tweets.

- *Trends* – Most popular topics on Twitter in real time.

- *Handle* – Your twitter's username that is identified by the "@" symbol in front of it and acts as a link to your account.

- *Mention* – Is triggered when someone uses your handle in his or her tweet.

---

[48] http://www.chrisbrogan.com/socialmediaetiquette/

- *Lists* – A quick way to group users to focus on specific users' tweets.

- *Favorites* – Tweets that have been marked as favorites.

Getting Started with Twitter

Getting started with a Twitter business account is straightforward and the following list will guide you through the steps:

1. *Set up an Account* – First, open a new Twitter account. Unlike Facebook, Twitter doesn't have any special types of account for businesses. Make sure the handle you use is consistent with your brand across other social networks.

2. *Customize Your Twitter Profile* – Customization options for Twitter include changing your photo and header images as well as the Twitter's signature full background image. Use the best marketing assets that you had created for your website. For the photo choose something that will make your tweets stand out. For the header image, include your company name as well as some descriptive taglines. Twitter's background images are famous for originality so you're your web developer or SMM partner prepare something creative. In addition, you can customize colors to match your company/website colors. Finally, thoroughly complete your bio.

3. *Follow and Build Network* – Start following other users in the industry right away. Because many will follow you back, this is the common strategy to acquire new followers. You can follow up to 2,000 users initially so try to follow as many as you can but do it gradually. Search for lists that contain top influencers in your industry. Use tools like Followerwonk (https://followerwonk.com/), Twitaholic (http://twitaholic.com/) and Tweepi (http://tweepi.com/) to target whom to follow. Reach out to them by retweeting and marking their tweets as favorites.

4. *Request Follows* – It is acceptable to request others to follow you. One of the best ways to do that is by complimenting them on their content and tweets and offering to follow you in order to share content in the future.

Proven Twitter Practices

Twitter is a community like no other. It takes time and practice to master. The following are some of the best Twitter practices for businesses:

- Not all content from your business Twitter account should be industry- or business-related. Share anything that's useful, newsworthy or informative.

- Twitter originally started as 140 character posts, but now you can also tweet photos and videos that can be far more effective than words alone.

- Focus on quality content and make every tweet count. Don't flood your followers with spammy content.

- Alternate between times of the day when you tweet and day of week.

- Send welcome tweets to your new followers. It's a great way to reinforce your connections as well as to attract new followers (people often retweet welcome messages)

- Always thank those who retweet your tweets for the same reasons as above. Retweet them in return.

- It goes for those who favorite your tweets as well. Remember, any time someone replies, retweets or favorites your tweet, it goes to all their followers.

- Make your tweets and responses personal. The Twitter community doesn't think highly of automated tweets.

- Listen and observe what others are tweeting before tweeting yourself.

- Summarize and curate useful and relevant content.

- Twitter considers it acceptable to tweet the same content multiple times but don't overdo it.

- Use a maximum of three hashtags per tweet. Any more than that could be overwhelming and annoying.

- Post daily thoughts or quotes of the day.

- Twitter is a great way to answer anyone's questions that are related to your industry. That's a sure way to gain credibility and attract new followers.

- By the same token, ask questions.

- Share useful information about industry trends and predictions.

- Share interesting facts and statistics.

- Share your passion about what you do.

- Always be authentic and believable with every tweet.

- Go behind the scenes about your company, as well as your team and projects. Make it personable.

- Reward your followers by offering them exclusive specials from your company.

- Tweet about general specials and promotions from company, but don't go overboard.

- Tweet about timely news and events relating to your business.

- Tell memorable stories and learning experiences from your business interactions.

- Share links to your articles and blog posts.

- Research hashtags and identify trending conversations so you can participate in them.

- Experiment with various tweets to see what works best.

LinkedIn Marketing Tactics

LinkedIn, the world's largest social network for professionals, is growing by an average of two new members every second. LinkedIn is a combination of an online resume and a contact list, allowing you to network and interact with other business professionals.

How Use LinkedIn for Marketing

Unlike Facebook and Twitter, which are primarily recreational, LinkedIn is all about business. With members ranging from small business owners and entrepreneurs to Fortune 500 executives, LinkedIn offers business networking opportunities like no other social network.

LinkedIn is a phenomenal tool to expand the list of your business connections. It allows you to connect with people you don't know through the people you do know. LinkedIn's concept is built around the famous "Six Degrees of Kevin Bacon"[49] idea, implying that every person on Earth is only six connections away from knowing someone who knows Kevin Bacon. With LinkedIn networking tools you can uncover new connections, request introductions and be discovered for up to three levels (3rd degree connections).

LinkedIn also has wide range of tools and features designed specifically for businesses: company profiles, member groups, career opportunities, member groups, etc. Many of these can be successfully utilized as part of your marketing, including demonstrating your expertise and helping with search engine optimization.

---

[49] http://en.wikipedia.org/wiki/Six_Degrees_of_Kevin_Bacon

LinkedIn Lingo You Should Know

The following basic LinkedIn lingo will help you get started:

- *Network* – The list of your contacts (connections)

- *Contacts / Connections* – LinkedIn members who are part of your network.

- *1st Degree Connections* – LinkedIn members with whom you are connected directly.

- *2nd Degree Connections* – LinkedIn members who are connected with your 1st level connections.

- *3rd Degree Connections* – LinkedIn members who are connected with your 2nd level connections.

- *InMail* – Private messages that can be used to contact any LinkedIn member while protecting privacy.

- *Groups* – Private communities within LinkedIn based on common interests or professional occupations. You can join multiple groups and participate in discussions. Any member can also start a new group.

- *Endorsements* – Nominations given by members in your network to help validate you for a specific skill.

- *Recommendations* – General comments written by contacts in your network to recommend you. They are typically associated with a position.

Getting Started with LinkedIn

LinkedIn has more tools and features for business than any other social network. It would be impossible to cover them all here, but the following guide will help you get started with a strong foundation for using LinkedIn for business:

1. *Set up a Strong Profile* – Your personal profile on LinkedIn will be instrumental to tap into its full potential, so spend some time setting up your own profile and add as much relevant information as possible. Your LinkedIn profile is your online resume, and without a strong profile, your other activities will not produce much traction. Beef up your profile. Focus on your professional summary and your background, education, languages you speak, and your skills and interests. Connect your Twitter account so your connections can follow your tweets. Finally, encourage all your colleagues to beef up their LinkedIn profiles as well.

2. *Consider a Premium Account* – Premium (paid) accounts have many more perks such as more search results, InMail (reaching out to members outside your network), better visibility and additional networking opportunities.

3. *Build Your Network* – As soon as your profile is created, start building your network. First, find your colleagues, friends and former classmates. LinkedIn will guide through this process. Second, tap into your address books to find and connect with as many people as you know, including your customers, vendors and other business associates. Building your network on LinkedIn is an ongoing process, so think of it as a work in progress, and update regularly.

4. *Ask for Introductions* – Whenever you see a 2nd level connection that is of potential interest to you, ask for an introduction from your direct (1st level) connection. This is quick way to not only expand your network but also a great way to connect with potential customers.

5. *Participate in Groups* – Find and join as many professional groups as possible. Focus on the largest groups with the most activity related to your industry. Become an active participant by engaging in discussions as well as by initiating new ones. Groups are also great for sharing your unique content, but don't spam groups.

6. *Create Your Own Groups* – Starting your own group is one of the best ways to market on LinkedIn. Groups can be public (anyone can join) or public where you will review each request to join. As a group owner, you have access to a number of great marketing tools such as sending messages group-wide, managing and moderating featured discussions, and even creating e-mail templates for users who request to join your group. You can also create subgroups, which is a great way to grow your parent groups (members of subgroups automatically become members of the main group).

7. *Grow Your Group* – The group's marketing potential is only fully realized if your group has a large number of members. That's why it is important to spend some time growing your group. You can do so by optimizing your group name and description for keywords (people search for groups on LinkedIn), inviting all your connections to join the group, as well as uploading e-mail lists using the "pre-approve people" tool under group management. By using these methods, I was able to grow one of my groups to one of the Top 20 groups on LinkedIn.

8. *Create a Company Page* – The next order of business is to create a page for your company. Company pages on LinkedIn are similar to the ones on Facebook. When you create a company page, it is automatically associated with your account and you can designate additional administrative users. Company pages allow you to feature your company's information, promote products and services, jobs as well as post updates. In my experience, marketing with company pages is not nearly as effective as with groups but I do recommend having a company page.

9. *Customize Company Page* – To maximize its effectiveness, customize your company page. This includes uploading logo and a header image, listing company specialties, multiple company locations. Also, take advantage of listing your

products and services (upload logos and images). Finally, you can associate groups with your company page.

10. *Ask for Endorsements and Recommendations* – A great way to add creditability to your LinkedIn profile is by requesting recommendations from your clients, colleagues and peers. When you endorse or recommend people, they will be more likely to recommend you in return. You can also request recommendations for your company page (even for specific services). Request customers for recommendations.

Best LinkedIn Practices

As mentioned earlier, because of the diverse number of tools on LinkedIn, it may take time to master it. Below is a list of some of the best practices will help you get started:

- Post regularly, at least once a week.

- Keep all your posts professional and business-related. Save personal posts for Facebook and Twitter.

- Connect with everyone you know professionally. Make an effort to reach out to new clients, prospects, vendors, partners or those you interact with in your personal life.

- It is against LinkedIn rules to connect with people you don't know, so reach out with messages or introductions first. If too many people report that they don't know you, LinkedIn has the prerogative to suspend your ability to send out connection requests.

- Many people are open to connecting, even if they don't know you. They are termed "open networkers." You can conduct searches for open networkers, or join groups in which they are members.

- It is considered acceptable to connect with someone based on interactions or exchanges in a group.

- Write recommendations for your connections as well as issue endorsements on a regular basis. You will find that many will respond by endorsing and recommending you.

- Ask for introductions through your connections.

- Take the time and effort to complete your profile. It will be easier for others to find you and connect with you.

- Post your unique and relevant content such is links to your latest blog posts. Share them with groups as well.

- Post company news and updates, such as press releases.

- Post any events such as tradeshows, seminars or conferences in which you participate.

- Participate in group discussions. Help others by answering their questions as well as request guidance from others.

- If you manage a group, don't lose sight of it. Keep all the content relevant, remove spam, kick out and block violators, approve new members, etc.

- Post regularly to your company page. Adopt the same habits as posting on your personal profile.

- Consider running paid ads to promote your content or your company's page. LinkedIn offers advertising that is laser-targeted by geographical location, company, occupation, position, etc.

Google Plus Marketing Tactics

Google+ (or Google Plus) is a relatively new network in the social media arena. However, you can't afford to ignore it in your social media marketing strategy. Its growth is primarily credited to the strong backing by Google that is determined to take this social network to the top. Google+ is becoming increasingly influential in the marketing world.

Using Google+ for Business

Google+ should be incorporated into your social media marketing strategy. Google is using its massive influence to promote and grow the platform. For example, the search giant is constantly rolling out new ways to integrate Google+ with search results. For one, it's been shown that Google search gives higher rankings to Google Plus posts, as well as displays authors' images next to blog posts that have authorship associated with Google Plus accounts, making their presence more prominent.

Many experts agree that Google Authorship will continue becoming one of the key criteria used in Google's search ranking algorithm. Using Google+ as part of your SEO and SMM strategies is becoming vital to pushing your content up the ranks in Google search results.

Finally, because Google+ is also tightly integrated with other services under the Google Account umbrella (such as Gmail, Google Docs, Picasa), it is easy for people to follow you and share content.

Google+ Lingo You Should Know

The following terminology from Google Plus will help you get started:

- *Home* – This is where you see updates from your network and where you can post your own updates.

- *Life Stream* – a chronological list of your updates, photos, videos or other content you have posted.

- *+1* – A way to like or recommend anything posted or shared on Google Plus.

- *Profile* – Your Google+ account. Profiles are for personal use and represent individuals

- *Page* – Pages are profiles for businesses, brands and organizations. Establishing a business presence on Google+ is done by creating a page.

- *Circles* – Groups of people you follow on Google+ who are typically defined by relationships (friends, family, work, etc.). You can choose to post updates to selected groups and filter the incoming updates by them as well.

- *To Circle* - Adding someone to a circle (i.e., following them); circling someone doesn't mean that they will "circle" you in return.

- *Hangouts* – A video chat feature that allows communicating with other participants. You can also use it for text chatting, voice or document sharing.

- *Cover* – The large image that is displayed across the top of your page.

- *Profile Photo* – your company's avatar, which is used to identify you throughout Google+ and on Google Search.

Getting Started with Google+

Your business presence on Google+ is vital to your long term SEO and SMM strategy. The following checklist will help you get started:

1. *Set up a Business Page* – The first order of business is to set up a business page on Google+. A business page is like a separate profile for your brand. You can also claim a vanity URL. (http://plus.google.com/+Company). Make sure you are using Google+ as the page (and not your personal account) to share, +1 and adding people or pages to your circles, (you can switch the account in the top right corner).

2. *Update your Local Listing* – It is also important to maintain brick and mortar business information and locations to ensure visibility in Google searches. Check the "Local"

section in the sidebar. Google replaced local pages with Google+ Local. This means that your Google+ page is also a venue for people to check in and find your business locations.

3. *Customize the Page* – You need to spend an adequate amount of time to make your page visually appealing. At the very least, change the avatar and the page's cover image. You can have your web developer or SMM partner help with the design that is consistent with your branding and identity, as well as helping to support important messages. Finally, make sure to thoroughly complete the information in the "About" section of the profile, and include your strategic keywords in your tagline and introduction. Also, link to your other social media accounts.

4. *Use Circles* – Set up and use circles to organize your connections for marketing purposes. This will allow you to concentrate your efforts on each "category" individually, from growing the network to segmenting your marketing with targeted messages. Your classification should be as simple or detailed as you want—Customers, Prospects, Employees, Associates, Partners, Influencers, VIPs, etc. After your circles are in place, search for Google+ users you can relate to, and add them to your circles.

5. *Circle Influencers* – Continue growing your circles by finding influential users in your industry and adding them to your circles. Similar to Twitter, some may follow you in return by adding you to their circles. Use the Google+ Discover tool (under People) to find influencers. Search for additional lists online. Websites like http://www.recommendedusers. com/ will give you a good starting point.

6. *Make Use of Hangouts* – Google Hangouts is a unique feature to Google+. Because you can use it to video chat and share your screen with up to 10 participants at a time, it provides a great platform for hosting webinars, Q&A events, presentations, training, etc. When joining these, others will be encouraged to connect with you and add you

to their circles. Also, consider organizing *Hangouts on Air* – live discussions and presentations that can be broadcast through your Google+ page and a YouTube channel.

7. *Join Communities* – Communities on Google+ are similar to groups on LinkedIn and form around specific issues or interests. Search for communities that align well with your company, and join them. Be an active member in the communities by contributing valuable content, helping others and participating in discussions. This is also a great way to meet new contacts.

8. *Create a Community* – Once you understand the nature of the community functionality, consider starting your own community to expand your reach and influence even further. Google+ has a number of great features to moderate and manage communities.

9. Claim Google+ Authorship – As stated earlier, it is important to associate your content with your Google+ account. First, your Google+ avatar will appear in Google search results drawing more attention. Another benefit is that Google tracks the quality of content from associated authors, and in the long run, it will help get better rankings in search results. Any content can be connected to your account by using the "rel=author" tag and by listing the website where the content is published on your profile.

Best Google+ Practices

The following are some of the tips and practices that have been proven to produce good long terms results on Google+:

- Keep your posts short, and make them visually appealing by using images and videos as much as possible.

- Share your latest content or posts from your blog, and ask you network for their views.

- Post valuable content that is exclusive to your Google+ account.

- Use hashtags where appropriate.

- Customize your posts by using bold or italics for emphasis. Surrounding your text by "_" for italics or "*" for bold. For example "*hello*" will display as **"hello"**.

- Offer discounts and promotions.

- Hold competitions to encourage members in your circles to participate.

- Respond to all comments. Never leave any comment unreasoned.

- Ask questions, and answer other peoples' questions.

- Encourage customers to write reviews, even if you are not a brick and mortar store.

- Join as many related communities as possible, and stay active in them.

- Tap into Hangouts as a conferencing / presentation / webinar tool to encourage others to add you to their circles. For example:

    o Use Hangouts to interact with customers for Q&A sessions, helping with problems or for training and support.
    o Use Hangouts for discussions, expert panels and guests.
    o Use Hangouts to interview Influencers for your blog.
    o Use Hangouts for webinars, product demos, launches and presentations.

Other Social Networks to Consider

The social networks arena is very crowded. Facebook, Twitter, LinkedIn and Google Plus are certainly dominating the field, but there are countless others. While it is still recommended you focus your energy and efforts on major social networks that provide the best ROI, you should at the very least take a look at what's "out there." Some social networks below may represent great opportunities, depending on your industry, the audience and the type of the content you produce:

Video Content

- **YouTube** (www.youtube.com) – Nothing compares to YouTube for sharing videos. If you have quality, original video content that was produced as part of your website project or is part of your SMM strategy, you should consider opening a YouTube channel and upload videos there regularly to build a following. YouTube marketing is a separate and unique topic.

- **Vimeo** (www.vimeo.com) – Vimeo is a popular alternative to YouTube that is favored by many in the creative community. If you have quality video content, you may share it through Vimeo as well.

Images / Visual Content

- **Pinterest** (www.pinterest.com) – is one of the fastest growing social networks that works as a pinboard for visual content. Any visual or multimedia content (photos, images, infographics) does well on Pinterest with users liking, commenting and repinning each other's content.

- **Instagram** (www.instagram.com) – Instagram has grown to be one of the most popular social networks for mobile photo sharing. If you produce quality visual content on the go, Instagram may be the perfect choice.

- **Flickr** (www.flickr.com) – Flickr is a social network that is designed specifically for sharing photographs. It is also a

446

good place to feature photographs of your facilities, team, events or products. Flickr has support for sharing video content as well.

Social Bookmarking

- **Reddit** (www.reddit.com) – Reddit is a strong and tight community that shares interesting materials by voting links up or down. If your content makes the front page, the exposure is huge. However, beware of overly promoting your content, as it is a quick recipe to get banned.

- **StumbleUpon** (www.stumbleupon.com) – StumbleUpon is another social bookmarking website that is designed to help people discover interesting content on the Web. You can submit your own pages as well as discover content based on specific categories of interest.

Blogging

- **Tumblr** (www.tumblr.com) – is another microblogging platform, but unlike Twitter, it is primarily focused on image sharing.

Location Based

- **Foursquare** (www.foursquare.com) – is a location-based social network that allows users to check-in to venues they visit. If you are a consumer business (like a store or a restaurant) you should consider setting up a presence.

Useful Social Media Tools

You may find the following tools helpful in managing your social media marketing:

- **Hootsuite** ( ) –industry's leading automation tool to manage and measure your multiple social networks. Manage Twitter, Facebook, LinkedIn and Google+ with one tool.

- **Mention** (www.mention.net) – tool to monitor and alert you for mentions of your name or brand online.

- **SocialMention** (www.socialmention.com) - tool for real-time chatter monitoring, social media search and analysis.

- **KnowEm** (www.knowem.com) - tool to check your brand or username across hundreds of popular and emerging social networks to help secure your brand before someone else does.

- **Klout** (www.klout.com) - a platform that helps people get discovered on Twitter for their passions.

- **Bufferapp** (www.bufferapp.com) - a service that allows you to easily share across multiple social media accounts (Facebook, Twitter, Google+ and LinkedIn).

- **Shoork** (www.shoork.com) a great Facebook page analytics tool that has a great deal of reports, let's you monitor your competitors and optimize your actions.

- **Hashtags.org** (www.hashtags.org) helps with research to help businesses improve and boost social marketing strategies.

- Topsy (www.topsy.com) a great research tool for searching and analyzing Twitter. Can be used to research tweets and find influencers.

Summary of Part III

You and your web developer shouldn't treat the project as completed when the website launches.

If you want to get the most from your website, you need to continue monitoring, marketing, improving and fine-tuning your website following its launch. Without this ongoing attention, your website will never realize its true potential or worse, inevitably diminish in its performance and competitive edge.

The following are the ten key points to address following your website's launch:

1. Select no more than 10 Key Performance Indicators (KPIs) that measure the performance of your website pertaining to business objectives. Have your web developer set up and configure Google Analytics and other tools to measure these KPIs.

2. Review reports weekly. Analyze the Acquisition-Behavior-Conversion (ABC) cycles to reveal shortcomings and opportunities for improvement. Create intelligence reports and attribution modeling for multi-channel funneling.

3. Schedule ongoing website performance reviews with your web developer. Continuously improve your website by collecting feedback, analyzing user behavior and monitoring competition. Maintain a wish list and follow a goal-oriented road map.

4. Hire experts to assist in search engine optimization and social media marketing in order to create and execute a solid marketing plan for your website.

5. Know your High Value Customers (HVC), who they are, what they want and how to attract them.

6. Set up tools and define KPIs to measure success of all your marketing campaigns and activities. Invest only in those that deliver ROI (Return on Investment).

7. Design an inbound marketing strategy based on content marketing. Understand the "Attract, Convert, Close and Delight" methodology, and design your strategy around it.

8. Invest in quality content and set up an infrastructure (blog, whitepapers, social media integration, etc.) to make the most of your content across multiple channels. Maintain best practices in blogging.

9. Avoid common Search Engine Optimization (SEO) mistakes and maintain best practices. Don't be tempted by engaging in risky, black-hat methods, and follow a safer, long-term strategy.

10. Avoid common Social Media Marketing (SMM) mistakes and use recommended tactics for each of the major social networks.

CONCLUSION

I decided to write this book because I became frustrated with a vast number of underperforming websites I see daily. I wanted to make a difference. I felt that I had much to give and much to share. After all, this book has been in the making for over eighteen years—the length of time I have been working in the industry.

Sixteen months and six hundred hours later, with a manuscript sitting on my desk, I realized something that was eloquently expressed by Socrates of ancient Greece: "I know that I know nothing."[50]

Michael Strokes, author of *Apology of Socrates,* argued that Socrates didn't literally mean that he knows nothing. What he meant is that one cannot know anything with absolute certainty but can feel confident about certain things.[51]

This is also true about the Internet.

This book cannot possibly give you answers to all your questions. In fact, no one can. The Internet today represents the combined knowledge of the entire human race that evolves and expands at an incomprehensible pace. That's why no expert knows it all. What worked for my clients may not work for you, and what is true today may not be the case tomorrow. That's the constantly evolving nature of the Internet.

What I can say with confidence, however, is that recommendations outlined in this book are a good place to start. They will save you much effort, time and money and will give you a solid foundation for continuous growth and improvement.

By finishing this book you have demonstrated your willingness to learn, and that gets you closer to the truth that took me eighteen years to assimilate: the ultimate secret of successful business websites was

---

[50] "Ipse se nihil scire id unum sciat" – derived from Plato's account of the Greek Philosopher Socrates.

[51] Stokes, Michael C. (1997). *Apology of Socrates.* Warminster: Aris & Phillips. p. 18

defined by Socrates almost 2,500 years ago. When it comes to success online, no one knows anything with absolute certainty—not you, not me, and certainly not your competition. Use that secret to your advantage. The more you learn, the more you will discover there is to learn. It is not the knowledge you have already acquired that made you successful; it is the discovery of new things of which your competition knows nothing. This is how, with every such turn, you will be putting more distance between you and everyone else.

And now you have a head start.

SPECIAL THANKS

I would like to extend special thanks and appreciation to my friends and colleagues without whom this book would have not been possible:

- Diane Pearson
- Dmitry Andrejev
- Sasha Berson
- Megan Teplitsky
- Safa Khudeira
- Miles Grundy
- Ryan Fitzer
- Grant Epstein
- Kristina Guzikova
- Anton Entin
- Alex Noio
- Alex Obuhovich
- Stas Filipov
- Valentin Poddubnyak
- Erik Snarski
- Anna Jeglova
- Danielle Kogan
- Andreas Shabelnikov
- Wojciech Lorenc
- Larry Minsky
- Tomas Hauck

INDEX

456

458